Avril Robarts LRC

Liverpool John Moores University

Space Grid Structures

SPACE GRID STRUCTURES

John Chilton

Architectural Press

OXFORD   AUCKLAND   BOSTON   JOHANNESBURG   MELBOURNE   NEW DELHI

Architectural Press
An imprint of Butterworth-Heinemann
Linacre House, Jordan Hill, Oxford OX2 8DP
225 Wildwood Avenue, Woburn, MA 01801-2041
A division of Reed Educational and Professional Publishing Ltd

 A member of the Reed Elsevier plc group

First published 2000

British Library Cataloguing in Publication Data
Chilton, John
    Space Grid Structures
    1. Space frame structures – Design and construction
    I. Title
    624.1'773

Library of Congress Cataloguing in Publication Data
A catalogue record for this book is available from the Library of Congress

ISBN 0 7506 3275 5

Composition by Scribe Design, Gillingham, Kent
Printed and bound in Great Britain

Contents

Preface

This book has been long in gestation. The original stimulus for it came about seven years ago out of my teaching about space structures to student architects, reinforced by my earlier doctoral research into space grid structures. When asked by students to suggest an appropriate text where they might encounter information about the geometry, design parameters, detailing and construction of space grids, I found the choice was rather limited (although there seemed to be many more books describing the structural behaviour and analysis of such structures). At that time a book that I consistently recommended was *Space Grid Structures* by John Borrego, which was published in 1968 by MIT Press (and, coincidentally, has the same title as this present volume). However, thirty years have passed since its publication and the technology of space grids has developed considerably over this period. Therefore, from the outset my intention has been to create a text of similar utility for architects, engineers and builders who wish to understand the basics of space grid design and construction in the late 1990s.

Encouragement to pursue this idea came in 1993, when I attended the 4th Space Structures Conference at the University of Surrey, where I tried to strike up a conversation with Stéphane du Château, one of the pioneers of space grid structures who sadly died this year, aged 92. He immediately asked if I was an engineer or an architect and when I responded 'engineer', he at first was not too keen to talk to me but when I added that I taught in a School of Architecture he became very communicative and eventually presented me with a signed copy of his own book on structural morphology in which he wrote:

'a Jean – John Chilton – pour l'inspirer des idées pas comme les autres – avec toute ma sympathie'
Guildford
10.9.93

It was after much consideration that the title 'Space Grid Structures' was chosen for this volume. Among architects, engineers and others in the building and construction industry the generic term 'space frame' is commonly used to describe three-dimensional structures that may be either frames or trusses in the engineering definition of the terms. In fact, practically all 'space frames' are space trusses in the engineering sense. However, space grid is a widely accepted alternative name that encompasses both structural systems and can be used when describing features common to both. The more correct terms, space frame and space truss, may then be used where it is important to distinguish the differences in their structural action.

Chapters 1 to 4 describe the history, geometry, design and construction of space grids. A selection of space grid structures of varying sizes, made from different materials, using different systems and constructed over the last thirty years are included in Chapter 5, in order to show the wide potential for the use of this structural form. Chapter 6 investigates the use of retractable, deployable and foldable space grids that, although having been developed early in the 1960s, have only recently been exploited to any great extent in architectural applications. Finally, in Chapter 7, some space grid concepts that have not yet been fully utilized are outlined together with some interesting developments that might be implemented in the near future.

Some people who consider that the use of space grids reached its zenith in the 1970s have commented that this might be a book of only historical interest. However, as the case studies in Chapter 5 demonstrate, space grids are still being used widely for medium and long-span structures of innovative form. Although their use may diminish in the more developed countries of the world, there is still a huge potential for their widespread use in developing countries where materials are expensive, labour is cheap and simple efficient structures are in demand.

Acknowledgements

First and most importantly I must give my heartfelt thanks to my wife Gloria Llanos for her unfailing support and encouragement without which I doubt whether I would have ever completed the task of writing this book. Not only has she endured many lonely evenings and weekends as I have laboured incarcerated in my study, but she has also carried out many corrections and revisions of the word-processed text.

Although I have ended this journey alone it did not start thus. Therefore, I also give my sincere thanks to Dr Richard McConnel, of Cambridge University Engineering Department, who was initially my co-author, for his assistance in acquiring some of the information included in the book and for the time that he spent reading and making very constructive comments on an early draft of the manuscript.

It would be difficult to produce a book of this character without the help and generosity of many people. Of those who have contributed I am particularly indebted to Graeme Barker for his excellent three-dimensional, computer-generated representations of space grid geometry used in Chapter 2 and to Glyn Halls, photographer in the School of the Built Environment at the University of Nottingham for his assistance in the production of many of the photographs. I am also extremely grateful to the following who have given their permission for drawings and/or photographs to be reproduced: ABBA Space Structures, Architectural Association Photo Library, British Steel Tubes Division, De Bondt, A. El-Sheikh, Félix Escrig, J. François Gabriel, Alastair Gardner, G. C. Giuliani/Redesco srl., Glyn Halls, H. Hendriks, Pieter Huybers, N. M. T. Jackson, Mamoru Kawaguchi, L. A. Kubik, Matthys Levy, Mai Sky System Inc., Carlos Márquez, J. Martinez-Calzón, R. E. McConnel, Mero (UK), Orona S. Coop. Ltda., Fundación Piñero, Tony Robbin, Scogin Elam and Bray, Shimizu Corporation, R. G. Satterwhite, Space Decks Ltd, Kyo Takenouchi, R. Taylor, Peter Trebilcock, Ture Wester and Yoh Architects.

Of those who have provided illustrations, listed above, a special mention must be made of Mamoru Kawaguchi who very generously provided copious amounts of information, diagrams and photographs of the projects with which he has been associated, in particular those constructed using the Pantadome system. In addition, I am very grateful to Roland Howarth and Richard Porada – Space Decks Ltd; Ane Yarza – Orona S. Coop. Ltda.; Eddie Hole – British Steel Tubes Division; Jane Wernick – Ove Arup; K. Sugizaki – Shimizu Corporation; and Stephen Morley – MODUS Consulting, all of whom have assisted me in the acquisition of drawings, photographs and information. If I have omitted anyone, I apologize.

Finally, I wish to thank my father who, although neither architect nor engineer, read and commented on the almost completed manuscript (without the benefit of the figures to aid his understanding) and my mother for her patience in listening as he read her sections of the text. I owe them the most, for without their nurture, support and encouragement I should never have embarked on my career as an engineer and would not have had the opportunity to write this book. It is dedicated to them both.

1 Early development of space grids

Architects and engineers are always seeking new ways of solving the problem of space enclosure. With the industrialization and development of the modern world there is a demand for efficient and adaptable long-span structures. Space grid structures are a valuable tool for the architect or engineer in the search for new forms, owing to their wide diversity and flexibility. Before entering into a discussion of the design and use of space grids in the late twentieth century, it is useful to look back at the early use of three-dimensional structures.

Until the middle of the eighteenth century the main construction materials available to architects and engineers were stone, wood and brick. Metals, being in relatively short supply, were used mainly for jointing of the other materials. Of the widely available materials, stone and brick are strong in compression but weak in tension. Thus they are suitable for three-dimensional structural forms such as domes and vaults. Impressive feats of vaulting were achieved by medieval masons but the largest span masonry domes, St Peter's Basilica in Rome (1588–93) and Santa Maria del Fiore in Florence (1420–34) are both approximately 42 m diameter at the base.[1] Good quality timber has strength in tension and compression but is naturally available only in limited lengths and with limited cross-section. For large-scale three-dimensional structures jointing of timber becomes a major problem. Nevertheless, the Todai-ji temple at Nara in Japan, the largest historic timber building in the world, is 57 m by 50 m and 47 m high. The present building dates from 1708 and replaces the original, even larger, structure which was destroyed by fire. Although these materials were used to produce impressive large-scale structures, the spans were limited and the construction heavy. However, with the Industrial Revolution came the wider production of iron and then steel, high-strength materials that permitted the construction of more delicate structures of longer span or greater height. At approximately the same time, mathematical techniques were being developed to describe and predict structural behaviour and understanding of the strength of materials was advancing rapidly. Equally, with the advent of the Railway Age and the industrialization of commodity production came an increasing demand for longer span structures for bridges, stations, storage buildings and factories. With the wider availability of iron and steel and the demand for larger spans, there came a period of development of new structural forms, initially a multiplicity of different truss configurations and eventually three-dimensional space grids.

Many structural forms including most space grid assemblies are modular. The concept and efficiency of modular building construction was dramatically illustrated, almost 150 years ago, by the design, fabrication and assembly of the metal framework of the Crystal Palace in Hyde Park, London, for the Great Exhibition of 1851. The whole process, from the submission of the tender by Fox Henderson & Co. and Joseph Paxton to the possession of the completed building, was accomplished in approximately six months – a feat that would probably tax the abilities of today's construction industry.

Landmark structures such as the Eiffel Tower in Paris constructed from wrought iron between 1897 and 1899, bear witness to the stability and durability of modular three-dimensional metal construction. The tower, built as a symbol for the centenary celebration of the French Revolution, and conceived as a temporary structure, has already survived over 100 years. Sadly, the magnificent 114 m span Galerie des Machines by Contamin and Dutert, built at the same time adjacent to the tower, has not. Such structures demonstrated the possibilities for the use of iron and steel in high-rise and long-span buildings and challenged the ingenuity of architects and engineers to discover new and more efficient ways for their construction.

Probably the earliest examples of what we now commonly call space frames or space grids (light, strong, three-dimensional, mass-produced, modular structures) were developed by the inventor of the telephone, Alexander Graham Bell (1847–1922). In the first decade of the twentieth century he experimented with space trusses composed of octahedral and tetrahedral units (Figure 1.1). In his article on kite construction in the *National Geographic Magazine*,[2] in 1903, Bell commented:

> Of course, the use of a tetrahedral cell is not limited to the construction of a framework for kites and flying-machines. It is applicable to any kind of structure whatever in which it is desirable to combine the qualities of strength and lightness. Just as we can build houses of all kinds out of bricks, so we can build structures of all sorts out of tetrahedral frames and the structures can be so formed as to possess the same qualities of strength and lightness which are characteristic of the individual cells.

1

As can be seen from this quotation, Bell appreciated the dual properties of high strength and light weight exhibited by the rigid three-dimensional tetrahedral forms and incorporated them into many of his projects. One of the first steel space grid structures, using cast nodes and tubular members, the observation tower at Beinn Bhreagh, USA, was constructed by Bell in 1907.

Despite Bell's development of lightweight three-dimensional space trusses early in the century, they were not used in architecture until the introduction of the MERO system, in 1943. This was the first space grid system widely available commercially and was developed in Germany by Dr Ing. Max Mengeringhausen (1903–88). Using what is still probably the most common method of space truss construction, the system consists of individual tubular members connected at 'ball'-shaped node joints. The aesthetic appeal and popularity of this system has endured to the present day, as confirmed by the many alternative tube and ball systems now available.

An alternative popular method of constructing double-layer grids uses prefabricated modules. In the UK, during the 1950s, Denings of Chard developed the Space Deck system, based on bolting together prefabricated steel pyramidal modules (1.22 m × 1.22 m in plan and 1.05 m or 0.61 m deep respectively). With only slight modifications to module dimensions and materials, Space Deck has been widely and successfully used for roof and floor structures ever since. The system is described in detail in Chapter 3. A similar module, with the same plan dimensions but overall depth of 600 mm, was adopted for roof and floor construction in the Nenk modular building system.[3] The Nenk system was developed by the former Ministry of Public Building and Works in the UK in collaboration with Denings and was used in the construction of army barrack blocks in the early 1960s. It could span 12.2 m (40 feet) with normal floor loads and 26.8 m (88 feet) with normal roof load. Space grids were used to allow freedom of column location and space planning on the floor below. Precast concrete floor

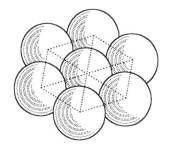 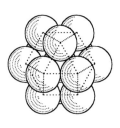 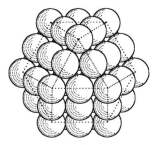 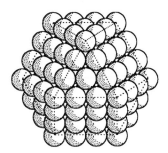

1.2
Close-packing of spheres as studied by R. Buckminster Fuller. (Drawing: John Chilton)

slabs, set on preformed strips of polystyrene or polyurethane, were used within the square upper grid of the modules to form the floor plates.

During the 1950s and 1960s, space grid systems were proliferating all over the world as architects explored the relatively new aesthetic of the modular grid and engineers experimented with alternative jointing systems, materials and configurations. In the USA, Richard Buckminster Fuller (1895–1981), following his study of the closest packing of spheres, developed the Octet Truss system.[4,5,6] The name Octet Truss derives from the octahedron-tetrahedron geometry formed by the lines linking the centres of spheres packed together in a continuum so that each sphere is surrounded by twelve more in close contact (see Figure 1.2). Members of the space grid then follow these lines. The Ford Rotunda Building, Ford River Rouge Plant, Dearborn, Michigan, constructed in 1953, used aluminium Octet Truss grids to form the faces of a 28.4 m diameter geodesic dome weighing only 8.5 tonnes (Figure 1.3). This space grid is of 'nodeless' construction as the X-shaped ends of the members allow them to be bolted directly to each other at the intersections without the use of a separate node component. An exhibition of Buckminster Fuller's work at the Museum of Modern Art, New York, in 1959, featured a 1.22 m deep Octet Truss structure 10.7 m wide and 30.5 m long (consisting of two cantilevers of 18.3 m and 12.2 m) made from 51 mm diameter aluminium tubes.

Konrad Wachsmann (1901–80) was appointed in 1959 to develop a space grid system for large span aircraft hangars, for the United States Air Force. The brief demanded great flexibility in construction, geometry and building type, whilst also asking that the components

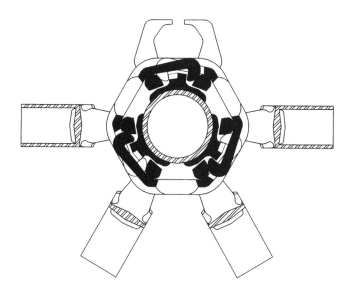

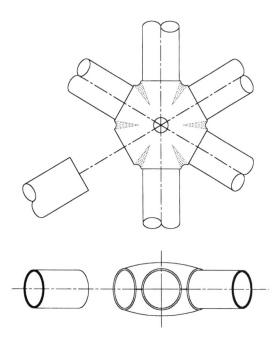

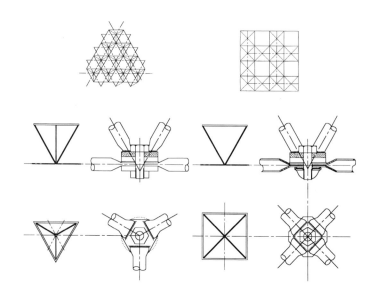

1.5(a)
Tridirectionelle S.D.C. (1957) which required workshop or site welding of tubular members to the connectors, developed by Stéphane du Château (Drawing: John Chilton after S. du Château)

1.5(b)
Pyramitec (1960) a system using triangular, square or hexagonal based pyramidal modules, developed by Stéphane du Château (Drawing: John Chilton after S. du Château)

should be demountable and reusable in the same or other configurations. Wachsmann's system[7] incorporated a relatively complicated universal connector made from a combination of four standard die forged elements which allowed up to twenty tubular members to be connected at each joint, (Figure 1.4). Two diameters of tube were employed, one for the continuous top and bottom chords of the grid made from 9.1 m lengths joined using a flush connector and smaller diameter tubes for the diagonals. The joints between chords and diagonals were designed in such a way that on site, only a hammer was required for assembly. This was necessary to drive three soft steel wedges through notches to lock the connectors into position on the main chord members.

In France, Stéphane du Château (1967–1999) developed Tridirectionelle S.D.C. (1957) which required workshop or site welding of tubular members to the connectors, (Figure 1.5(a)). Subsequently, du Château also developed a system using triangular, square or hexagonal based pyramidal modules, Pyramitec (1960), (Figure 1.5(b)). This was the forerunner of the Unibat system (1962; see Figure 1.6) which used similar modules, but in this case was bolted together only at the corners.[8,9] Du Château also developed Tridimatic (1965), a system of interconnected prefabricated plane trusses and Spherobat (1984), which uses two-part hollow spherical nodes through which bolts connect to the end of tubular members.

In Canada, the Triodetic system, predominantly using aluminium as the material for the bars and joints, was introduced on a commercial basis in 1960, by Fentiman Bros. of Ottawa, Ontario, Canada.[10] The system, was innovative in its use of extruded tubular members, flattened or coined at their ends and a solid extruded aluminium hub with slots that matched the coining of the tubes (Figure 1.7). Development started in 1953 following the construction of a prototype, in wood, of an octahedral-tetrahedral grid. An early experimental use was for a totally demountable aircraft hangar (21 m wide, 20 m deep and 9.8 m high) that was developed for the Royal Canadian Air Force and which could be packed into three crates 1.5 m by 1.5 m by 3.7 m long. The fully demountable Netherlands Pavilion at Expo '67, Montreal, 74 m long, 22.5 m wide and 18.3 m high and erected without scaffolding, was constructed using an external structure of Triodetic space grid. It used approximately 52 000 aluminium tubes of 38, 51 and 76 mm diameter, 5000 steel tubes of 76 mm diameter for highly loaded members and around 17 500 aluminium connectors.

Recognition of the innovative work of Richard Buckminster Fuller and the growing acceptance of space grid structures came in the adoption of a 76 m diameter, three-quarter sphere, geodesic dome for the US pavilion for Expo '67 in Montreal, Canada. Designed by Fuller in conjunction with Sadao Inc., Geometrics Inc., and Simpson, Gumpertz and Heger Inc., the dome was a dou-

1.6
The pyramidal modules of Unibat are bolted together at the corners (Photograph courtesy R. Taylor)

1.7
Triodetic system introduced in 1960, by Fentiman Bros. of Ottawa, using aluminium for the bars and solid hub joints (Photograph courtesy Glyn Halls)

ble-layer tubular steel space grid having a triangular geodesic grid for the outer layer and a hexagonal grid for the inner layer (Figure 1.8). At the same Montreal Expo, two massive theme pavilions, 'Man the Explorer' and 'Man the Producer' (Architects: Affleck, Desbarats, Dimakopoulos, Lebensold, Sise (CCWE)) were also constructed using modular three-dimensional space grids. These multi-layer grids were one of the early attempts to demonstrate the feasibility of inhabited mega-structures

constructed from a modular system of small elements. The pavilions (Figure 1.9) were constructed from around 400 000 members composed of paired steel angles, using 2.5 million bolts and 100 000 connecting nodes, totalling approximately 7500 tonnes of steelwork. Large wall and floor sections were assembled using grids based on the geometry of a regular truncated tetrahedron of side length 1 m (see Figure 1.10(a)). The truncated tetrahedron is one of the few regular space-filling polyhedra thus these

1.8
Richard Buckminster
Fuller's 76 m diameter,
three-quarter sphere,
double-layer space
grid geodesic dome
for the US pavilion at
Expo '67 in Montreal,
Canada (Photograph
courtesy Alastair
Gardner)

1.9
Modular multi-layer
space grid pavilion
'Man the Producer', at
Expo '67, Montreal,
Canada. (Photograph
Kamlesh Parikh,
Architectural
Association Photo
Library)

basic modules could be nested in such a way that two parallel surfaces were formed (see Figure 1.10(b)). The resulting buildings had floors configured as shown in the plan view of Figure 1.10(c) and walls that were inclined inwards at an angle of 71 degrees to the horizontal. A typical elevation is shown in Figure 1.11.

The centrepiece of the Fairground at Expo '67, in Montreal, was a multi-layer space grid 65.5 m high

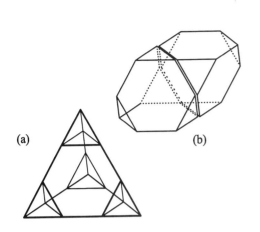

(a)

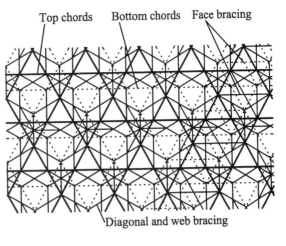

(b)

Top chords   Bottom chords   Face bracing

Diagonal and web bracing

(c) Typical floor grid

*1.10
(a) Truncation of
tetrahedron to form
geometry of the grid
(b) nesting of
truncated tetrahedra
to form parallel
surfaces and (c)
configuration of floor
grids for the pavilions
'Man the Explorer'
and 'Man the
Producer', at Expo
'67, Montreal, Canada
(Drawing: John
Chilton)*

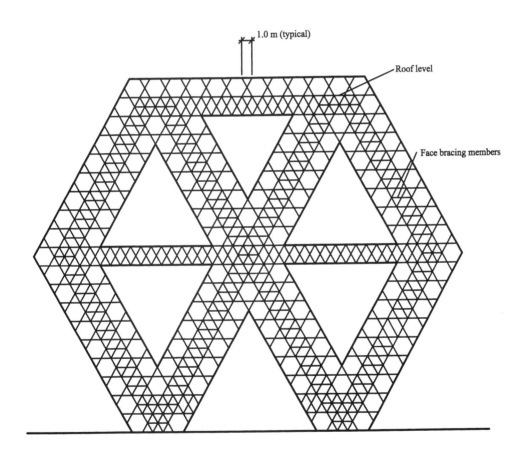

1.0 m (typical)

Roof level

Face bracing members

*1.11
Elevation of typical
wall construction for
the pavilions 'Man the
Explorer' and 'Man
the Producer', at
Expo '67, Montreal,
Canada (Drawing:
John Chilton)*

connected by a space grid bridge to an adjacent smaller structure of similar form (both were octahedra with the longer axis vertical and truncated at the base).[11] The Pyramid and Volcano (also known as the Gyrotron), in Figure 1.12, are shown in plan and section in Figure 1.13 (Architects: Sean Kenny, George Djurkovic;

Engineer: Boyd Auger). The contract to supply the space grid was won by the Aluminium Company of Canada Ltd (ALCAN) who have their head office in Montreal. Over 8500 aluminium tubes 4.9 m long, 152 mm diameter and having four different wall thicknesses were used in the structures. Cladding was

1.12
Pyramid and Volcano (Gyrotron) multi-layer aluminium space trusses at Expo '67, Montreal, Canada (Photograph E.H. Robinson, Architectural Association Photo Library)

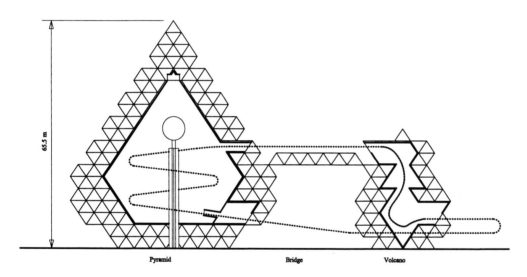

65.5 m

Pyramid   Bridge   Volcano

ELEVATION

1.13
Plan and section of the Pyramid and Volcano (Gyrotron) multi-layer aluminium space trusses at Expo '67, Montreal, Canada (Drawing: John Chilton)

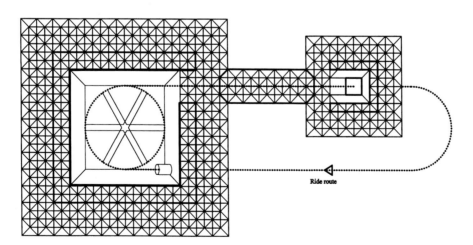

Ride route

PLAN AT BRIDGE LEVEL

1.14
Prototype Nodus
space truss, Corby
(Photograph courtesy
British Steel Tubes &
Pipes)

applied to the internal surface thus fully exposing the external space grid.

At around the same time, the wider use of electronic computers and the development of programs to enable space grid structures to be analysed more accurately increased confidence in their use for larger and longer span structures. It is interesting to note that, due to the inefficiency of the structural analysis computer software existing at the time, a completely new program capable of dealing with large structural configurations was written in order to analyse the multi-layer grid of the Pyramid and Volcano described above.

During the late 1960s and early 1970s many of the pioneering space grid systems were superseded by second generation systems. British Steel Corporation (Tubes Division), now British Steel Tubes & Pipes, developed the Nodus system with a small range of sophisticated standard node joints, designed to suit their tubular section products, and produced in different sizes with varying load capacities. All of the standard joints were tested to failure in a special rig, at their research centre in Corby, to prove their effectiveness, and a full size 30.5 m by 30.5 m, 1.52 m deep space grid (Figure 1.14) was also built and tested. This structure was dismantled after testing and re-erected for use as the Space Structures Research Laboratory at the University of Surrey, in Guildford, UK (Figure 1.15).

For the Olympiad held in Mexico City in 1968, the architects Felix Candela, Antoni Peyri and Castenada Tamborrel designed a Sports Palace covered by a dimpled copper-clad dome. The supporting structure was a series of orthogonal intersecting trussed arches that formed a double-curved, double-layer space grid of 132 m span.[12]

Expo '70 in Osaka, Japan also featured several space grid structures. Significantly, the centrepiece was the huge 291.6 m by 108 m space truss, supported on only six columns at a height of 30 m above the ground, which covered the Festival Plaza (shown later in Figure 5.1). The design and erection of this space grid, designed by architect Kenzo Tange and engineer Yoshikatsu Tsuboi, is described in more detail in Chapter 5. Pods containing exhibits, including a capsule house designed by Kisho Kurokawa,[13] were suspended within the 7.6 m deep roof structure. Several of the pavilions were designed by Metabolist architects and incorporated space grids, for example, the Expo Tower by Kiyonori Kikutake and the Toshiba IHI and Takara Beautilion also by Kurokawa.[13] A total of 1444 tetrahedral modular units were used in the Toshiba IHI pavilion (Figure 1.16) and only four types of module of different strength were incorporated in the structure. The Takara Beautilion (Figure 1.17) was constructed using a space frame with a cubic multi-layer grid, assembled from rigid jointed modules that were bolted together at the mid-length of each member. Each module was fabricated from twelve tubes (100 mm in diameter) bent through right angles and connected by gusset plates and circular flange plates to form six arms

of equal length, each consisting of four tubes. Around 200 modules were used, each with overall dimensions 3.3 m by 3.3 m. Assembly was accomplished in only a few days. Prefabricated stainless steel capsules containing exhibits were inserted within the repetitive grid. As a result of the prefabrication of space grid modules and capsules, the whole of this pavilion was erected in one week.

Notable examples of long-span space grids constructed in 1970 and 1973 were the British Airways maintenance hangars (formerly owned by BOAC) at Heathrow Airport, London, designed by Z. S. Makowski and Associates.[14] The hangar roofs were diagonal double-layer grids 3.66 m deep and provided a column-free covered area 67 m by 138 m in plan. In this case, the space grids were not constructed from a proprietary system but were manufactured from tubular steel prefabricated elements joined on site with bolted grid connectors.

In the 1980s the use of continuous cold-formed steel sections for the top and bottom chord members of 'nodeless' space trusses led to the development of cheaper, lightweight systems, such as Harley, which originated in Australia, that can compete against well-established portal frame construction for medium span buildings. In this type of space grid, which is described in more detail in Chapter 3, the continuous chords in the two orthogonal directions are of 'C' section bolted back-to-back at the nodes.

In the 1980s and early 1990s the CUBIC Space Frame, SPACEgrid and Conder Harley space grid systems emerged in the UK being respectively a modular space frame, a development of the UNIBAT space truss system and a modified version of the Australian Harley space truss system.

1.15
Prototype Nodus space truss re-erected as the Space Structures Research Laboratory, University of Surrey, Guildford, UK (Photograph courtesy British Steel Tubes & Pipes)

1.16
Toshiba IHI pavilion, Expo '70, Osaka, Japan composed of tetrahedral space grid modules. Architect: Kisho Kurokawa (Photograph Dennis Crompton, Architectural Association Photo Library)

1.17
Takara Beautilion, Expo '70, Osaka, Japan, assembled from six branched, rigid-jointed modules to form a cubic space grid. Architect: Kisho Kurokawa (Photograph Richard Ronald, Architectural Association Photo Library)

recent developments. The story continues in Chapter 5 where a series of studies of interesting projects, completed over the last thirty years, are presented, commencing with the space grid of the Festival Plaza at Expo '70.

Notes

1 Melaragno, M. (1991). *An Introduction to Shell Structures: The Art and Science of Vaulting*. Van Nostrand Reinhold, p. 87.
2 Bell, A. G. (1903). The tetrahedral principle in kite structure. *National Geographic*, **14** (6), June, 231.
3 Walters, R. and Iredale, R. (1964). The Nenk method of building. *RIBA Journal*, June, 259.
4 Marks, R. W. (1960) *The Dymaxion World of Buckminster Fuller*. Southern Illinois University Press.
5 McHale, J. (1962). *R. Buckminster Fuller*. Prentice Hall, pp. 30, 32, photos 60–64 and 83.
6 Baldwin, J. (1996). *Bucky Works-Buckminster Fuller's Ideas for Today*. Wiley.
7 Wachsmann, K. (1961). *The Turning Point of Building*. Reinhold.
8 Du Château, S. (1995). Space structure – structure space. In *Lightweight Structures in Civil Engineering* (J. B. Obrebski, ed.) pp. 756–66, magat®, Magdalena Burska, Warsaw.
9 Makowski, Z. S. (1975). Space structures of Stéphane du Château. *Building Specification*, **6** (5), 31–40.
10 Fentiman, H. G. (1966). Developments in Canada in the fabrication and construction of three-dimensional structures using the Triodetic system. In *Space Structures* (R. M. Davies, ed.), pp. 1073–82, Blackwell Scientific.
11 Auger, B., Solomon, E. W. and Alcock, D. G. (1966). An aluminium space frame construction. In *International Conference on Space Structures*, Department of Civil Engineering, University of Surrey, Paper J2.
12 Gordon, B. F. (1983). *Olympic Architecture: building for the Summer Games*. Wiley.
13 Kurokawa, K. (1977). *Metabolism in Architecture*. Studio Vista.
14 Makowski, Z. S. (ed.) (1981). *Analysis, Design and Construction of Double Layer Grids*. Applied Science Publishers.

Although by no means an exhaustive review of the historical development of space grid structures, this chapter has served to introduce the work of some of the engineers and architects who have influenced the advancement of this efficient, usually modular, structural form. Several of the systems mentioned above are described in more detail in Chapter 3 together with more

2 Space grid geometry – thinking in three dimensions

There is often a tendency for architects, and possibly more so engineers, to think in terms of planar structures such as beams, trusses and portal frames when considering methods of spanning space. However, in many cases there are advantages to be gained from thinking in three dimensions and adopting spatial structures for medium to long spans. This is particularly true where heavy point loads or moving loads are to be supported.

Of course, all structures are three-dimensional in the sense that they have length, depth and thickness. However, planar beams and trusses are predominantly two-dimensional in their structural action, as they effectively resist loads applied only in one direction between their supports (usually in the vertical plane). Nevertheless, even for these simple structures it is unwise to neglect their stability in three-dimensions. For example, beams and trusses, in bending, are made deeper with increasing span and this, in turn, increases the tendency for the compression zone to buckle sideways, perpendicular to the vertical plane. To counteract this tendency, lateral bracing of the compression zone must be provided. With a system of multiple parallel beams with bracing systems at right angles to the span, it may become economical to take advantage of the benefits of three-dimensional structural action described below. Because of the planar nature of individual beams or trusses, they must be designed to resist the full magnitude of any point or moving load applied to them. However, with some modification of the lateral bracing system provided to maintain stability of typical beams and trusses, it may be employed to distribute loads between adjacent beams. This forms a three-dimensional structure where loads are rapidly distributed throughout the whole system. Every member usually contributes some resistance to the applied load unless the load is located at or very near a support.

Why two-way spanning structures?

To demonstrate the principle and benefit of using a two-way spanning structure we can consider a familiar example in the home, the woven canvas webbing often used for seats of stools or to support chair cushions. If webbing strips are used only in one direction, a load applied to one strip will cause it to sag and transfer load to only two sides of the supporting frame. However, if the webbing strips are interwoven in two orthogonal directions the loaded strip is partly supported by all of the others. This reduces the sag of the loaded strip and distributes the applied load more evenly to all sides of the frame. In the second case, each strip does not have to be capable of carrying the full applied load on its own and a lighter structure can be used for the supporting frame. Another advantage is that, if one of the webbing strips breaks, the seat as a whole will still support loads.

Similar benefits may accrue from the use of two-way spanning structures in architecture and engineering. For example, a load applied to a simple one-way spanning beam or plane truss, must be transmitted through the structure directly to its supports (Figures 2.1(a) and 2.1(b)). If, however, a grid of connected intersecting beams or trusses is formed in the horizontal plane, a vertical load applied to any one beam or truss will be distributed, in part, to all the other elements in the grid and thus to all of the supports. Figure 2.1(c) shows this for a small grid of intersecting trusses. Although, in these cases, the structural action differs from that described above for the woven webbing (bending and shear for the beams, axial forces for the trusses and pure tension for the webbing), an analogous, more efficient, load-sharing system has been produced. A configuration of intersecting beams is usually described as a single-layer grid and a very common example of its use in buildings is the coffered reinforced concrete slab where the orthogonal ribs produced by the coffering effectively form a grid of intersecting beams supporting a thin floor slab.

When the span of the structure exceeds about 10 m, the use of beam elements in a single layer grid becomes less economical and open web trusses or Vierendeel girders may be substituted for the solid beams. The structure then effectively consists of two parallel horizontal grids of 'chord' elements connected with a pattern of vertical and/or inclined 'web' elements between the two plane grids. This three-dimensional structure is generally described as a double-layer or space grid, and is also commonly known as a space frame or space truss depending on the type of bracing between the two layers and the method of connecting the members. Double-layer grids are one of the most efficient and lightweight

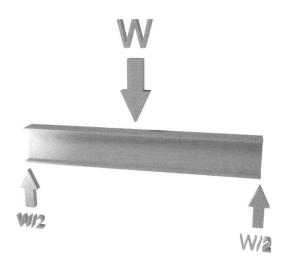

2.1(a)
A point load supported by a simply supported beam (Drawing by Graeme Barker © John Chilton)

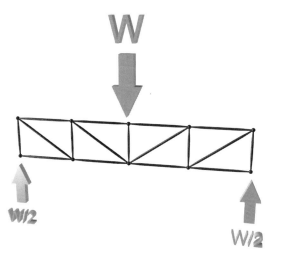

2.1(b)
A point load supported by a simply supported truss (Drawing by Graeme Barker © John Chilton)

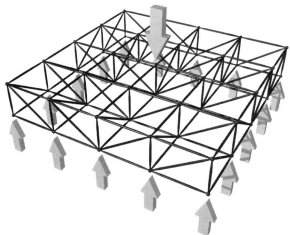

2.1(c)
A point load supported by a small space grid of intersecting trusses (Drawing by Graeme Barker © John Chilton)

structural systems due to their ability to share the task of load carrying through the whole structure; see Figures 2.2(a) and 2.2(b).

The term 'space frame' is often used loosely by both engineers and architects, to describe many different types of double-layer grid even though they may carry loads by quite different structural actions. The principal difference is between:

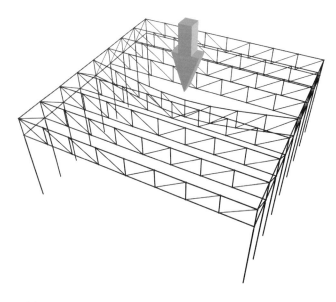

2.2(a)
Deflection of a system of individual trusses (Drawing by Graeme Barker © John Chilton)

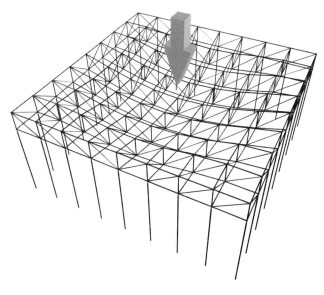

2.2(b)
Deflection of a two-way spanning double-layer grid of intersecting trusses demonstrating the load distribution advantage of the latter (Drawing by Graeme Barker © John Chilton)

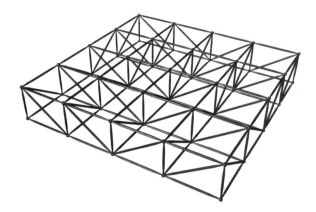

2.3(a)
Basic double-layer grid of intersecting trusses (Drawing by Graeme Barker © John Chilton)

2.3(b)
Basic double-layer grid of intersecting Vierendeel girders (Drawing by Graeme Barker © John Chilton)

1 double-layer grids with inclined web elements, such as the grid shown in Figure 2.3(a), and
2 double-layer grids generally with no inclined web elements, such as the grid with only horizontal chords and vertical web elements shown in Figure 2.3(b).

The former (1) rely primarily on truss action achieved through full triangulation of the structure, which is commonly composed of nominally 'pin-ended' bars or members connected between 'node' joints. In this type of structure, which should be more correctly called a space truss, if the loads are applied directly to the node joints, the bars within the space grid carry predominantly either axial tension or compression forces. However, some bending is always present due to the self-weight of the bars spanning between the nodes, and secondary bending effects may be introduced depending on the rigidity and form of the connection between the bars and nodes.

Frames, in the more specific engineering sense, are generally not triangulated, have some or all joints fully rigid, and resist the applied loads by a combination of bending, shear and axial forces in all elements, even when loads are only applied at the joints. The intersecting elements in the latter type of double-layer grid (2) are frames, in the same specific sense, as they also contain fully rigid joints and rely on frame action to resist the applied loads. They are genuine space frames and are usually either constructed from prefabricated, three-dimensional modules or they may be fabricated in situ by welding individual elements together. Modular systems have rigid joints within the components which are then connected by site bolting (e.g the CUBIC Space Frame described in Chapter 3 or the multi-layer frame of the Takara Beautilion referred to in Chapter 1). Systems fabricated by welding on site usually form a three-dimensional, completely rigid-jointed structure.

To be able to distinguish between space trusses and 'true' space frames is arguably not as important for an architect as it is for an engineer, although there are situations when an understanding of the difference may be of benefit (e.g. from an aesthetic point of view given the more open nature of the 'true' space frame, which has no diagonal members). In common usage the term 'space frame' is often applied to all space grids, including most proprietary modular systems that are actually space trusses. Even the proprietary name and/or the technical literature issued by manufacturers may refer to space truss systems as space frames. However, the use here of the broader term 'space grid', when speaking generally, will allow the distinction between space trusses and 'true' space frames to be made when discussing aspects limited to just one of these structural types.

Aspect ratio

The decision whether to use a three-dimensional space grid or a one-way spanning structure is often influenced by the plan form of the building and the location of the supporting structure. For instance, it may only be possible to provide support along two opposing sides of a rectangular building, in which case a one-way spanning primary structure will almost certainly be more economical, especially if the applied loads are uniformly distributed over the plan area of the roof or floor. However, when supports can be provided along all sides of a square or rectangular plan, a two-way spanning grid may be considered and it is then more difficult to decide which type of structure is more appropriate. One consideration influencing the choice will be the degree of load distribution expected in the three-dimensional structure. This depends on several factors, in particular the ratio of the spans in each direction of the two-way grid – the span *aspect ratio*.

The influence of the span aspect ratio on load distribution within a two-way spanning structure may be illustrated simply by considering a point load, W, applied at the intersection of two orthogonal beams of span L_1 and L_2. If these beams are connected at their midpoints they will form a very simple single-layer beam grid. Initially, it is assumed that both beams have the same material and cross-sectional properties (i.e. the modulus of elasticity or Young's Modulus (E) and the second moment of area (I) are the same for both). The relationship between the span aspect ratio (L_2/L_1) and the loads carried by each beam W_1 and W_2 can easily be found by a series of calculations for different ratios of beam span. The equations are given in Appendix 1 and the relationship is shown in Figure 2.4 where L_2 is the longer span and L_1 the shorter span.

It can be noted from Figure 2.4 that, with $I_2/I_1 = 1$, the beam with the longer span carries the least load, the shorter span carries the greater proportion of the load W and that (as would be expected) equal load is carried by each beam when they are both the same length. It can also be seen that when the ratio of the two spans (L_2/L_1) exceeds 2.0 the load is primarily carried by the shorter beam (89 per cent of the applied load when the aspect ratio equals 2.0). This simple example demonstrates that the benefit of two-way spanning grids is greatest, if the structure can be broken down into approximately square bays in plan and that this benefit reduces rapidly as the ratio between the two spans increases. Of course, in large space grid structures, a double-layer grid is more usual and there are many more intersecting members but the basic principle of using aspect ratios close to 1.0 still applies if an economical solution is to be obtained. If the aspect ratio is much greater than 1.0 the possibility of dividing the longer span by introducing intermediate columns should be considered. Where a clear span is absolutely essential, additional lines of support, in the form of stiff edge or intermediate beams on grid lines between columns, may be used to break the structure into approximately square bays. This can be achieved within the depth of the space grid itself, by locally using stiffer members along lines between opposing perimeter columns. It can also be accomplished by locally increasing the depth of the space grid at appropriate intervals.

A property of all structures, including three-dimensional grids, is that applied load is attracted towards the stiffest parts. Therefore, it is possible to modify the proportion of the load carried by elements in the two directions of a typical space grid by altering the stiffness of elements appropriately. For example, in the simple two-beam system described above, it is possible to increase the stiffness of the longer beam to balance the load distribution between the two beams when they have different spans. This could be achieved by increasing the depth of the longer beam and thus the magnitude of its second

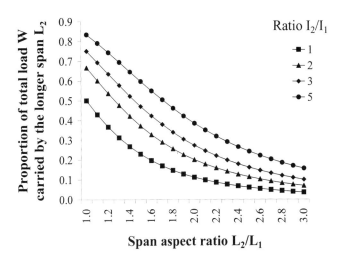

2.4
Relationship between span aspect ratio and proportion of total load carried by the longer span beam, L_2, of the simple two-beam intersecting grid with ratio I_2/I_1 equal to 1, 2, 3 and 5 (Graph: John Chilton)

moment of area I. Figure 2.4 also shows how the proportion of total load, W, carried by the longer beam varies for different aspect ratios and for different beam stiffness. Although expensive, in full-scale space grids with rectangular bays, a similar modification of member properties can be employed to modify the load distribution characteristics, for instance, by increasing the size of chord members in the long span direction.

Space truss stability

The stability of rigid jointed space frames depends on the bending resistance of the joints for its structural integrity. However, space truss structures depend on their geometrical configuration to ensure stability. To form a stable pin-jointed truss structure composed of nodes interconnected by axially loaded bars only, a fully triangulated structure must be formed. In a three-dimensional pin-jointed space truss structure, it is a necessary condition for stability, (variously known as Maxwell's Equation or Foppl's Principle), that,

$n = 3j - 6$, where   n = number of bars in the structure
j = number of joints in the structure
6 is the minimum number of support reactions.

There are many double-layer space truss geometries that comply with this condition. Some common ones are described later in this chapter. From this equation, it also

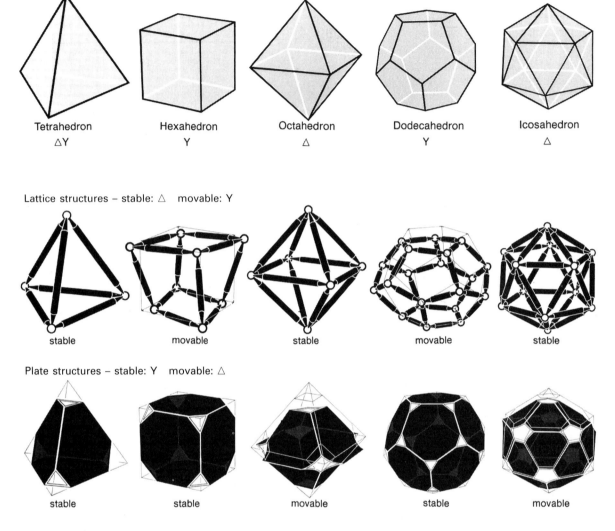

Tetrahedron
△Y

Hexahedron
Y

Octahedron
△

Dodecahedron
Y

Icosahedron
△

Lattice structures – stable: △   movable: Y

stable   movable   stable   movable   stable

Plate structures – stable: Y   movable: △

stable   stable   movable   stable   movable

2.5
Platonic polyhedra as bar and node or pure plate structures (a) tetrahedron, (b) cube or hexahedron, (c) octahedron, (d) dodecahedron and (e) icosahedron. (Diagram courtesy: Ture Wester)

follows that a structure that is not fully triangulated can be made stable if suitable and sufficient additional external supports are provided.

Alternatively, the stability of common space grid geometries can be related to the stability of simple polyhedra. Therefore, we shall briefly look at the behaviour of these forms.

Stable polyhedral forms

Polyhedral forms are bodies in three-dimensional space. From well before the time of the ancient Greek civilization, mathematicians have studied and ascribed special properties to them. The most basic of these forms are termed the regular or Platonic polyhedra (Figure 2.5) and consist of the tetrahedron, cube (or hexahedron), octahedron,

dodecahedron and icosahedron. Each of these is composed of similar faces of regular polygons (i.e. the sides of each face are the same length and each polyhedron has faces of only one polygonal shape). In the study of space grids we are primarily concerned with bar and node structures. However, to understand the stability of three-dimensional structures in general, it is advantageous to study the behaviour of simple, regular, polyhedral shapes (composed as either bar and node or plate structures) when loads are applied to their vertices (or nodes).

Bar and node structures

The tetrahedron is the minimum stable, three-dimensional, pin-jointed bar and node structure. It has four joints or nodes connected by six bars or members. Provided that the necessary support conditions can be satisfied, this structure complies with the equation above and is a stable form which generates only axial forces in the bars when loads are applied at the nodes (i.e. $j = 4$, $n = 6$ and $3j - 6 = (3 \times 4) - 6 = 6$). The cube or hexahedron has eight joints and twelve bars and provided that only the minimum of six support reactions are present, we find that $n = 12$ but $3j - 6 = (3 \times 8) - 6 = 18$. Thus the pin-jointed cube structure is unstable unless additional bars are inserted between the nodes or further support reactions are introduced. In the case of the octahedron $n = 12$, $j = 6$ and $3j - 6 = (3 \times 6) - 6 = 12$ and it is a stable pin-jointed bar structure. Following similar reasoning, it may be demonstrated that the pin-jointed dodecahedron is unstable as a bar structure but that the icosahedron is stable. Therefore, as they are composed of bars and nodes, most double-layer space truss geometries are based on the stable polyhedral forms (usually tetrahedral and octahedral or half-octahedral modules linked together).

Polyhedra as plate structures

Forming the same polyhedra from flat plate surfaces rather than from individual bars connected by pinned joints, and again applying loads at the vertices, the tetrahedron, cube and the dodecahedron are found to be stable structures whilst the octahedron and icosahedron are not. The sole Platonic polyhedron that is stable both as a bar and node structure and as a plate structure is the tetrahedron. If one tries to demonstrate the plate behaviour using card models it is necessary to cut off all the vertices to prevent the edges of the plates from acting like bars between nodes. Once this is done the instability of the octahedron and the icosahedron can easily be seen.[1]

Combined bar and plate structures

Research has been carried out, in particular by Ture Wester at the Royal Academy of Fine Arts, in Copenhagen, into the stability and structural duality of polyhedra composed exclusively of bars connected at nodes or of plates connected at their edges.[1] His work has demonstrated that the two structural actions may be combined to form stable space grids composed of bar elements and plate elements. The ability to combine the two types of structure might be exploited in metal space trusses combined with structural plate elements of glass or plastic.

Advantages of using space grids

Some of the benefits to be gained from the use of space grid structures have already been outlined. These, and

other advantages, illustrated with appropriate built examples, are described below.

Load sharing

As described above, the prime advantage of space grid structures is that generally all elements contribute to the load carrying capacity. Planar beams or trusses must be capable, individually, of carrying any possible concentrated or heavy moving loads (e.g. overhead cranes). However, in space grids such concentrated loads are distributed more evenly throughout the structure and to all the supports. This can also reduce the cost of the supporting structures as maximum column and foundation loads may be less. Maximum deflections are reduced compared to plane structures of equivalent span, depth and applied loading, assuming that the structural elements are of similar size. Alternatively, a lighter or shallower three-dimensional structure may be used to carry the same loads, resulting in maximum deflections no greater than those of a planar structure.

Installation of services

In space grids, the reasonably open nature of the structure between the two plane grids allows easy installation of mechanical and electrical services and air-handling ducts within the structural depth. Their fixing is simplified as there is a regular system of supports available, thus greatly reducing or even eliminating the need for secondary steelwork. If heavy equipment is to be installed within a space grid, the loads should ideally be supported at node joints. This is particularly necessary in space trusses in order to minimize bending moments in the chords. Otherwise, due account must be taken of such loading in the initial design of the nominally axially loaded members.

A good example of the load distribution properties of a space grid, as well as the freedom to install plant and machinery within the roof depth, being exploited to the full, is in a food-processing factory in Nottingham, England, which was constructed with a CUBIC Space Frame roof. It was expected that, at different times during the life of the building, various areas of the factory floor would be used as refrigerated stores. To aid this flexibility, 100 mm thick insulated panels were fixed to the whole of the lower layer of the space grid roof and the 75 m by 75 m structure (with just three internal supports) was designed to take point loads totalling approximately 600 tonnes. This permitted almost total adaptability of the refrigeration plant configuration within the 3 m deep roof space over the production and storage areas (Figure 2.6).

*2.6
Equipment in the roof
space of the CUBIC
Space Frame,
Northern Foods,
Nottingham
(Photograph courtesy
David Hague
Photography Ltd)*

Robustness

Space grids are highly redundant structures, which means that, in general, failure of one or a limited number of elements – for instance, the buckling of a compression member under excessive loading – does not necessarily lead to overall collapse of the structure. There have, however, been exceptions to this; notably, the collapse of the space truss roof of the Hartford Civic Centre, Coliseum, in January 1978.[2,3] This roof collapsed under snow and ice loading early in the morning of 18 January 1978, only a few hours after it had been occupied by a crowd of 5500 spectators at a basketball match. The subsequent investigations concluded that a fold line had developed in the roof in a north–south direction (roughly perpendicular to direction of the longer roof span) due to progressive buckling failure of the top chords of the truss. The failure occurred with a snow load of 78 to 88 kg/m^2 (16 to 18 lb/ft^2). It was concluded that the space truss failed 'at about one-half the total load which would have caused first yielding in the weakest member' (see Ref. 3, p. 636).

In space trusses supported at the bottom nodes there are usually four diagonal web members converging on each support and these are in compression. Failure of only one of these due to accidental damage or buckling under excessive compression owing to an unforeseen load can lead to the partial or total collapse of the whole structure, as the load originally carried by the failed member transfers to the remaining three and in turn causes their failure. The redundancy of space grid structures also assists with their resistance to damage from fire, explosion or seismic activity. In the case of fire or explosion there may be localized damage of the space grid, which allows the heat and smoke (in fire) or the force of the blast (in explosion) to escape. Unless critical elements (e.g. highly stressed compression chords, or web members adjacent to individual column supports as previously mentioned) are removed or weakened, total collapse is unlikely. The behaviour of space grids in fire and earthquake is discussed in more detail in the following chapter.

Modular components

Space grids are highly modular structures assembled from components that are almost exclusively factory fabricated. The components therefore, are usually produced with high dimensional accuracy, with a high quality of surface finish and they are generally easily transportable, requiring little further work except assembly on site. Because of their modular nature, space grids may be extended without difficulty and even taken down and reassembled elsewhere. The Mero space grid stand for the Edinburgh Tattoo (Figure 2.7) is an example of a space truss that has been taken down and re-erected annually, since 1973.

2.7
The Mero stand for the Edinburgh Tattoo has been taken down and re-erected at Edinburgh Castle, annually, since 1973 (Photograph: John Chilton)

Sadly, some architects seem to exhibit a resistance to the use of standard modular grid components. Perhaps they feel that their creativity is somehow restrained. However, just as an amazing diversity of masonry architecture has been produced using the standard modular component of the brick, so, with imagination, the standard components of a space grid system may be combined to generate exciting architectural forms. Some examples are shown in Chapter 5.

Freedom of choice of support locations

Great choice in the location of supports is offered by space grid structures. Within reason, space grids can be supported at any node of the grid and at practically any location in plan. This gives the architect considerable freedom in space planning beneath the grid. For instance, columns can be concealed on the lines of internal partitions. However, as discussed previously, approximately square structural bays are preferable as they lead to a more efficient use of material. The appropriate location of grid support and the effect that this can have on the structural efficiency is considered in more detail later in this chapter.

Regular geometry

For ease of construction, most space grids have a regular pattern that may be exploited architecturally to some effect. Particularly striking effects can be achieved if the colour chosen for the structural members contrasts with the colour of the decking, or with the sky in the case of unclad grids or fully glazed applications. The white double-layer space grid of the simple glass-covered entrance canopy at the Georgia Dome, Atlanta, USA, shown in Figure 2.8 contrasts beautifully with the blue of the cloudless sky. In fact, the colour chosen for a grid, as well as the grid pattern itself, can influence considerably the perceived weight of the exposed structure. The effect may be even more important than the actual member sizes or density of the grid. For instance, with appropriate lighting, a white space grid set against a white metal liner tray will not be particularly noticeable but the same grid set against a deep blue sky will be quite dramatic.

Ease of erection

A further advantage of the use of space grids is the efficiency of erection for large-span roof structures and especially on sites with limited access. In the former case, the whole roof can be assembled safely at or near ground level, complete with decking and services, and then jacked into its final position. In the latter case, the small components of a space grid can be assembled at almost any location using only manual labour and simple lightweight tools, even inside existing buildings. An example of the advantage of ease of erection of the small com-

2.8
Glass-covered canopy, Georgia Dome, Atlanta, USA (Photograph: John Chilton)

ponents of a space grid, was the very first commercial use of the CUBIC Space Frame in the Waverley Building, Nottingham Trent University, UK. Here an existing roof of a Victorian building was to be replaced in order to provide a rehearsal theatre. Alternative schemes using standard planar trusses and the CUBIC Space Frame were drawn up. However, the tender for the space frame included a full-scale load test to prove the adequacy of the new system. Despite this additional expense, the space frame solution was cheaper overall as the modules could be manually handled into the building and raised using simple lifting gear, whilst the planar trusses required a large (and expensive) mobile crane to lift them into position over the front of the building. Space grid erection methods are considered in more detail in Chapter 4.

Disadvantages

There are also some disadvantages in the use of space grids that must be offset against the considerable number of advantages described above.

Cost

Of the disadvantages associated with space grid construction, perhaps the main one is the cost, which can sometimes be high when compared with alternative structural systems such as portal frames. This disparity in cost is particularly evident when space grids are used for relatively short spans, although the definition of a short span is very dependent on the system under consideration. However, spans of less than 20 to 30 m can probably be considered short, for most space grids. Often a direct comparison of like with like is not made. For instance, increased frame-spacing in a portal framed structure will usually require additional or heavier purlins to support the roof decking and secondary steelwork may be necessary to carry services and equipment, neither of which may be needed if a space grid were used instead.

Regular geometry

Although the regular geometry of space grids is generally cited as one of their appealing features, to some eyes they can appear very 'busy'. In real buildings they are rarely seen in plan or in true elevation (as they generally appear on the architect's drawings) but more typically they are viewed from quite close up and in perspective. Consequently, the regular nature of the geometry is lost and at some viewing angles, the 'lightweight' structure can appear to be very dense indeed. The upper and lower grid size, the grid depth, as well as the grid configuration, can have a considerable influence on the perceived density of the double-layer structure. These factors are discussed in more detail later in this chapter.

Erection time

Again, this is a topic that also appears under the list of advantages. However, another common criticism of space grids is that the number and complexity of joints can lead to longer erection times on site. The erection time obviously depends on the system being used for a particular application as well as other factors such as the chosen grid module. Designing the grid to contain the most practical minimum number of nodes is good practice as they are usually the most expensive components. This leads to economy of material costs and faster erection times.

Fire protection

Space grids are mainly used in roof construction where, depending on the materials involved, nominal or no fire

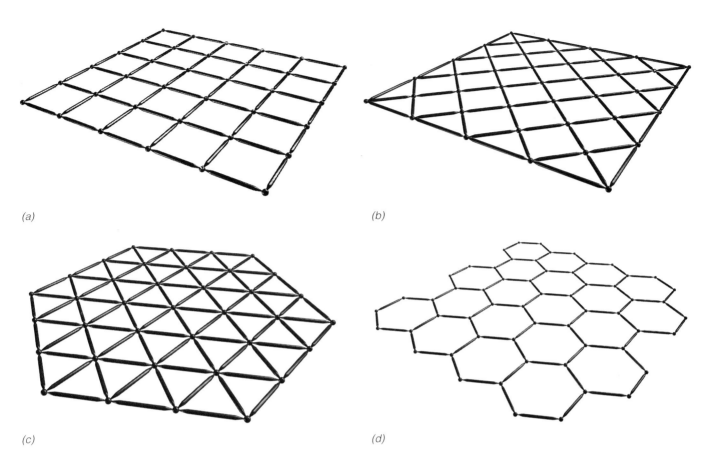

(a)

(b)

(c)

(d)

2.9
Tessellations of a flat plane with regular (a) squares, (b) rotated squares, (c) triangles and (d) hexagons (Drawing by Graeme Barker © John Chilton)

resistance is normally required. However, when they are used to support floors, some form of protection is usually demanded to provide the necessary fire resistance, if they are exposed. This protection is difficult to achieve economically due to the high number and relatively large surface area of the space grid elements, but intumescent coatings can be applied. The effect of fire on space grids is considered in more detail in Chapter 4.

Grid configurations

There are many possible ways of dividing a flat plane using a grid of lines connecting points in a regular or irregular pattern but this may produce considerable variation in the length of the lines and the angles between them. In modular structural systems such as single or double-layer grids it is normally considered advantageous if, in any particular structure, the number of different member lengths can be limited and connection angles at the joints standardized. However, with modern computer controlled cutting, drilling and machining equipment, it is now almost as simple to produce members

with many different lengths and nodes with many different connection angles without excessive cost penalty. Until recently, therefore, regular patterns were usually adopted for both the upper and lower layers of space grids. This approach can be rather restrictive as there are only three regular polygons (i.e. polygons with all sides of equal length) that can be used exclusively to completely fill a plane. These are the equilateral triangle, square and hexagon. The regular plane tessellations are shown in Figure 2.9(a)–(d) and these form the most common chord configurations.

Using square configurations the grid lines can be parallel to the edges of the grid (Figure 2.9(a)) or set on the diagonal, usually at 45° to the edges (Figure 2.9(b)). Both of these are described as two-way grids as they have members orientated in only two directions. However, plane grids of triangles and hexagons produce three-way grids with members orientated in three directions (Figure 2.9(c) and (d)). More complex grid geometries may be produced by combining the regular polygons or by using them in combination with other polygonal shapes (e.g. triangles and squares, triangles and hexagons, squares and octagons).

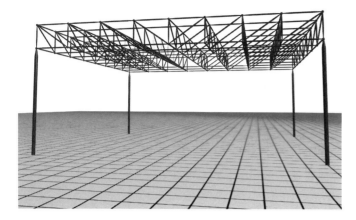

2.10
Square on square grid configuration (Drawing by Graeme Barker © John Chilton)

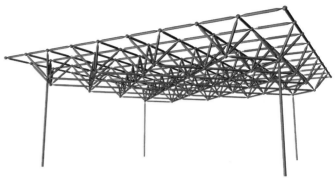

2.12
Square on diagonal square grid configuration (Drawing by Graeme Barker © John Chilton)

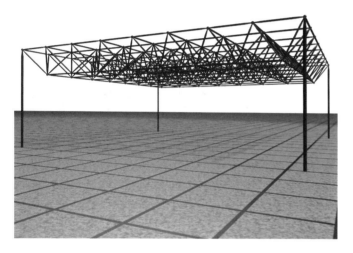

2.11
Square on square offset grid configuration (Drawing by Graeme Barker © John Chilton)

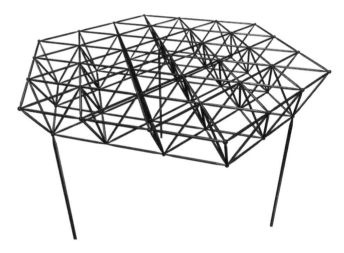

2.13
Triangle on triangle offset grid configuration (Drawing by Graeme Barker © John Chilton)

Double-layer space grid structures, where two plane grids are separated by web members, do not necessarily have to have the same pattern or orientation in the upper and lower grids. In practice, for reasons of cost and facility of connection of web members, the number of common configurations is usually quite limited.

In the description of the more common forms of double-layer grid configurations that follows, the reference to square grids also encompasses rectangular grids with different spacing in each direction, as well as the possibility of rhombic grids:

1   Square on square: where the upper chord grid is directly above the lower chord grid and the web members connect the layers in the vertical plane between the upper and lower grids. When viewed in plan only the top square grid is seen (see Figure 2.10).

2   Square on square offset: where the top chord grid is offset, usually by half a grid square in both directions, relative to the lower chord grid. In this configuration the web members connect the intersection points in the upper grid with the adjacent intersections in the lower grid and a continuum of tetrahedral and half-octahedral cells is generated (see Figure 2.11). This is the most commonly used configuration.

3   Square on diagonal square: where the lower chord grid is set at 45° to, and is usually at a greater spacing than, the top chord grid. Again the web members connect the intersection points on the top and bottom grids (see Figure 2.12). A further alternative version of this grid configuration is diagonal on square where the upper grid is at 45° to the lines of support and the lower grid is parallel to the supports.

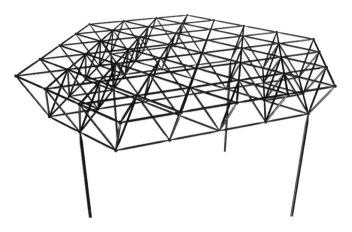

2.14
Triangle on hexagon grid configuration (Drawing by Graeme Barker © John Chilton)

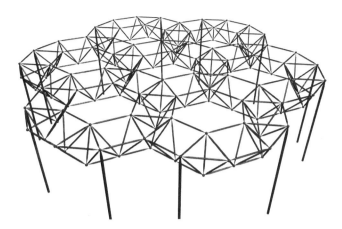

2.16
Non-regular grid for upper and lower chords (Drawing by Graeme Barker © John Chilton)

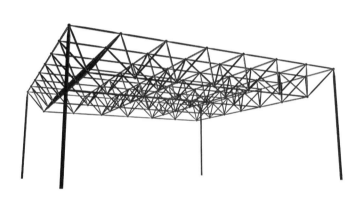

2.15
Sparse modular grid with modules omitted on a chequer-board pattern to reduce its self-weight (Drawing by Graeme Barker © John Chilton)

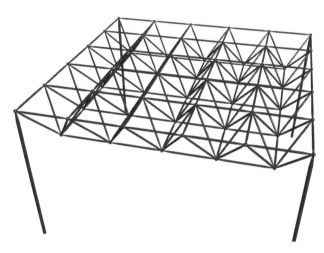

2.17
Visual effect of the variation in grid spacing node density and web inclination – typical space grid (Drawing by Graeme Barker © John Chilton)

4 Triangle on triangle offset: where both chord grids are triangular but the intersections in the lower grid occur below the centres of alternate triangles in the upper grid. In this case also, the web members connect the intersection points on the top grid with the adjacent intersections in the lower grid (see Figure 2.13).

5 Triangle on hexagon: where the upper (denser) grid is triangular and the lower (more open) grid is hexagonal due to removal of some lower chord and web elements from the triangle on triangle grid described in 4 above (see Figure 2.14).

More open grid geometries are often possible in the lower layer of a double-layer grid because the members are normally in tension (i.e. not subject to member buckling). The lower (tension) chords may, therefore, be longer than the upper (compression) members even though the forces within them may be greater. In modular space grid systems, for the same reason, complete modules can sometimes be omitted in a regular pattern to produce a more open geometry and thus to reduce the self-weight of the structure. Figure 2.15 shows a grid where pyramidal modules have been removed on a chequer-board pattern. This may be compared with the full grid of Figure 2.11. An open grid with a non-regular tessellation is shown in Figure 2.16. Such economies are not always feasible and before removing modules or reducing the density of the lower chord grid, the effect of the disposition of grid supports and the degree of load reversal that may occur due to wind action should be assessed. Space grid roofs are usually flat or of low pitch and the action of a wind passing over the building causes negative pressure or suction over the whole roof area.

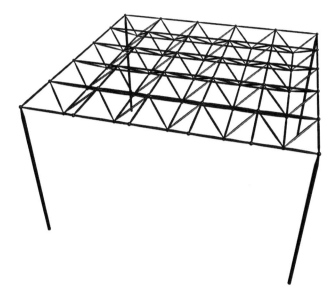

2.18
Visual effect of the variation in grid spacing node density and web inclination – shallow space grid with web members at an inefficient angle (Drawing by Graeme Barker © John Chilton)

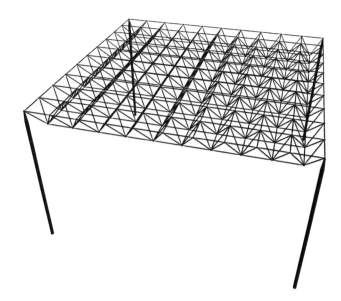

2.19
Visual effect of the variation in grid spacing node density and web inclination – shallow space grid with high density of nodes and members (Drawing by Graeme Barker © John Chilton)

When there are also large openings in the building (e.g. aircraft hangar doors) large internal pressures may also be generated by a strong wind blowing directly into the opening. The combined external suction and internal pressure act in the same direction, opposing and sometimes exceeding the gravity loads on the roof. When the gravity loads are exceeded, the net loading on the roof is upwards, reversing the forces generated in the space grid by loads such as self-weight and snow. Thus members usually in tension may have to resist compression under wind action and this may be the critical design load for the chords of the lower grid.

Choice of grid configuration and the depth between the chord layers will affect the economy of the space grid. For space trusses and frames constructed from pre-fabricated modules there is often less freedom to vary the grid geometry without cost penalty as modules will usually be produced only in a limited number of standard sizes and depths. For bar- and node-type space trusses, the member lengths can be varied at will and there is usually a range of node sizes and strengths to choose from. Hence, the geometrical possibilities are almost limitless. However, the node joints are normally the most expensive components, therefore, the more nodes that there are in a given plan area the higher the material cost is likely to be. Also, with more nodes in the structure, erection times are increased and, thus, overall construction costs will be higher. Increasing the upper and lower grid spacing reduces the number of joints for a given plan area but there may be disadvantages. For example, in space trusses with a larger upper and lower

grid spacing, the depth between the two grid layers may have to be increased to accommodate the inclined web members at an appropriate angle – usually between 30° and 70° to the horizontal chords – and individual members will inevitably be longer. When the longer members are subject to compressive forces, they may need to be larger in cross-section or wall thickness to avoid buckling if they are laterally unrestrained. Consequently, the space truss may become heavier and more costly.

The visual effect of these variations can be seen in Figures 2.17 to 2.20 which illustrate structures of the same span but with different grid densities and depth. A grid of typical proportion is shown in Figure 2.17 and a grid of similar density but reduced depth is shown in Figure 2.18. The latter appears more open but chord and web elements would need to be bigger because of the reduced structural depth. Figures 2.19 and 2.20 show the same span with a grid spacing half that of Figures 2.17 and 2.18 and different depths. The structures seem much denser and the number of joints and members has increased dramatically.

Defining the grid

The behaviour of space grid structures is analogous to that of flat plates and before the widespread availability of fast digital computing and suitable three-dimensional structural analysis software, the forces within space grids were determined using approximate hand calculation based on plate theory. Computer technology has moved quickly during the 1980s and 1990s: processing speed

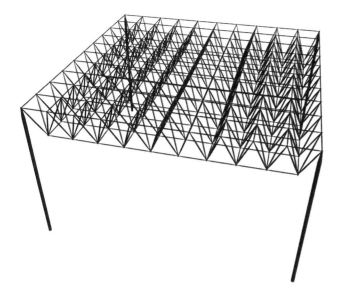

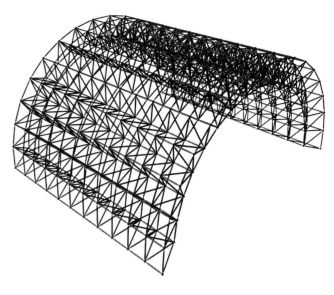

2.20
Visual effect of the variation in grid spacing node density and web inclination – deep space grid with close grid spacing, high density of nodes and members (Drawing by Graeme Barker © John Chilton)

2.21
Double-layer barrel vault space grid (Drawing by Graeme Barker © John Chilton)

has increased dramatically and memory and storage capacities have expanded rapidly whilst their cost has decreased. Consequently, it is now possible to analyse many space grids, modelled as individual bar and node structures, on a desktop (or even notebook) computer in a few hours or even minutes depending on the size and complexity of the configuration and loading. To carry out the analysis it is necessary to define the structure unambiguously by specifying the positions of the nodes (for instance by using Cartesian coordinates relative to three mutually perpendicular axes). Also the location, orientation and physical properties of each member, the type of connection between bars and nodes ('pinned', fully rigid or semi-rigid joints) and the position and degree of restraint for each support must be stipulated. Subsequently, a series of load cases can be defined for the grid, including its self-weight, imposed loads such as cladding and installed services, the loads imposed in use such as floor loads, snow loads, wind loads and the effect of temperature changes. In fact, defining the disposition of the separate parts of a space grid – its configuration – is often the most time-consuming aspect of performing an analysis. However, space grid manufacturers usually have pre-processing computer programs, particular to their product, to automatically generate node coordinates, member lists and the description of which members are connected to which nodes, for simple grids.

Once a numerical description of the configuration of a space grid structure has been established, further processing can be used to create more complex structural forms. Configuration processing, as this is called, may

use additional computer programs developed by manufacturers specifically for their products, or may use programs such as Formian, based on Formex algebra developed by Professor H. Nooshin at the University of Surrey, Guildford, UK.[4] Further advances in the generation of data to define grid configurations have evolved from the exchange of data between computer-aided design (CAD) software, used for engineering and architectural drawings, and structural analysis software.

Complex geometries

As the majority of space grids are constructed as flat (or near flat) planes, it is sometimes assumed that they may only be used in such circumstances. However, space grids are not limited to planar surfaces and more complex geometries such as barrel vaults, domes, hyperbolic paraboloids or even free-form surfaces may be generated. These are usually formed from two parallel single- or double-curved surfaces, which define the upper and lower chord layers, separated by a constant dimension. If required, the two curved surfaces can be different, so that the distance between the upper and lower chord layers varies across the space grid. Figures 2.21 shows a space grid barrel vault and Figure 2.22 (a) and (b) show the plan and three-dimensional view of the space grid roof of the Anoeta Stadium, San Sebastián, Spain. Some built examples are described in Chapter 5 (for example, the Sant Jordi Sports Palace, Palafolls Sports Hall and Bentall Centre).

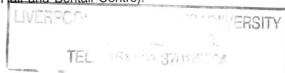

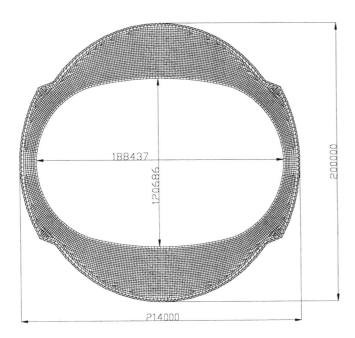

2.22 (a)
Plan of wave form space grid roof, Anoeta Stadium, San Sebastián, Spain (Courtesy Orona S. Coop., San Sebastián).

Support locations

The choice of the most advantageous support locations for the space grid will, of course, depend on the plan form of the structure and architectural considerations. Nevertheless, the positions chosen may have a significant influence on the structural efficiency. Depending on the grid configuration, it is possible to support either top or bottom node joints. In the former case, the web members immediately adjacent to the supports will usually be in tension and in the later case in compression. For a grid supported at the lower nodes in only a few loca-

tions, it may result that the web members around each support are the most critical of the whole structure and failure of one compression diagonal may result in progressive collapse of the whole structure. For this reason, the potential for collapse of the grid can be reduced if it is supported at the upper nodes, maintaining the most heavily loaded diagonals in tension, although the supporting columns, being longer, then themselves become more vulnerable to buckling failure.

Some alternative support positions for a uniformly loaded, square plan, square on square offset grid roof structure, supported at the upper node joints, are shown in Figures 2.23 to 2.26. Intuitively, it can be appreciated that the provision of supports at each node along the full perimeter (Figure 2.23), is likely to be a more efficient arrangement for the space grid, than having supports only at the corner nodes (Figure 2.24). With full edge support, the applied loads have a shorter load path to the ground although, because of the greater number of columns, additional foundation costs may be incurred. For similar space grids subject to the same loading, the maximum member forces are lowest in the fully edge-supported case and the maximum vertical deflections are also much smaller. However, slightly modifying the corner-supported condition, with the introduction of one or more intermediate supports along each edge (Figure 2.25) will greatly improve the space grid performance at little extra cost for columns and foundations. With this support configuration an efficient space grid structure is achieved, whilst keeping the number of columns to a sensible minimum.

Single columns located at the middle of each side (Figure 2.26) may also produce an efficient support system. In this case, the corners of the space grid are cantilevered and counterbalance the central area; thus the vertical deflections and the member forces at the centre are reduced. Most of the bottom chord members will be in compression and most of the top chords in tension.

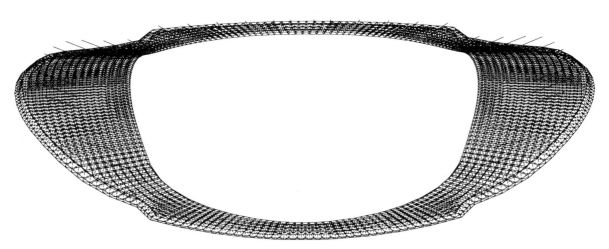

2.22 (b)
Three-dimensional view of wave form space grid roof, Anoeta Stadium, San Sebastián, Spain (Courtesy Orona S. Coop., San Sebastián)

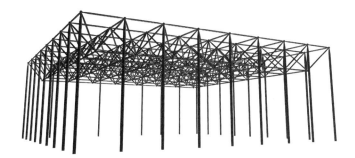

2.23
Square on square offset grid with full edge node support (Drawing by Graeme Barker © John Chilton)

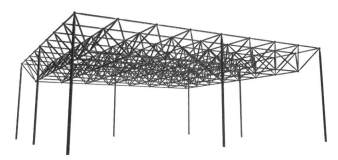

2.25
Square on square offset grid with corner and intermediate edge node support (Drawing by Graeme Barker © John Chilton)

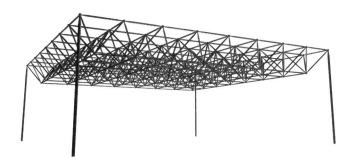

2.24
Square on square offset grid with corner support only (Drawing by Graeme Barker © John Chilton)

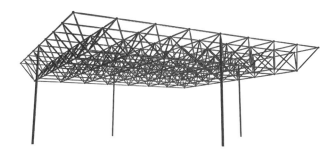

2.26
Square on square offset grid with mid-side support only (Drawing by Graeme Barker © John Chilton)

Maximum vertical deflections and chord forces can be reduced still further, in most of the above cases, if the supports are located slightly inward from the edges of the space grid so that a short cantilever is produced around the whole structure. Although this may introduce columns into the main volume of the building, it can be advantageous architecturally, giving the opportunity to define circulation spaces around the periphery behind fully glazed, column-free elevations or a canopy to provide shelter or shading around the full building perimeter if desired. With some space truss systems the ability to cantilever is limited as they are not usually designed to accept large compressive forces in the lower grid (for example, the Space Deck pyramidal modules are generally connected in the lower grid by slender rods that have a relatively low compression resistance). These cantilevered support configurations should, therefore, be used with care. With excessive length of cantilever, the limiting vertical deflections at the perimeter, under variations in load, may become the critical design case.

In most books and product literature about space grids, it is usual to show supports on a uniform grid and, because of this, it is commonly assumed that space grids must be supported in such a regular manner. None the less, as long as sufficient supports are provided, it is possible to place them under any node within the grid (see Figure 2.27). For an irregular plan form, the cost of the structure will only be increased marginally if supports are not on a rigidly defined grid pattern.

'Tree' supports

Up to this point it has been assumed that the grid is supported at discrete nodes along its edges or at individual internal columns. However, an alternative method of reducing both maximum vertical deflections and member forces in the space grid is to use 'tree' supports instead of individual columns. This is commonly achieved by providing a square-based inverted pyramid of 'branches' at each support location. These may be composed of space truss members using the standard joints or specially fabricated elements. As the grid is supported on several nodes at each column location, the forces in the adjacent web bracing members are less than they would have been with the grid supported on simple columns. Effectively, the span of the space grid is reduced. Tree supports can also be used to architectural effect (Figure 2.28) as they replicate the flow of forces from the space grid into the supporting columns. With

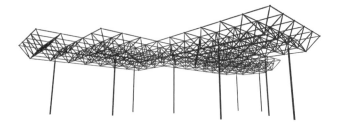

2.27
Square on square offset grid of variable plan form supported on columns at irregular centres (Drawing by Graeme Barker © John Chilton)

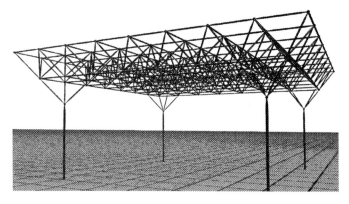

2.28
Tree supports mimicking the flow of forces to the column base (Drawing by Graeme Barker © John Chilton)

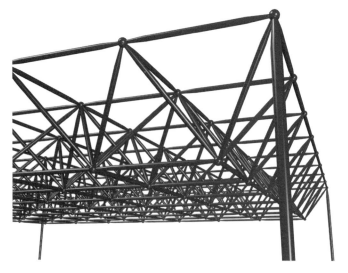

2.29
Cornice edge profile (Drawing by Graeme Barker © John Chilton)

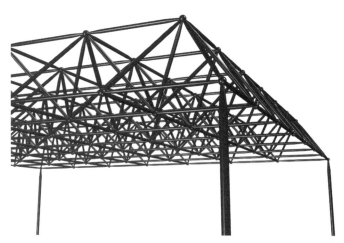

2.30
Mansard edge profile (Drawing by Graeme Barker © John Chilton)

multi-span space grids, the economy derived from using tree form columns is increased.

Edge profiles

From the outside of a building having a space grid roof, it is often only the eave profile that gives any clue as to the form of the structure within. There are three common edge profiles that derive from the inherent geometry of space grids. Two alternatives result from the geometry of square on square offset space trusses. In one case, the top chord grid extends beyond the bottom chord grid and the web bracing between the two plane grids generates an inclined cornice edge profile (Figure 2.29). On the other hand, if the lower grid extends beyond the upper grid, the bracing forms a mansard edge (Figure 2.30). Other space grids such as systems of intersecting planar trusses and the CUBIC Space Frame lend

themselves to the use of vertical edge profiles (Figure 2.31). A vertical edge can also be achieved with standard space trusses by using a half-bay at the edges. The architect is not limited to these profiles as special edge details (Figure 2.32) can be manufactured to order and fixed to the standard space grid nodes or modules.

Multi-layer space grids

Where a flat double-layer space truss is spanning a considerable distance (over, say, 100 m) and/or the applied loads are particularly heavy, it becomes necessary to greatly increase the depth between the upper and lower grids, to limit the maximum deflection or resist high bending moments. As the grid depth is increased, either the angle of the diagonal bracing becomes more vertical and/or the grid spacing of the two horizontal layers must also be increased. Eventually the depth and grid spacing

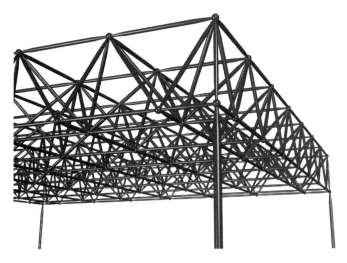

2.31
Square edge profile (Drawing by Graeme Barker © John Chilton)

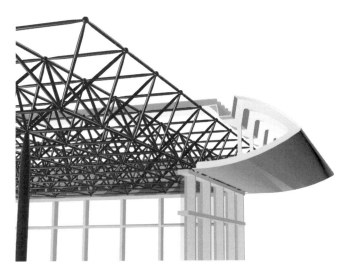

2.32
Special edge profile (Drawing by Graeme Barker © John Chilton)

may be enlarged to such an extent that the compression members (the top chords and many web bracing elements) become excessively long. Long, highly loaded compression elements tend to be large in diameter with thick walls. Thus they are heavy and uneconomical, contrary to the philosophy of lightness and economy of materials behind the use of space grids. In such situations it is possible to introduce an intermediate horizontal grid between the normal upper and lower chord layers. This additional layer allows the grid spacing of both outer layers to be reduced. Consequently, the length of the top compression chord members and the unrestrained length of the web compression members are reduced, with an appropriate reduction in member cross-section. A further benefit is that the horizontal grid layers can each have different configurations so that the most efficient chord layout may be selected.

The intermediate layer is usually at or near the mid-depth of the grid, and in this location it is only lightly stressed (by analogy with the material at the mid-depth or neutral axis of a solid beam) and can therefore be composed of lightweight elements and/or use a sparse grid configuration. Although the additional layer increases the number of bars and nodes in the space truss structure, it allows lighter compression members to be used. The extra cost of the additional lightly stressed bars and nodes is presumed to be less than the cost of the materials saved from the other components.

Multi-layer grids may also be used when only moderate distances are to be spanned by lightweight space truss systems that use cold-formed steel sections of limited strength in compression. In this case, there are often standard member lengths and longer span structures are

produced by assembling three (or more) layers from the regular kit of parts. A quite recent example of a deep three-layer Mero space truss, the roof of the National Indoor Arena for Sport, constructed in 1990, in Birmingham, UK, is described in detail in Chapter 5.

Over the years, there has been much interest among architects in the exploitation of multi-layer grids in the urban environment. Proposals have been made for the construction of gigantic space truss mega-cities in which the interstices of the multi-layer grid are inhabited by the citizens of the twenty-first century and beyond. These concepts have yet to be realized, despite the current availability of the necessary technology that has to some extent already been proven in the harsh environment of deep-sea oil rig construction. Inhabited space grids on both the small and large scale are reviewed in Chapter 7.

Notes

1　Wester, T. (1983). *Structural Order in Space: The Plate-Lattice Dualism.* Royal Academy of Fine Arts, School of Architecture, Copenhagen.

2　Smith, E. A. and Epstein, H. I. (1980). Hartford Coliseum roof collapse: structural collapse sequence and lessons learned. *Civil Engineering – ASCE,* April, pp. 59–62.

3　Thornton, C. H. and Lew, P. I. (1984). Investigation of the causes of Hartford Coliseum collapse. In *Third International Conference on Space Structures* (H. Nooshin, ed.) pp. 636–41, Elsevier.

4　Nooshin, H. and Disney, P. L. (1997). *Formian 2.* Multi-Science.

3 Materials and systems

In this chapter, the materials that are used for space grid construction are briefly reviewed, various space grid types are categorized and representative commercial systems are described for each category. As this book is intended to present a general overview of space grid structures and is not meant to be a design manual, detailed material specifications are not included. To categorize the bar and node type space grids that form the majority of available systems, they are grouped according to the type of node joint that is used.

Materials for space grids

Most space grid systems for building structures are manufactured from steel, although aluminium has been used fairly extensively and timber, concrete and reinforced plastics have also been used. More exotically, experimental structures using bamboo poles[1] have been investigated and glass has also been incorporated into space trusses but only in sculptural objects.

High yield and mild steel tubes and sections, elements cold-formed from steel strip and castings from spheroidal graphite iron are used. These are usually galvanized and/or painted (known as the duplex system if both are used). Alternatively, aluminium alloy nodes and members may be employed. Although the typical density of aluminium alloy (around 2700 kg/m^3) is only approximately one third that of steel (7865 kg/m^3), it also has a lower modulus of elasticity, or Young's Modulus ($E_{aluminium}$ = 70 000 N/mm^2 whilst E_{steel} = 205 000 N/mm^2). The modulus of elasticity of the components of a structure govern its overall deflection. Therefore, because of the relative moduli of elasticity, for an aluminium alloy space grid of approximately equivalent load capacity to a steel space grid with equal span and imposed loading, the resulting aluminium structure may be lighter, unless deflections are critical. In which case, additional material may be required to keep deflections within acceptable limits. As the material cost for aluminium alloy is greater than that of steel the choice of material will depend very much on individual circumstances. The coefficients of thermal expansion for steel and aluminium are 0.000012 /°C and 0.000024 /°C respectively, thus aluminium structures require more allowance to be made for thermal movements caused by normal ambient temperature changes (see Chapter 4). Greater care is required to weld aluminium than steel and as many space grid systems involve at least some welding in their manufacture, steel is the most commonly used material for the members. Many systems use cast steel for end connectors and node joints.

Timber is also used in space trusses in the form of roundwood poles, solid sawn timber and in the refined form of glued laminated timber. As with most timber structures, one of the principal design considerations is the transfer of forces (particularly tensile forces) between members at the joints. Because of the high axial forces experienced by space grid members, individual members usually have metal inserts introduced at the ends so that the forces can be transferred over a greater length of the member. These metal inserts are connected to metal nodes (as in the Mero Holz system) or directly to each other (as in systems designed by Pieter Huybers at TU Delft, described in detail in Chapter 5).

Concrete space grids, although much heavier (both visually and in actual weight) can become an economic proposition in countries where steel is relatively scarce and expensive and labour is cheap. This is often the case in developing nations. For example, large reinforced concrete space truss pavilions were built for a permanent trade fair site at New Delhi, India, in 1982 where five pyramidal pavilions were constructed from in situ reinforced concrete using multi-layer grids of octahedral and tetrahedral geometry.[2,3]

Some experimental space grid structures have been made using reinforced plastics, the most common being glass reinforced polyester (GRP). However, the use of these materials is still in its infancy. Although having a more favourable strength to weight ratio than many traditional structural materials, reinforced polymers display characteristics such as higher coefficient of thermal expansion, higher modulus of elasticity, deterioration with exposure to ultraviolet light and creep due to the viscoelastic nature of the polymers used to bond the fibres that can detract from their utility for many structures.

Space grid systems

Literally hundreds of different space grid systems have been developed since they were first introduced commercially over fifty years ago. Throughout the world new systems are brought on to the market almost every year.

Of these, some are used only once or last for only a few projects before their demise. Practically all are space trusses with diagonal web bracing between the chord layers.

Commercial space grid systems can generally be divided into three types: those that are assembled from discrete members running between node joints (often referred to as 'piece-small' systems), those that are assembled using continuous chords and those that are assembled from factory prefabricated modules. In the following sections, examples taken from some of the many systems currently available commercially are used to illustrate the variety of products at the disposal of the designer. Some manufacturers market more than one system, in which case the most commonly used of their systems is described in the appropriate category. Addresses of a selection of space grid manufacturers, including those mentioned in this chapter, are given in Appendix 2.

'Piece-small' systems

The 'piece-small' systems primarily differ in the jointing method. Most use circular or square hollow tube members because of their better performance in resisting the forces present in space trusses (normally pure axial tension or compression, with only secondary bending effects). Tubular members are also considered to have a superior aesthetic appearance. To architects this is especially important, as space grids are normally left exposed to view so that the building's users can appreciate the pattern of the regular grid geometry. The main difference between tubular members in the alternative systems is the detailing of their ends for connection to the nodes. In most types there is some addition to the basic tubular member. For instance, in the Mero KK system in the form of a cone, in the Nodus system as solid ribbed castings or in the KT Space Truss as capping and jointing plates. These additions are welded to the ends of the pre-cut tubular members. In other systems the tube itself is modified at the ends, usually by flattening with a plain or crimped profile (e.g. Triodetic). There are some lightweight systems such as Unistrut/Moduspan that use cold-formed channel section members that are bent to shape and have bolt holes punched at the ends.

The distinguishing features of the 'piece-small' systems are the shape of the nodes and method of member connection at those nodes. The tremendous variety of node jointing systems (e.g. 'ball' joints, hollow spheres, profiled plates, etc.), illustrates the difficulty of achieving a simple, aesthetically pleasing joint. Joop Gerrits of TU Delft has carried out a detailed study of the morphology of the available node jointing systems in which he classified them by node type.[4] The categorization of various 'piece-small' space truss systems used here is based on his proposals with, where necessary, further subdivision of the categories. These are as follows:

1 Spherical nodes:
   (a) solid
   (b) hollow.
2 Cylindrical.
3 Prismatic.
4 Plates.
5 'Nodeless'.

Spherical nodes

Nodes based on a sphere are probably the most aesthetically pleasing. Depending on the form of connection of the adjacent members, they can provide a very clear and uncluttered appearance to the space grid. The class, which is taken to include 'pure' and faceted spheres, can be further divided into solid and hollow types.

3.1
Typical node of tubular bamboo stem as studied by Dr Max Mengeringhausen (Photograph: John Chilton)

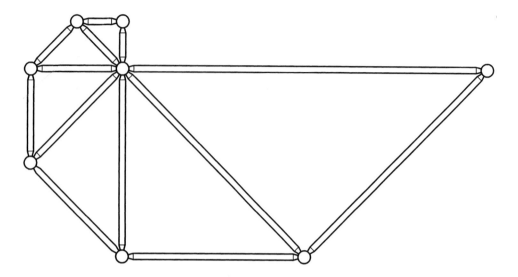

3.2(a)
Comparison of a modular structural system and growth in nature: Mero members with a factor of √2 between sequential sizes radiating from a central node (Drawing: John Chilton)

3.2(b)
Comparison of a modular structural system and growth in nature: section through a Nautilus shell (Photograph: John Chilton)

Solid spherical nodes

Solid cast steel spheres are drilled with threaded holes at the appropriate angle for connection of the adjacent members and are machined to provide appropriate bearing surfaces. The attachment of each member is usually achieved with a single bolt on its central axis. In some systems the ends of the members come into direct contact with the nodes, whilst in others the axial forces are transmitted solely through the connecting bolts. The representative systems described in this section are (Mero KK, Germany, and Orona SEO, Spain).

MERO KK

The *Mero KK* space truss system, the first commercially available, is still considered to be one of the most elegant solutions for the construction of space grid structures. The elegance and simplicity of the Mero system

means that it is not only used in buildings but also for shop displays and exhibition stands using lightweight materials. Circular tube members are connected to cast 'ball' joints at the nodes by a single concealed bolt for each tube. The concept developed from studies of natural structures, carried out in the 1930s, by the system's originator, Dr Max Mengeringhausen. His investigation of slender but strong natural structures such as wheat stalks and bamboo stems (Figure 3.1) revealed how they derive their strength from the use of tubular cross-sections stabilized by nodes at regular intervals along their length. The name Mero, by which the system is now well known, derives from an abbreviation of the original name Mengeringhausen Rohrbauweise.

Initially conceived as a system based on a fixed module, the Mero space truss had a universal node connector and a series of standard length members, starting at 1 m and progressing with a factor of √2 between

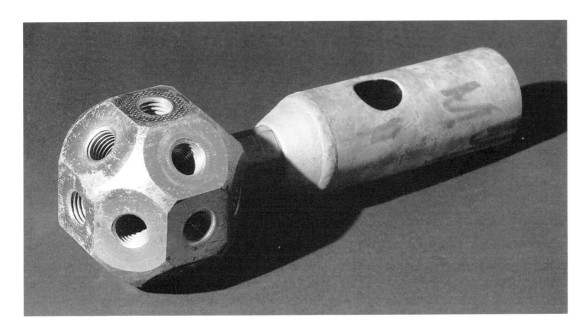

3.3
Standard Mero KK node with 18 threaded holes and machined bearing surfaces at angles of 45°, 60° and 90° relative to each other (Photograph: Glyn Halls)

sequential sizes (i.e 1.0, 1.41, 2.0, 2.82 m ... etc.). The growth of member lengths drawn radiating from a central node creates a spiral form (Figure 3.2(a)) that, as Mengeringhausen pointed out, echoes the spiral growth of the Nautilus shell (Figure 3.2(b)). However, there are now several different types of node connector available from Mero for a range of applications, in single and double-layer space grids and members are fabricated to any required length. The original 'ball' joint, now known as the KK system, is a hot-forged solid steel sphere finished with 18 threaded holes and machined bearing sur-

faces at angles of 45°, 60° and 90° relative to each other (see Figure 3.3). Standard nodes are produced in bulk in a range of sizes suitable for the transmission of member forces of different magnitude. Stock nodes, with fewer holes, are also produced for common applications such as standard support nodes.

With modern computer numerically controlled precision drilling techniques, holes may now be drilled at almost any required angle rather than only at the standard angles, although there is a minimum angle of 35° specified between adjacent holes. This ability to drill and

3.4
Mero standard member tapered cone sections welded to each end (complete with connection bolt and sleeve) (Photograph: John Chilton)

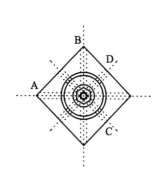

*3.5
Mero Holz metal
insert to the ends of
laminated timber
members (Redrawn
from Mero technical
literature: John
Chilton)*

tap threaded holes at non-standard angles gives the designer much greater flexibility in selecting the geometry of the space grid.

Standard members are circular hollow steel (or aluminium) tubes that have tapered cone sections welded to each end (see Figure 3.4). Integral with each cone there is a connection bolt and a sleeve with slotted hole and pin to allow the bolt to be rotated and to indicate when it has been fully tightened. For corrosion protection the tubes are galvanized inside and out, and finishes include a polyester powder-coated or two-part urethane wet process. The Mero Holz system uses laminated timber members that have short tubular steel inserts at the ends for connection to the nodes (see Figure 3.5).

The size of the connecting bolt between tubes and nodes depends on the forces to be transmitted. Tension forces have to be transmitted from the member end cone to the bolt by the internal bearing surface of the cone, then through the bolt in tension to the threads in the node. Compression forces, however, are transmitted through the sleeve surrounding the connecting bolt by direct contact of machined bearing faces and the bolt effectively only locates the member in the correct position on the node. The form of the spherical joint is such that the line of action of all member forces intersect at the centre of the node so there are no eccentricities to induce bending in the tubes that carry primarily axial tension and compression forces. Manufacturer's tables are available to show the relationship between node, tube and connecting bolt capacities.

Generally Mero space trusses are supported using a variation of the standard node connector, depending on the type of restraint required. Figure 4.3, in the following chapter, shows one of the sliding bearings support-

ing the Mero space truss roof at the National Indoor Arena for Sport, Birmingham, UK.

As one would expect for a system has been in use for over fifty years, there are, worldwide, thousands of examples of Mero space grids, both large and small. Nowadays, there are alternative node joints and member cross-sections to suit various applications such as direct glazing of single-layer dome grids. However, single-layer grids, and therefore many of these new applications, are beyond the scope of this study which is primarily concerned with double or multi-layer grids. One of the most dramatic uses of the Mero system is for the grandstand roofs at the stadium in Split (see the plan and section shown in Figure 3.6). Constructed in 1978, in former Yugoslavia (now Croatia), these roofs are segments of a 452 m diameter cylinder inclined at 11.2° to the horizontal. The free edge spans 215 m with an arc length of 220 m (Figure 3.7). Together the two areas of space grid cover approximately 13 600 m² with a double-layer square on square offset system, having grid dimensions of 3.0 × 3.0 m, a structural depth of 2.3 m and a maximum cantilever of 45 m from the elliptical perimeter of the stadium. The two areas of roof are symmetrical only about the long axis of the stadium; thus there are 12 832 members of 1143 different types and 3460 nodes of 1678 types (839 configurations mirrored because of the symmetry). Translucent polycarbonate barrel-vaulted ribs run parallel to the top chords of the space grid from the perimeter to the free edge, with secondary framing supported only at the nodes.

There are now worldwide many space truss systems based on the concept of cast ball joints and tubular members. For instance, the 'TM Truss' produced by Taiyo Kogyo Co. in Japan, and 'ABBA Space' produced by ABBA Space Structures in South Africa. The variation is

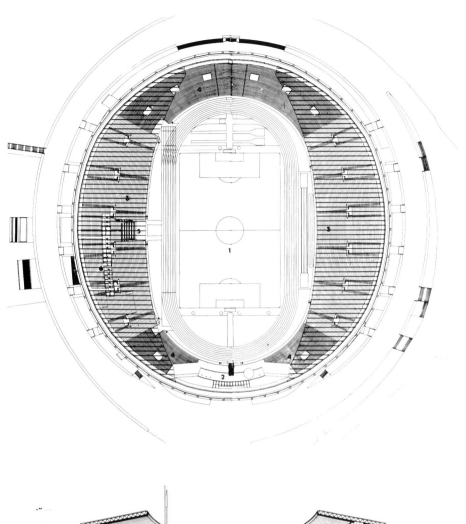

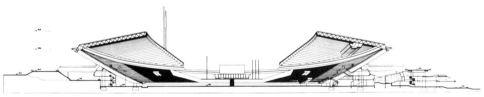

3.6
Plan and section of
the Mero grandstand
roofs at the stadium
in Split, in former
Yugoslavia (now
Croatia). These roofs
are segments of a
452 m diameter
cylinder inclined at
11.2° to the horizontal
(Courtesy Mero)

3.7
Mero grandstand
roofs at the stadium
in Split, Croatia with a
free edge spanning
215 m with an arc
length of 220 m
(Photograph courtesy
R. E. McConnel)

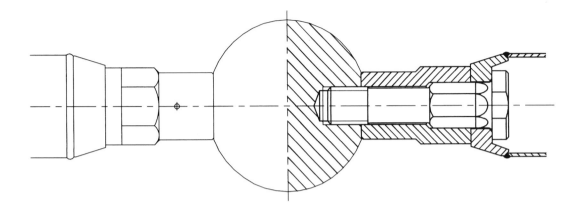

3.8
Section through a typical Orona SEO space grid joint (Courtesy Orona S. Coop., San Sebastián, Spain)

mainly in the method of connection between the tube ends and the ball joints, although some systems are very close to the original Mero system.

ORONA SEO

The *Orona SEO* space grid manufactured by Orona S. Coop., San Sebastián, Spain, is a ball and tube system that was introduced in the 1980s and used for the roof of the Sant Jordi Sports Palace, constructed in Barcelona for the 1992 Olympics.

In the SEO system, the solid forged spherical joint has a number of threaded holes, drilled according to the node location within the grid and the geometry of the connecting members. The number and position of the holes is limited only by the interference of adjacent connected bars. Truncated conical end pieces are welded to the normally cold-formed, longitudinally welded, steel tube members. The cones hold the connecting bolt which has a hexagonal shank for the section near to the head and a normal plain/threaded section for the rest of the bolt shank (see the typical section shown in Figure 3.8). A capping sleeve, that maintains the correct distance between the end of the member and the node, surrounds the hexagonal and the plain shank section of the bolt. The inner profile of the sleeve follows that of the bolt and the outer profile also has hexagonal and plain sections. To tighten the bolt, the hexagonal part of the sleeve is rotated so that the threaded length of the bolt enters the node. This connection system allows any bar to be removed easily from a completed grid at any time. By unscrewing the sleeves at both ends of a member, the bolts retract inside the tube sufficiently to enable its removal and replacement. Thus damaged bars can be restored or it may be possible to increase the load capacity of a grid by upgrading the most critically loaded elements.

During manufacture, the tubular members are assembled complete with end cones, bolts and sleeves, on an adjustable bed, ready for welding. The overall length of the component is fixed on this bed by the correct posi-

tioning of the end bolts so that tolerances in the individual member parts do not lead to accumulated errors. Following welding the length of each bar has a tolerance of ± 0.5 mm. The threaded holes in the spherical nodes are drilled and machined by a purpose-designed robot that can be programmed manually, but is generally controlled by numerical data produced by post-processing of the structural analysis. A list of materials, node sizes and hole geometry, bars sizes and lengths is presented in a form that can be read by the numerical control (NC) machines.

Normally an electrostatic polyester powder-coating finish is applied to the tubes with a minimum thickness of 70 microns. This is oven cured at 210 °C for twenty minutes. A minimum surface treatment of degreasing and phosphating is applied prior to the application of the coating. Further pre-treatments such as mechanical brushing, shot-blasting and galvanizing may also be applied, depending on the degree of oxidation of the surface and the corrosion protection specified. The polyester finish has good impact and scratch resistance and produces a lacquer-like surface. For the small diameter spheres the same process as that used on the tubes can be applied, however, with large diameters the greater thickness of the node material creates problems. Therefore, the larger nodes are shot-blasted, primed and then finished with a two-coat epoxy or chlorinated rubber paint.

Hollow spherical nodes

Hollow spherical nodes are of two general types. Some are cast hollow as almost complete spheres and these are subsequently pierced by drilled or punched holes in predetermined locations (e.g. Spherobat, France; NS Truss, Japan; Tuball, Netherlands; Orbik, UK). Others are composed of two pressed steel approximate hemispheres with or without an intermediate central disc (e.g. SDC, France; Oktaplatte, Germany; Vestrut, Italy; Nodus, UK). In the former type, connecting bolts are introduced through an access hole and screwed from inside the sphere into the adjacent members. Subsequently the access hole may be closed with a cap. In the latter case, there are various means of connection of the members. For example, Vestrut uses two near hemispherical parts and intermediate plates to clamp solid 'T'-shaped connectors that are welded to the ends of the members.

NODUS

The *Nodus* system, a 'piece-small' space truss, was developed during the late 1960s by the Tubes Division of the British Steel Corporation and introduced commercially in the early 1970s. Since 1985, Nodus has been owned by Space Decks Ltd of Chard.

During development of the system, a series of standard joints were evolved. Samples of each size and type of joint were tested to failure, in purpose-designed testing rigs, at the British Steel Research Centre in Corby. Two series of tests were undertaken, the joints being modified after the first series in order to improve their performance. The second series confirmed the improvement and allowed strength design charts to be compiled. Following the laboratory tests a complete 30.5 by 30.5 m space grid 1.52 m deep was fabricated and assembled by an independent company to ascertain the ease of construction. A test load of 1.8 kN/m^2 (equivalent to the design dead load plus 1.5 times the design imposed load) was applied to the structure for twenty-four hours, in accordance with the then current British Standard for steel structures, BS 449. The residual strains measured after the test were well within the limits specified in the standard.

The Nodus joint (Figure 3.9) uses a relatively complex assembly of parts. Special cast steel end connectors are butt-welded to the chord and web bracing members in fabrication jigs, to ensure dimensional accuracy of the space truss components. The node itself is composed of two half-casings (one plain and one with lugs for attachment of the web bracing, Figure 3.10) and a spacing piece. Those are joined using a single high-strength friction grip bolt, nut and washer. As the bolt is tightened the ribbed end connectors of the chord members are clamped between the two half-casings. Web members are joined by steel pins through the forked end connectors of the bracing to the lugs on the node casing. Standard edge joints are also produced. Two configurations of lug are available, one for connection of the bracing members on the same grid lines as the chords and the other with the bracings oriented at 45° to the chord grid. The plain casing has a hexagonal recess to receive the bolt head so that it does not protrude above the level of the top chord members, thus enabling decking to be fixed directly to the chords where square hollow sections are used. Therefore, there can be a saving as secondary purlins may not then be required. A result of the joint configuration is that chord members can be considered

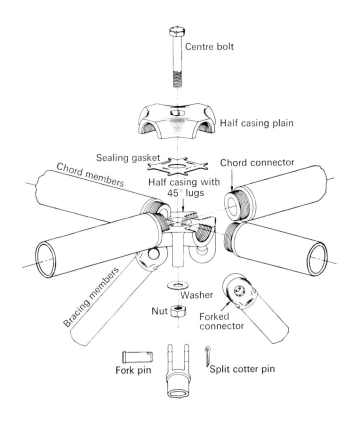

3.9
The Nodus node joint developed by British Steel Tubes Division, now British Steel Tubes & Pipes (Courtesy Space Decks Ltd)

continuous for local bending due to the decking loads. This reduces the magnitude of design bending moments in the chords, but they must still be designed for the combined effect of local bending and axial forces.

Four standard joints (reference 24, 30, 35 and 45) use half-casings of different size related to the chord section dimensions. The smallest joint (reference 24) is used for circular hollow section (CHS) chords 60.3 mm in diameter and rectangular hollow section (RHS) chords 60 by 60 mm, whilst the largest joints (reference 45) accommodate circular sections of 114.3 mm diameter and rectangular sections 120 by 120 mm. Circular CHS in section bracing members have a minimum size of 42.4 mm for all joints, whilst for rectangular bracings the minimum size is 40 by 40 mm (except for joint type 45 where the minimum is 50 by 50 mm). The maximum sizes of bracing members that can be accommodated respectively by the standard joints are 60.3, 60.3, 76.1 and 88.9 mm diameter for CHS and 50, 60, 80 and 90 mm for RHS.

Pinned connection of the bracing members permits variation of the space frame depth limited only by the requirements of structural efficiency or interference between members at the joint. A consequence of the geometry of the joint is that the centrelines of bracing

3.10
Typical node castings for standard Nodus joints (Photograph: John Chilton)

members and chords do not intersect at one single point within the node thus generating small secondary bending moments within the grid. The smaller the angle between the diagonal bracings and the plane of the chords, the greater is the eccentricity of the two intersection points. Consequently, the secondary moments are greater and the grid becomes less efficient.

Because the joints are only produced with two lug orientations, the possible grid configurations are limited to variations of the square on square, square on square offset, or square on diagonal square layouts. Within this limitation it is still possible to generate slightly cambered, barrel-vaulted and domed structures using the standard joint. The use of Nodus in the National Exhibition Centre in Birmingham, UK, and the atrium roof and entrance canopy of Terminal 2 at Manchester Airport, UK, are described in detail in Chapter 5.

Cylindrical nodes

The most well known solid cylindrical node is that of the Triodetic system. This consists of an extruded aluminium section with longitudinal slots into which the crimped ends of the hollow tubular bars are slotted. Clamping retains the bars in position between two end plates held by a single bolt passing through the centre of the node. A similar type of node made from steel has been used by Triodetic.

Triodetic

The Triodetic system of space grid construction is also a 'piece-small' system but uses a totally different concept for the connection of the individual members at the nodes. Developed during the 1950s by Fentiman Bros. of Ottawa, Canada, it was introduced commercially in 1960. Recognizing that the key problem in space grids is the efficient and simple connection of many elements at the nodes, experimental assemblies and nodes were produced based initially on the 'dovetail' joint used in timber construction. However, the eventual solution came from H. G. Fentiman's[5] observation of the effectiveness of the gripping jaws in tensile testing machines. He reasoned that, by providing matching indentations in the tubes of the space grid and in the node components, an efficient joint would result. The flattening (or coining) of the tubes does not remove any material and thus maintains the strength of the cross-section.

This is one of the few systems that predominantly uses aluminium as the material for the bars and nodes, and was developed at a time when there were restrictions on the use of steel in Canada. Circular drawn or seamwelded tube members have their ends crimped with a corrugated profile at the appropriate angle for connection to the node and, at the same time, the members are cut to the correct length with a tolerance of ± 0.13 mm. Nodes (or hubs) are extruded in generally cylindrical sections with longitudinal profiled slots ready

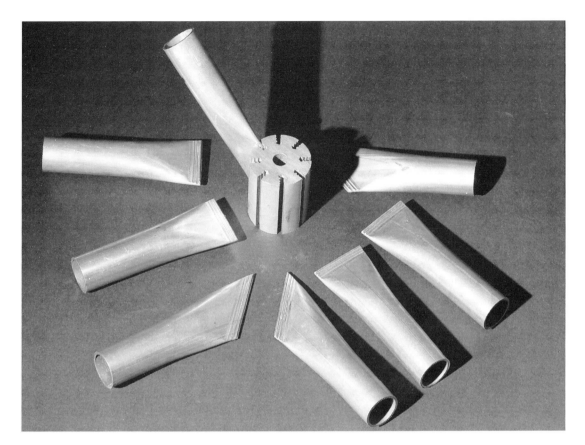

3.11
Triodetic nodes (or hubs) are extruded in generally cylindrical sections with longitudinal profiled slots ready to receive the crimped ends of the members (Photograph courtesy Glyn Halls)

to receive the crimped ends of the members (see Figure 3.11). Once all the members have been slid into place in the slots of the node, a bolt is passed through a central longitudinal hole and is tightened to hold retaining plates at each end of the cylinder. This is a very simple method of assembly but requires high precision in the manufacture of the nodes and members. At the time of the initial development of the system, the tolerances in the standard aluminium extrusion processes did not produce hubs of the necessary precision and improved methods of extrusion die production had to be established.

Although the system was originally developed with aluminium tubes and hubs, in subsequent development steel tubes have been used in combination with aluminium hubs. With correct selection of materials and suitable paint finishes it is possible to combine aluminium and steel without encountering the usual problems of electrolytic action between the two metals.

Plates

Flat or pressed plates are frequently used as the node connectors in lightweight systems composed of cold-rolled steel channels (e.g. the original Unistrut, now called Moduspan, USA). They are also used as con-

nectors in the timber roundwood pole space grids developed by Pieter Huybers at TU Delft, in the Netherlands described in Chapter 5.

Moduspan (formerly Unistrut)

Moduspan market a variety of 'piece-small' space truss systems, of which System I is the current version of the system originally invented and patented by Charles W. Attwood. In the basic system, five standard components, as shown in Figure 3.12, are assembled by simple bolting. There are two types of node connector both press-formed from 6 mm thick hot-rolled steel plate and having punched shear lugs and bolt holes for connection of the members. The 'in-strut' connector, used in the top layer of the grid, has lugs located on the inner faces of its diagonal planes while the 'out-strut' connector, used in the bottom layer, has lugs located on the outer faces of its diagonal planes. Members having standard modular lengths of 1.22 m and 1.52 m connect the nodes and the same members are used for the chords and diagonals. These members are roll-formed 12 gauge (0.27 mm) thick hot-rolled steel in a lipped channel section, typically 41.3 mm wide by 41.3 or 61.9 mm deep, with holes punched near the ends for bolting to the nodes and to provide the necessary shear connection. The last two standard components are a high-strength steel bolt

3.12
Typical Moduspan
(Unistrut) node
showing the cold-
formed members
bolted to the node
plate (Photograph:
John Chilton)

3.13
Entrance canopy,
Georgia Dome,
Atlanta, USA, using
Moduspan
(Photograph: John
Chilton)

(which has a shoulder to act as a shear lug) and a steel nut with counter-bored hole (to receive the shoulder of the bolt).

In addition to these five basic components, there are reinforcing struts to increase the capacity of the standard members in highly loaded locations (such as adjacent to columns), bearing seatings to transfer the load from the space grid to the supporting structure, half connectors to accommodate abutment against a wall or the

use of a vertical fascia, etc. An example of the use of Moduspan for an entrance canopy at the Georgia Dome, Atlanta, is shown in Figure 3.13.

'Nodeless' joints

Because the special separate node components usually represent a considerable proportion of the cost of a space grid, some systems eliminate these completely, relying instead on direct connection between the ends of the grid members. Although this saves in overall cost, it tends to limit the possible configurations of the grid as the end connections of members are often designed to accommodate standard angles between the parts.

The Octet Truss developed by Buckminster Fuller, used extruded members with an X cross-section and with the ends cut at the angles appropriate for tetrahedral and octahedral geometry (70.53° and 109.47° respectively). In the Multi-hinge system developed in the USA by Peter Pearce, fin plates with pre-drilled bolt holes are welded to tubular members for assembly in predetermined configurations. An example of the use of the system is for Biosphere 2, in Arizona, USA, which is described in Chapter 5.

Continuous chord systems

Systems with continuous chords could be considered as a halfway stage between the 'piece-small' and modular types as, although they are assembled from relatively small pieces, they generally have no special node component. The Unibat and SPACEgrid systems described below, to some extent use continuous chords for the bottom layer of the grid. However, there are other systems that use both top and bottom chords that are continuous through the node joints. Although this can sometimes lead to eccentricity of member forces at the joints, that in turn produce secondary bending in the members,

there are also benefits: there are no expensive nodes, fewer components are necessary and chords can be joined by simple splices at positions between the chord intersections.

Harley/Conder Harley

The Harley system was introduced into Europe by Conder Group plc in 1989. It was manufactured under licence from the patent holders in Australia where it has been available since 1980. After preliminary trials and the construction of a test structure, it was estimated that the system was highly competitive against more traditional portal frame construction for industrial and storage buildings. The series 80 Conder Harley space truss system is suitable for structures with plan areas of 250 m² upwards.

There are fundamental differences between this and the other space truss systems described above. The chord members are made from cold rolled steel continuously formed and cut to lengths up to 12.5 m. Therefore, in general, the chord members pass through the intersections with the diagonals rather than being broken by a separate nodal connector. To achieve this, the chords in orthogonal directions are placed in slightly different horizontal planes. For instance, 'C' section chords can be set back-to-back, thereby avoiding direct intersection of the members. Web bracing members are circular tube sections. At each end they are crimped, bent to the required bracing angle and drilled for bolting to the chord intersection. A typical joint layout is shown in Figure 3.14.

3.14
A typical Harley Type 80 node joint (Photograph: John Chilton)

As the centroids of the chord sections do not pass directly through the centre of the node, neither do the member axial forces. There is, therefore, an eccentricity inherent in the Harley Series 80 connection that generates bending moments in the grid elements. These are dealt with by local reinforcement at the joints.

Manufacture from cold-formed strip allows production of elements ranging in thickness from 1.5 to 8 mm in a wide variety of chord profiles. Chords are cut to length and precision drilled for bolting at the predetermined intersection points with a tolerance of (± 0.5 mm). Typical UK grid dimensions are around 3 m in plan. For long-span applications, the Harley system is adaptable for use in multi-layer grids or, alternatively, the basic member section sizes can be increased and a greater grid spacing adopted.

Mai Sky System

The patented Mai Sky System resulted from a desire to produce an economical method of space grid construction. Top grid geometry is square or rectangular with an offset bottom layer. Chord members in one direction are continuous and have angled fin plates, with pre-drilled bolt holes, shop-welded to them at intervals appropriate for the grid geometry. In the orthogonal direction the chords are discontinuous and have profiled end/fin plates welded to them. These match those of the continuous chords. Diagonal bracing members have simple end fin plates. Generally, square or circular hollow tubular sections are used for all members. Figure 3.15 shows the typical Mai Sky System joint.

Assembly of the system is by site bolting and is usually carried out at ground level. The continuous chords of the bottom layer are laid out and automatically spaced by connection of the discontinuous chords sections in the orthogonal direction. At the same time as the chords are bolted together, the diagonals are fixed between the angled plates. A similar process is used for the assembly of the top layer of the grid.

A continuous edge beam is normally used to support the grids at the top layer nodes. This is in turn supported on columns at intervals suitable to limit deflection of the grid supports. The roof decking and preliminary service installation can be carried out before the grid is lifted into position by crane.

Catrus

Catrus is described as 'a low-cost answer to the problems of traditionally expensive structural systems'.[6] Developed by Dr Ahmed El-Sheikh, of Dundee University, in Scotland, and recently introduced in the

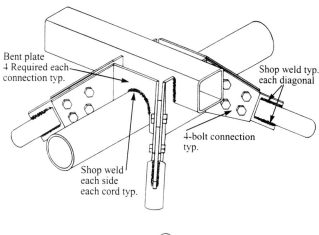

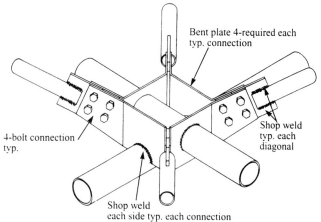

3.15
Typical Mai Sky System joint (Courtesy Mai Sky Inc.)

UK, it is now licensed to Technitube, in South Yorkshire. Primary considerations in the development of the truss system were low-cost, reliability and construction benefits. Research by Dr El-Sheikh showed that there was only limited use of space trusses mainly due to cost of 'node connectors to provide the concentric member connections'.[7] Usually, such systems are sophisticated, expensive and cost more than simple beams or frames, even though the latter might require the use of more material. Space trusses are also vulnerable to 'brittle' behaviour (i.e. they can in some cases collapse with little or no warning due to the failure of one or two members) and they also require good dimensional tolerances. However, they do benefit from lightness, high stiffness, ease of manufacture and ease of assembly. It is estimated that Catrus offers more strength and ductility than many other space truss systems. The eccentricities inherent in the node connections provide ductile failure modes for the grid elements, which provide a better reserve of strength after the initial buckling of a member and increased warning of failure.

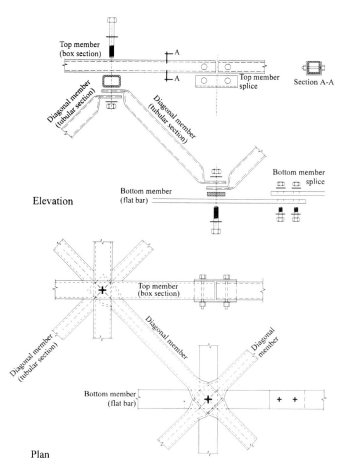

Elevation

Plan

3.16
The connecting bolt of the Catrus passes vertically through the two chord members, and the flattened and drilled ends of the four web bracing members. Top members are spliced using a tight fitting channel piece cut from an RHS whilst bottom members have a simple lap splice. (Courtesy A. El-Sheikh)

The system uses rectangular hollow section (RHS) top chords, tubular diagonals (with flattened and bent ends) and flat steel strip lower chords. Both the upper and lower chords run continuously across the node joints which are assembled using simple bolted connections (obviating the need for a special node joint). The RHS top chords are drilled on the centreline of the cross-section and, as can be seen in Figure 3.16, the connecting bolt passes vertically through the two chord members and the flattened and drilled ends of the four web bracing members. Chord members are produced in lengths to suit the particular grid dimensions of the space truss and they are spliced at suitable locations, usually midway between the nodes. This maintains member continuity and stability, and simplifies joint details. The splices in the top (compression) chords use a short length of a larger-section RHS (with the top face removed to form a U section), which is then bolted to

both chord sections. Bottom chord splices can be made in three forms; by clamping the two chord sections between two short jointing plates; by a simple lapped splice (with no additional cover plates) or, at the bottom nodes; by using a flat jointing plate. In proving tests during development of the system, splices with just two bolts were found to be as effective as those with four bolts and the members to be almost as efficient as an unspliced chord. Introduction of the splices produced an observed reduction in strength of 2 per cent and in stiffness of 12 per cent compared to fully continuous members.

Modules

There is more variation in the form of the modular units that distinguish different prefabricated types. The square-based pyramid is the most common modular unit and is used to construct space trusses, however, other modular systems, may, once assembled, form rigid-jointed space frames. Modular systems may also use angle, channel, Universal Beam, or Universal Column sections for the bars or members, as these are often cheaper than hollow sections. Such sections can be connected by simple bolting and welding.

Some space grid systems take advantage of the benefits of prefabrication to produce larger-scale modules that can be simply bolted together on site. This reduces the amount of site assembly, speeding the erection process. Depending on the shape of the module, there may be an increase in transportation cost as some modules can be stacked and nested easily (e.g. the square-based pyramids or half-octahedra of Space Deck, as shown in Figure 3.20) whilst others (e.g. CUBIC Space Frame modules, shown in Figure 3.28) require more space.

Typically, the Unibat, Space Deck, ABBA Dekspace and Mero DE systems use pyramidal modules, usually consisting of angle or channel sections welded together to form a square base frame for the pyramid. Tubular web elements are then welded to each corner of the frame on the diagonal and are also welded to a central boss or connector. Straight bars or tubes are then used to join the pyramid bosses to form the bottom chords of a three-dimensional grid.

Other systems may use flat truss modules of different configuration that can be assembled in a variety of ways, depending on the system. For instance, it is possible to form a two-way square on square space grid from basic flat rectangular truss modules connected by plate nodes in the upper and lower grids. The CUBIC Space Frame described below uses modules with upper and lower chord configurations, T- or L-shaped in plan.

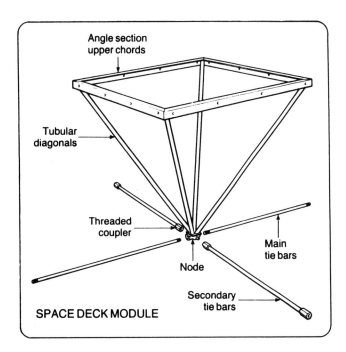

3.17
Space Deck modules and connecting bars (Courtesy Space Decks Ltd)

3.18
Cast boss at the apex of the Space Deck pyramids (Photograph: John Chilton)

Modular space trusses

Space Deck

Space Deck (Figure 3.17) is a modular system that was developed in the early 1950s by Denings of Chard,UK. There are thousands of examples of Space Deck structures all over the world, as the modular system has been available for almost fifty years in essentially the same form, with only minor changes in materials and metrication of module dimensions.

The system is based on pyramidal units that are assembled from a square frame of steel angles connected by circular steel tube bracing members to a central cast steel boss. All elements of the pyramids are welded together in a fabrication jig to ensure consistent dimensional accuracy. The cast boss at the apex of the pyramids (Figure 3.18) has a threaded hole on each side in one horizontal direction and a threaded stud protruding from each side in the orthogonal direction. High-tensile steel rod tie bars are used to connect the bosses of adjacent pyramids. In one direction of the lower grid the tie bars have threaded ends (one left-hand and one right-hand) which screw directly into the tapped holes in the pyramid bosses. Tapped hexagonal coupling pieces are used at the ends of tie bars in the other orthogonal direction to screw on to the protruding studs. of the bosses.

Standard modules are produced having grid dimensions of 1200 × 1200 mm with depths of either 750 or 1200 mm, 1500 × 1500 mm with depths of 1200 and 1500 mm and also 2000 × 2000 mm with a depth of 2000 mm. Different strength modules are available within the same overall dimensions. The variation in strength is in the size of bracing members, the stronger sections being used mainly to accommodate the high shear forces present in the space truss around column supports. By its nature, assembly of a Space Deck grid produces a cornice edge profile (as the standard modules are inverted pyramids). Therefore, in addition to the stock modules, standard half-modules are available to give a mansard edge where required. Special pyramid modules with varying grid dimensions are also available, made to order.

During manufacture of the modules the top frame angles are cut to the required length, mitred and have the holes for connecting bolts punched into what will be the downstand leg of the frame. Diagonals are also cut to length with ends at the appropriate angle for subsequent welding to the top frames and forged steel boss. The cast bosses are drilled and machined. All components are then degreased and the angles and diagonals are also shot-blasted prior to the application of a paint or lacquer finish. Angles are then welded in a jig to produce square frames that can either be used for the standard modules or infill (top chord) trays in sparse grids, where some of the pyramidal units are omitted (usually on a chequer-board pattern). Standard pyramid modules are assembled from an angle tray, boss and four diagonals, in a jig, to close dimensional and angular tolerances, and welded together.

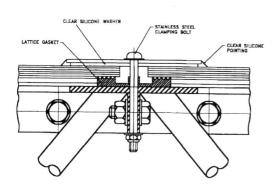

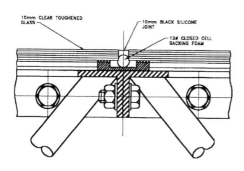

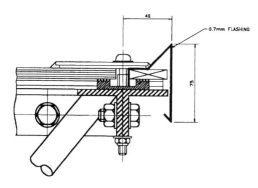

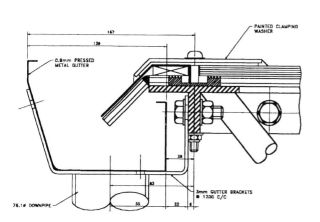

To assemble the Space Deck, the upper frames of the pyramids are bolted together through the downstand legs of the angles. The cast steel bosses are then joined with the tie bars. Because of the combination of opposing screw threads at each end of the tie bars, rotation of the bar screws it simultaneously into the boss (or on to the stud) at each end. This allows the distance between lower node centres to be easily adjusted to produce a small camber in one or both directions; thus a slightly domed or barrel-vaulted surface may be generated. The final grid has a square on square offset configuration.

Space Deck grids can be supported at either the top or bottom layer either on a regular pattern or at random. Typical span to depth ratios are around 25 to 30 for full edge supported roofs, although these ratios must be reduced if the roof is only supported at the corners. Cladding may be fixed directly to the space truss modules that provide convenient support at 1.2 m, 1.5 m or 2.0 m centres across the whole upper layer of the grid. Normally, a Space Deck roof has a perimeter angle trimming member but in situations where the overall plan dimensions of a building do not relate directly to the standard module dimensions, perimeter channels up to

3.20
Efficient stacking of Space Deck modules (Photograph: John Chilton)

3.19
Typical edge and glazing fixing details for Space Deck modules (Courtesy Space Decks Ltd)

*3.21
Space Deck used for
a new roof installed
over a 6400 m² area
of existing roof for
PSA Projects,
Edinburgh
(Photograph courtesy
Space Decks Ltd)*

200 mm wide or perimeter trays up to 375 mm wide can be added. Some typical edge and glazing fixing details are shown in Figure 3.19.

Transportation of the Space Deck space truss is very economical as the standard lightweight modules are easily stacked together (Figure 3.20) and the tie rods are simply bundled together. Large areas of Space Deck can be carried on one standard lorry trailer.

The advantage of a lightweight modular roofing system such as Space Deck is demonstrated by the project shown in Figure 3.21 where a new roof was installed over an existing 6400 m² area for PSA Projects, Edinburgh. Construction of a new slightly pitched roof over the existing flat roof of limited load capacity was a problem. To carry out such a project in only eight weeks, over such a large area, where cranage was difficult and the work had to be carried out whilst the building was still functioning as normal, demanded the use of a lightweight modular structure where the standard components were readily available. The space truss was able to accommodate to the irregular column grid of the existing structure and to work within the remaining load capacity of the existing columns.

Unibat and SPACEgrid

One of the great innovators in the field of space grid structures was architect/engineer Stéphane du Château. Following a system of gradual development and refinement, his Unibat system appeared in 1962. It also is comprised of pyramidal modules with rigid frames forming the upper chord layer, but in this variation, high-tensile steel bolts are used to connect the upper frames of the modules through their corners only. This is a much

*3.22
ABBA Cubicspace system used for a multi-layer grid at the
Highgate Shopping Centre, Johannesburg, South Africa
(Photograph courtesy ABBA Space Structures)*

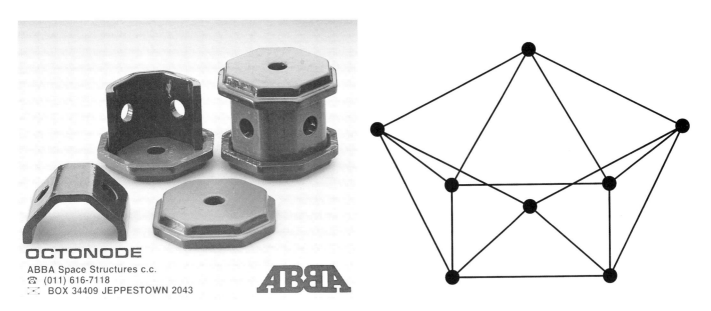

3.23
ABBA Cubicspace system with patented Octanode connection (Photograph courtesy ABBA Space Structures)

simpler and quicker method of assembly and consequently leads to economies in erection time and costs.

SPACEgrid is a space truss modular system that was developed by Ronald G. Taylor from the Unibat system that he originally developed together with S. du Château. To refer to SPACEgrid as a system is perhaps a misnomer as there is no standard module or joint, these being considered unnecessary restrictions for both engineering and architectural design. It is based on the concept that the most economical grid should be selected according to the plan dimensions and loading. Further, that the most economical member sections, hot-rolled or cold formed steel or alternatively aluminium, should be chosen depending on the member forces present. Finally, it is considered that the joints should be designed specifically to suit the chosen grid layout and the size and section of the members that have been selected.

The most common grid used by SPACEgrid is the diagonal square on square using, as with Unibat, pyramidal modules that are often connected by only a single bolt at the corners of the upper grid. Bottom chords may be individual bars between the lower nodes or, in preference, continuous members. This reduces the problems associated with connecting several elements in tension at each node as, with continuous chords, the connections do not necessarily have to be designed for the full force in the chord (only for the portion of the chord force transferred to or from the diagonals at the node).

ABBA

Since 1983 ABBA Space Structures of Jeppestown, South Africa, have developed several 'substructure' sys-

3.24
ABBA Dekspace system used for a space truss barrel vault at the Southgate Shopping Centre, Johannesburg, South Africa (Photograph courtesy ABBA Space Structures)

3.25
Detail of special 'pass through' chords for the Dekspace space truss barrel vault at the Southgate Shopping Centre, Johannesburg, South Africa (Photograph courtesy ABBA Space Structures)

tems of space truss construction. The high cost of traditional space grids of linear members connected by a universal node encouraged A. H. Noble to search for economic alternatives.

Cubicspace was developed by ABBA in 1983 and consists of square and triangular sub-frames that are assembled to form square on diagonal grids. At the Highgate Shopping Centre, Johannesburg, South Africa, in 1985, the Cubicspace system was used to construct a multi-layer space grid (Figure 3.22) and in 1986 the same system was used for a Geotechnic Centre built for Gold Fields. Individual space grid units in the second structure were connected using the patented Octanode (Figure 3.23) which was originally conceived as an octagonal cylinder with top and bottom plates. By splitting the octagon in half it became possible to preassemble manageable sub-units on the ground, ready to be craned into position and connected into the structure later.

The Dekspace system, introduced in 1987, consists of pyramidal units with angle top frames and tubular diagonals, and was first used for a 32 m diameter barrel vault at the Apostolic Faith Mission at Vereeniging. As in the original Space Deck system, the pyramids are bolted together through the angle frames but in this case they are connected by tubular members in the lower grid. Consisting of two separate barrel vaults, each terminating with a semi-dome and separated by an office block, the structure is known locally as the 'Hot-Dog' Church. Assembled in two halves, the barrel vaults were hinged at the supports, swung into position and spliced in the air along their centreline, whilst the semi-dome sections were built in successive layers from the ground up.

A 67.5 m long, 15 m diameter barrel vault was also constructed, using Dekspace, at the Southgate Shopping Centre, Johannesburg (Figure 3.24). The space truss vault, constructed from around 2000 apparently identical

pyramids, is supported on walls also of space grid. The whole structure is supported on only four pairs of columns and has a maximum clear span of 30 m along the axis

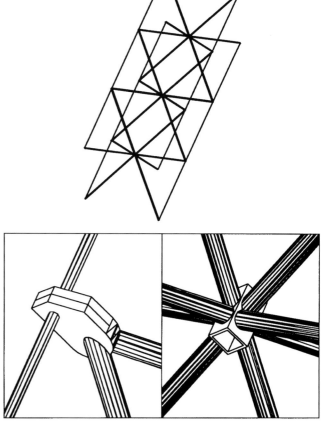

3.26
ABBA Spider Frame module and connection details (Courtesy ABBA Space Structures)

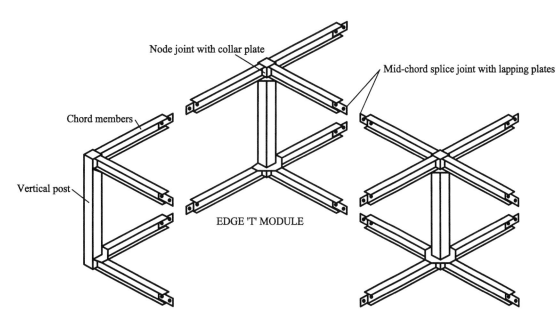

Chord members

Node joint with collar plate

Mid-chord splice joint with lapping plates

Vertical post

EDGE 'T' MODULE

CORNER 'L' MODULE

INTERNAL 'X' MODULE

3.27
Standard CUBIC
Space Frame
modules of 'X', 'T'
and 'L' shape in plan
showing typical node
and splice
configuration
(Drawing: John
Chilton)

of the vault. In order to keep the number of pyramids to a minimum, and to maintain the bottom chords parallel to the top chords, it was originally envisaged that the lower chords would form a cruciform. Problems of geometry at the junction between the barrel vault and the vertical walls meant that these crossed members did not intersect directly. The solution was to allow one bar to pass through a hole in the other and this arrangement (Figure 3.25) was, in the end, adopted for the whole structure. Cruciform units were, therefore, replaced by two straight tubular members.

Most recently, Spider Frame has been developed and used in a few small projects, e.g. a single beam 12 m long and 1.2 m deep at the Johannesburg German School and an entrance canopy composed of four 14.9 m long beams, 1.36 m deep connected side by side. This latter structure includes a 6.8 m cantilever and is covered with Ferrari Architectural Fabric. Based on cubic scaffolding, the spider units have eight arms extending from a tubular section node out to the vertices of a cube. The units are then joined end to end by connecting the arms and threading them on to longitudinal rods (Figure 3.26). It is envisaged that the concept could easily be applied to other close-packing solids.

Modular space frames

CUBIC Space Frame

Developed during the late 1970s by Leszek Kubik and his son Leslie, the CUBIC Space Frame system is marketed by Kubik Enterprises. As this is a modular system

containing no triangulation, the applied loads are resisted by frame action and the chords and vertical members are subjected to bending moments and shear forces, in addition to axial forces. It is, therefore, a 'true' space frame system.

The concept of the CUBIC Space Frame is based on the method used by engineers in the past to calculate, by hand, the forces and moments in Vierendeel girders. These girders have top and bottom chords spaced apart and connected only by rigid-jointed, vertical web members. Therefore, as they have no diagonal web members, they have to rely on frame action for their stability and strength. Approximately halfway between each of the verticals in the Vierendeel girder, there is a point of contraflexure (zero bending moment) in the top and bottom chord members. In the original hand calculation methods for the analysis of Vierendeel girders, fully rotationally free 'pinned' joints (that have zero bending resistance) were assumed to exist at the middle of each bay of the girder in order to simplify the solution of member actions. If a double-layer grid is formed from a network of intersecting Vierendeel girders arranged in two orthogonal directions and physical 'pin' joints (rather than the assumed pin joints) are inserted in the upper and lower chords midway between each chord intersection, the grid can be broken down into similar modules that are 'X', 'T' or 'L' shaped in plan. These are the basic modules of the CUBIC Space Frame system (see Figure 3.27). Although the modules 'nest' together quite well for transportation when they are relatively small (Figure 3.28), larger modules, such as those used in the roof structure of the FFV Aerotech Hangar at Stansted Airport, UK, with chord lengths of 3.5 m and 2 m in the two orthog-

3.28
CUBIC Space Frame
modules nested for
transportation
(Photograph: John
Chilton)

3.29
CUBIC Space Frame
roof for Hall 3 at the
International
Convention Centre in
Birmingham, UK
(Photograph: Douglas
Turner Convention
Centre JV, R.M.
Douglas and Turner
International)

onal directions, 4 m deep and weighing up to one tonne, are not so easy to handle or transport.

No special components are required to manufacture the CUBIC Space Frame modules as they are assembled from standard hot-rolled steel sections and plates welded together in a fabrication jig using standard cutting, drilling and welding techniques. In both orthogonal directions, the fully welded node joint, which is assumed to be rigid, is at the point of maximum bending in each module and it must also transfer the chord axial forces across the intersection. Consequently failure of the node could jeopardize the integrity of the structure. Therefore, the quality of welding at the joint must be well monitored by non-destructive means (e.g., by ultrasonic testing). Welding of the lap plates at the mid-chord splice joints must also be well controlled. Final assembly of the CUBIC Space Frame is by site bolting of the lap joint (usually with high-strength bolts) in the upper and lower chords.

The CUBIC Space Frame system was first used for re-roofing a rehearsal theatre 12 m × 20 m at Trent Polytechnic (now Nottingham Trent University), UK, in 1979. Because it was a previously untried system, a full load test was carried out to the then current British Standard, BS 449, at the fabricator's works before delivery to site. It is interesting to note that the contract was won because the modular space frame could be assembled in situ, without heavy cranage. The cost of lifting the originally proposed planar roof trusses over the façade of the existing building was more than the additional cost of the space frame, including the load test. Since then, the CUBIC Space Frame has been used successfully to roof several building types, including factory units and supermarkets where the absence of bracing members has allowed installation of plant, services and even offices within the depth of the space frame (see Figure 2.6 in the previous chapter).

The largest space grid constructed to date using the CUBIC Space Frame is the roof of a FFV Aerotech maintenance hangar for Boeing 747 aircraft at Stansted Airport, near London. The design, fabrication and erection of this building, completed in 1988, are described in detail in Chapter 5. In 1990 the system was used in Hall 3 at the International Convention Centre in Birmingham, UK (Figure 3.29). The exhibition hall, a non-regular octagon in plan and approximately 55 m in span, was covered by a CUBIC Space Frame capable of carrying a point load of 30 tonnes at any of the nodes. Because of the prominent position of the roof structure, a very high quality of detailing was used throughout for the fabricated nodes and splices.

A modification of the CUBIC Space Frame has more recently been developed for medium-span composite floor construction in office buildings. This system exploits the facility of service installation within the structural depth that is unobstructed by diagonal bracing or beam webs.

Notes

1 Ghavrami, K. and Moreira, L. E. (1993). Double-layer bamboo space structures. In *Space Structures 4* (G. A. R. Parke and C. M. Howard, eds), vol. 1, pp. 573–81, Thomas Telford.

2 Anon (1982). Concrete Space. *Architects Journal*, **175**(7), 20–1.

3 Anon (1982). Concrete Space Frame for Delhi Exhibition Halls. *RIBA Journal*, **89**(7), 50–1.

4 Gerrits, J.M. (1998). An architectomic approach to choosing a space frame system. In *Lightweight Structures in Architecture, Engineering and Construction* (R. Hough and R. Melcher, eds), vol. 2, pp. 992–999, LSAA, Australia.

5 'Impressed by the gripping strength of the jaws of the testing machine on test specimens, he reasoned that similar indentations on a node or connector of similar strength should provide reasonable efficiency' Fentinan, H. G. (1966). Developments in Canada in the fabrication and construction of three-dimensional structures using the Triodetic system. In *Space Structures* (R. M. Davies, ed.), p. 1074, Blackwell Scientific.

6 Purvis, G. (1995). Cover price. *Building*, Number 7911, **260**(40), p. 68.

7 Ibid.

4 Design and construction

The factors that affect the design and construction of space grids, such as, element structural behaviour, span to depth ratios, support details, dimensional accuracy, pre-camber, cladding and glazing, erection, behaviour in fire and behaviour under seismic loading are considered in this chapter.

Element structural behaviour

The two most important structural consideration in the design of space truss elements are the buckling of compression chords and web bracing members, and the design of joints to effectively and efficiently transmit axial forces between the bars and nodes whilst minimizing

secondary bending effects. A diagram showing the typical buckling failure mode of a corner-supported space truss is shown in Figure 4.1(a). Overloading of one top chord member may cause it to buckle and the force that it was previously transmitting is then transferred to the adjacent top chords. These, in turn, may fail due to the extra loading until a full or partial 'hinge' is formed across the whole structure and it collapses. Excessive shear load around the supporting columns may in a similar way induce progressive buckling of the web diagonals in compression (see Figure 4.1(b)). Space frames (with rigid node joints and no diagonal bracing elements) have to be designed for the bending moments induced by the frame action. In the majority of space truss systems, the connection of member to node is effected so that the

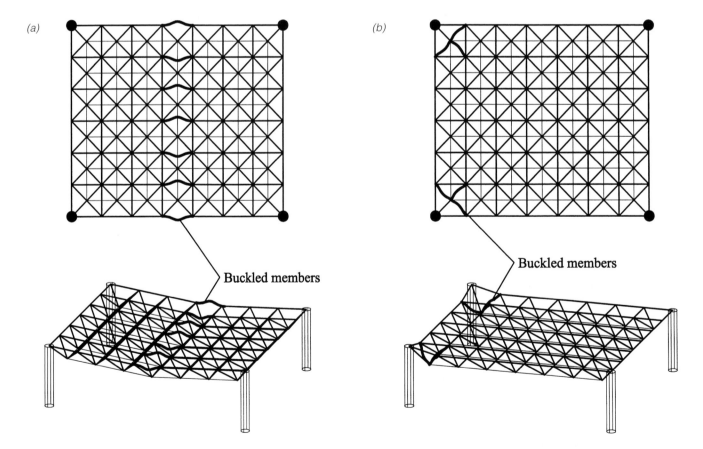

(a)

(b)

Buckled members

Buckled members

4.1
Buckling of compression elements in a corner-supported space grid (a) mid-span top chords and (b) web members near supports (Drawing: John Chilton)

axial forces pass through the centre of the joint, in order that secondary bending does not occur due to eccentricity of the forces. However, in some systems such as Harley (see previous chapter) the cold-formed channel section chord members in the two orthogonal directions in each layer are connected back-to-back. The line of action of the member axial forces is therefore displaced slightly from the centroid of the joint and secondary bending effects have to be taken into account in the analysis and design.

Span/depth ratios for various support conditions

It is difficult to generalize about the most economical span/depth ratio for space grid structures, as it is influenced by the method of support, type of loading and, to a large extent, on the system being considered. It has been suggested by Z. S. Makowski[1] that span/depth ratios may vary from 20 to 40 depending on the rigidity of the system used. Higher span/depth ratios can be achieved if all (or most) of the perimeter nodes are supported. However, the ratio should be reduced to about 15 to 20 when the grid is only supported at or near the corners.

An optimization study carried out by René Motro[2] considered a square grid 25.2 m × 25.2 m supported at 3.6 m intervals along the full perimeter, with the objective of minimizing the self-weight of the grid. Seven different grid configurations were studied with span/depth ratios ranging from 9 to 35. Although there was a difference in self-weight of 35 per cent between different configurations, the study concluded that the optimum grid

depth was approximately 1/15 of the clear span in all cases. However, it must be remembered that in terms of overall economy of the roof construction the minimum self-weight of the grid may not be of prime importance. For example, when there is a planning restriction on the overall height of a building, minimum depth might be the optimum solution.

Manufacturers usually supply tables of typical span/depth ratios, for their products, with different support conditions and a range of representative loadings. Span tables produced by Space Deck Ltd indicate that, for typical roof loadings in the UK, span/depth ratios of about 30 are possible using their standard modules. For example, a Space Deck roof supported on all edges, with a total imposed, decking and services load of 1.30 kN/m² in addition to its own weight will span up to 39 × 39 m with a module only 1200 mm deep.

Support details and thermal movement

Space grids usually form structurally rigid plates, therefore it is important that any potential movements are suitably accommodated in the support details. As with the majority of structures, this is usually achieved by the provision of an appropriate combination of fixed and sliding bearings. Sliding bearings usually incorporate polytetrafluoroethylene (PTFE) surfaces fixed to separate parts of the bearing assembly in such a way that they are free to slide relative to each other. Guide plates at the sides usually restrict the movement to one direction and lipping of the bearing plates ensures that the two parts of the bearing cannot normally be separated. The base of

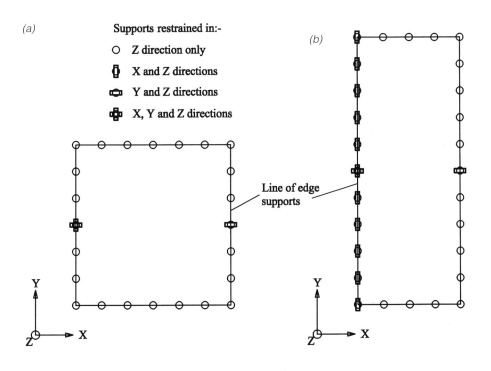

(a)

Supports restrained in:-

○   Z direction only

⬙   X and Z directions

⬒   Y and Z directions

⬚   X, Y and Z directions

(b)

Line of edge supports

4.2
Alternative lateral restraint positions to control the movement of a space grid subject to lateral forces whilst permitting restricted movements due to temperature changes (a) typical layout for a grid with large aspect ratio generating greater lateral force due to wind in one direction (Drawing: John Chilton)

4.3
Sliding bearing
supporting one
perimeter node of the
Mero space grid roof
at the National Indoor
Arena for Sport,
Birmingham, UK
(Photograph: John
Chilton)

the bearing is bolted to the supporting structure and the upper part of the bearing is bolted to the space grid. Thus, the grid and its support are connected in such a way that restricted relative movement can take place.

A major source of movement in metal structures is change of ambient temperature and this is especially true when very long clear spans are involved. The effect of expansion or contraction of the space grid depends very much on the way in which the structure is supported, in particular, the position and direction of horizontal restraints at the bearings. Besides movement due to changes in ambient temperature, the bearings may also have to transfer horizontal forces, due to wind loads or seismic activity, between the space grid and its supports. To hold the space grid structure against lateral loads a minimum of three lateral restraints is required. The position of these restraints will depend on the distribution and rigidity of the supporting structure and the supporting structure must in turn be designed to resist the lateral forces. Figure 4.2 shows alternative ways of restraining a space grid against lateral force, whilst permitting restricted movements due to temperature changes. A typical bearing which allows movement in one direction whilst restraining movement in the orthogonal direction, and supports the Mero space grid roof of the National Indoor Arena for Sport, in Birmingham, UK, is shown in Figure 4.3.

Alternatively, the space grid may be rigidly fixed in terms of horizontal movement to some or all of its sup-

ports. In this case, both the space grid and the substructure must be designed to cater for the forces generated by temperature change. This alternative solution was used for the Boeing 747 maintenance hangar at Stansted Airport, UK, described in detail in Chapter 5, where the CUBIC Space Frame was rigidly fixed in position at the top of the four main corner columns, which acted as vertical cantilevers when resisting lateral forces. Thermal expansion and contraction was assumed to occur relative to a notional fixed point at the centre of the roof structure, whilst the tops of the columns were considered to bend away from or towards this notional point as dictated by the change in roof dimensions. The three-dimensional trussed columns and their foundations were then designed to accommodate the forces induced by the movements in columns around 23 m high.

Dimensional accuracy

In three-dimensional space grid structures in general, and long-span structures in particular, dimensional accuracy is of paramount importance, as small variations in element dimensions may accumulate to produce gross errors in the dimensions of the final structure. As described in more detail below, this property can be exploited to produce a small pre-camber of space grids by controlled variation of element dimensions.

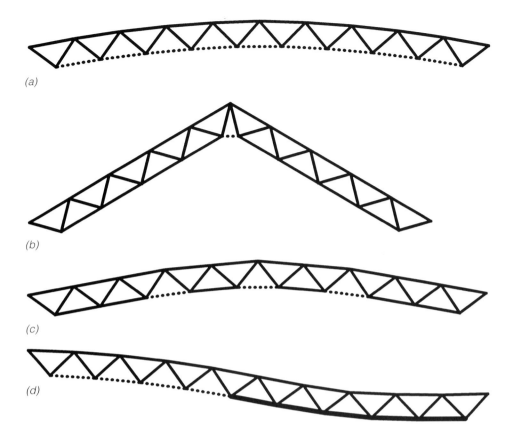

4.4
Camber of space grids: (a) uniform curved camber formed by slightly shortening all of the lower chord members in one direction, (b) ridge camber formed by shortening one lower chord member in one direction under the ridge, (c) stepped curved camber formed by slightly shortening the lower chord members in one direction at regular bay intervals and (d) freeform curve generated by suitable manipulation of top and bottom chord lengths in one direction (Drawing: John Chilton)

During the manufacturing process, components are typically cut to length to tolerances better than 0.5 to 1 mm. Many systems have parts that are fabricated from tubes and cast metal end connector components (e.g the Nodus and Mero KK systems) and these elements must be welded together to form complete members in accurately dimensioned jigs, to ensure that the overall length is within the required tolerance. In systems that use nodes to connect the individual members, these must be made to the same or better accuracy, with holes drilled in the correct position and at the correct angle, with bearing faces precisely machined. Other systems do not have separate nodes, for example, the Multi-hinge system developed by Peter Pearce and used in the construction of Biosphere 2 (see the case study in Chapter 5). In such 'nodeless' systems, the members are attached to each other directly at the ends and they have to be precisely pre-drilled in the correct positions to receive the connecting bolts. In the Triodetic system the tubular members are crimped at the correct angle and location, and simultaneously cut accurately to the correct length at the same time.

Fully modular systems such as Space Deck, the CUBIC Space Frame, ABBA Dekspace and SPACEgrid are also welded up from accurately cut components in precisely dimensioned jigs. This ensures overall dimensional accuracy for the modules, in this case, in three dimensions. Because of the necessity for three-dimensional jigs for these modules, it is preferable if one (or just a few) standard modules, if possible, are used for any structure as this reduces the number of adjustments that must be made to the jig, and hence the cost of fabrication.

Pre-camber

Most space grid applications are for roof structures. Therefore, it is necessary to provide adequate falls for rainwater run-off and an additional pre-camber may also be incorporated to counteract the predicted vertical deflection of the structure under imposed loading. In the majority of systems it is possible to achieve any required camber by varying the chord lengths very slightly. For instance, if the upper chord members in one direction of a grid pattern are all longer than the lower chords in the same direction, a barrel vault (or arch) of any required radius can be generated (Figure 4.4(a)). Similarly, an angular ridge can be formed by shortening (or by eliminating totally) one of the lower chord members (Figure 4.4(b)). A stepped arch as in Figure 4.4(c) can be achieved by reducing the length of lower chords at regular intervals along the section and free-form curves may also be produced by suitable manipulation of top and

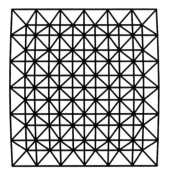

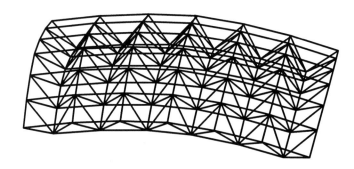

*4.5
Domed camber
formed by slightly
shortening all of the
lower chord members
(i.e, in both
directions) (Drawing:
John Chilton)*

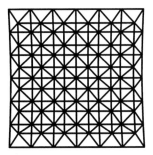

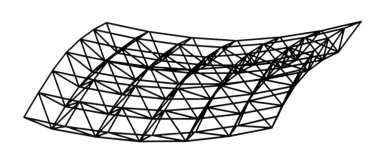

*4.6
Saddle surface
formed by slightly
shortening all of the
lower chord members
in one direction and
the top chords in the
other direction
(Drawing: John
Chilton)*

bottom chord lengths (Figure 4.4(d)). To achieve limited double-curved surfaces in three dimensions, it is possible to have lower chords shorter in both directions of a square grid and this generates a domed structure (Figure 4.5). However, only shallow domes can be achieved in this manner as geometrically incompatible internal deformations are generated if this approach is taken too far. In a similar fashion, shortening lower chords in one direction and upper chords in the other direction of a square grid produces a saddle-type surface (Figure 4.6). As noted above, from the construction point of view, it must be realized that very small variations in length may cause large differences in geometry of the space grid.

Cladding and glazing

Depending on the space grid system used, cladding and glazing elements may be supported directly by the top (or occasionally the bottom) chord members. If this is the case, the local bending and shear induced in the chords by dead and imposed loads on the cladding have to be considered in determining the member sizes. This may increase the size or thickness of the chords, and hence the cost of the grid. However, there will also be a saving, as separate purlins and purlin supports will not then normally be necessary. The alternative is to provide suitable brackets, or stools, at the node joints for purlin fixing, hence ensuring that the self-weight of the roof decking and the imposed loads are transmitted to

the space grid as point loads at the nodes. In this case, the self-weight of the chord members is generally small in comparison to the loads applied by the cladding in the former case; thus only limited bending is induced. An assessment of the cost of providing and installing a separate purlin system compared with the additional material costs associated with loads being applied directly to the chords (where the chosen space grid system permits) should be carried out to determine the most economical solution.

If cladding or glazing is fixed directly to the chords, then appropriate drainage falls must be provided by cambering or inclining the structural grid, as described in the previous section. But if separate purlins are used, the required gradient can be achieved by varying the height of the purlin fixing stools. However, this may not be acceptable for very long span structures, as the height of the purlin stools becomes excessive near the centre of the span, and therefore, cambering may still be necessary.

Methods of erection

There are several methods of erection for space grids and more than one may be used in the construction of a single grid. To some extent the method chosen will depend on the system being used but overall grid size, site access, and component size, will also be determining factors. In some cases erection can constitute a significant proportion of the overall cost of a space grid, therefore, it is important that the most efficient procedure is selected for each situation. This is one of the areas in which modular space grids have an advantage over 'piece-small' bar and node systems, as each module is an assembly of several individual members, therefore, the number of site connections is reduced.

The most commonly used techniques are:

1 Assembly of all the individual space grid elements or modules on a temporary staging or scaffolding, in their permanent position.
2 Assembly of space grid elements or modules in the air, by cantilevering from existing portions of the roof. Usually, individual or small subsets of members are lifted into position by crane.
3 Assembly of space grid elements or modules into larger panels (usually on the ground or a floor slab) before lifting them by crane and connecting them in the air to areas of the grid that have already been installed.
4 Assembly of the whole grid on the ground before lifting it on to the permanent supports by crane in one operation.
5 Assembly of a part or the whole space grid on the ground before jacking or winching it into its final position over temporary or permanent supports.

The area of the construction site available to the space frame subcontractor is often a deciding factor when choosing the erection technique. For instance, when an acceptably flat unobstructed area is available adjacent to (or even directly below) the final location of the space grid and there is good access for cranes, it is often much easier to completely assemble a small grid on the ground or floor slab and then lift it by crane into its final position (method 4). This is particularly suitable if the individual pieces or modules can be manoeuvred by hand, as cranage is only required for a few hours. Of course, it is essential that the lifting points on the space grid are correctly selected so that individual members are not over-stressed and the structure is not permanently damaged during the lifting process.

Where the area directly under the space grid is available for assembly but access is difficult for mobile cranes, method 5 may be preferred. The overall size of the space grid or the location of the assembly area may limit crane access. An example of the use of this erection method was the space grid of the Exhibition Centre, Anhembi Park, Sao Paulo, Brazil. The complete 260 × 260 m, 650 tonne, double-layer grid was lifted 14 m vertically, using this method. Twenty-five temporary supports were used for the twenty-seven hour operation. When such a large area of space grid is being raised in one operation at multiple locations, it is essential to control very

accurately the rate of vertical movement at all of the lifting points so that within specific predetermined limits the grid remains horizontal. Excessive relative differences in level of the lifting points on the space grid could induce forces in some elements of the structure that may exceed the forces experienced by those members under normal dead and imposed loading. It is generally much easier to control and monitor hydraulic jacking devices than cranes, therefore, the progress of a large-scale lifting operation is better accomplished using such equipment. In recent years, computer control has greatly increased the ease with which such manoeuvres can be carried out.

In situations where it would be difficult to lift the whole space grid as one piece, or where it is not possible to assemble the whole grid on the ground, due to lack of space, the preassembly of units into a manageable area of space grid is a good compromise (method 3). This technique was used for the erection of the Nodus space grid roof at Terminal 2, Manchester Airport, UK where the total 6000 m² area was divided into eleven sections, up to 25 tonnes in weight, which were placed by a 500-tonne mobile crane (see detailed study in Chapter 5).

Assembly by the connection of individual components in the air (method 2) is more appropriate for heavier modules (or members) particularly when the site may not be obstructed by erection of the grid at ground level. To accelerate the overall construction schedule on a very restricted site, this technique was used for the majority of the erection of the CUBIC Space Frame hangar roof at Stansted Airport. Consequently, other construction operations could be carried out simultaneously under the roof grid.

Usually, method 1 is only used when no other means are possible, as staging and scaffolding are expensive. However, it may be necessary to use temporary supporting structures under some areas of large grids to establish a structurally stable section of space grid for subsequent connection, in the air, of larger preassembled sections or modules.

An important advantage may be gained from assembling the grid at or slightly above ground level prior to lifting it to its final position (methods 4 and 5). It is much easier, cheaper and safer to install building services and/or roof decking when this can be carried out from the ground. Expensive temporary access scaffolding may be dispensed with and installation can proceed at the same time as space grid assembly. A further advantage is that protection from the weather is available as soon as the space grid is raised into its final position, allowing other construction operations to be undertaken in the dry (in wet climates) or in the shade (in hot climates).

For the 1992 Olympics in Barcelona, the roof of the Sant Jordi Sports Palace was constructed with the Orona system. It was erected using the innovative 'Pantadome' method proposed by engineer Mamoru Kawaguchi. As a variation of method 5, the 'Pantadome' method allows space grids having complex double curvature to be assembled near to the ground, following a different cross-section from that of the permanent structure, before being jacked vertically at the appropriate locations to transform their shape to the final profile. This is an exciting development in erection techniques for space grid structures as it permits more complex three-dimensional forms to be constructed economically. In Chapter 5 the design and construction of the Sant Jordi Sports Palace is reported in detail, and in Chapter 6 the principle of the 'Pantadome' system is described at length and further examples of its use are given.

Fire resistance of space grids

Space grid structures are predominantly, but not exclusively, constructed using steel members and joints. The incremental reduction in the strength of steel with increasing temperature is a well-known phenomenon which, in the event of fire, can lead to catastrophic collapse of building structures unless suitable protective measures are taken to prevent overheating of the steelwork. In common with all steel structures, therefore, the effect of fire on space grids must be considered

In a typical building structure, most or all members may be considered critical for the adequate performance of the whole (or part) of the structural framework generally, therefore, most members must be suitably protected. Space grids, however, are redundant structures in which the failure of one (or even several) elements does not necessarily result in distress or collapse of the structure. In certain circumstances the failure of one or more members, through loss of strength or plastic buckling, might possibly be accommodated by a redistribution of forces within the space grid although, for instance, the failure of highly loaded elements near supports in corner-supported structures would be very likely to induce general collapse. Although not provoked by fire, the collapse of the roof of the Hartford Coliseum in 1978, described in Chapter 2, demonstrated the possibility of progressive collapse of the whole of a space grid due to failure of one element.

In most countries Standard Fire Models are used to assess the effect of fire in buildings. However, there are many parameters that influence the severity of a fire within a building compartment and this, in turn, determines the effect of the fire on the structure. The most important parameters are:

1 Fire load and distribution within a compartment (or how much material there is to burn, how well it burns and where it is).

2 The thermal characteristics of the compartment boundaries (how easy it is for the heat to escape).
3 The geometry of the compartment.
4 The area, position and shape of openings in the boundaries.
5 The rate at which the flammable material in the compartment burns (influences the rate of increase of temperature and possibly the duration of the fire).
6 Ventilation rate (vents hot gases but can also fan flames).
7 Heat transfer within the compartment.

Normally the Standard Fire Models are not particularly refined due to the number and variability of the parameters to be considered, although currently there is a tendency to move towards more detailed computer simulation of real fires (Natural Fire Models). The traditional fire models tend to consider that the gas temperature is the same in the whole compartment. This is an unrealistic assumption in the large-volume enclosures for which space grid structures are frequently used. In such large volumes it is unlikely that all of the enclosing structure will be affected and even less likely that it will be subjected to a uniform temperature throughout. Also, the space grid may be well above the fire and therefore subject to a smaller rise in temperature. Space grid structures are, therefore, considered to be more vulnerable to localized fires in critical areas where members are highly loaded or where redistribution of member loads after, for instance, the buckling of a compression member could lead to progressive collapse.

A procedure for the fire analysis of space grids has been described by Ane Yarza.[3] First, it involves the description of a fire model to determine the gas temperature distribution within the compartment under consideration over time. Once this has been found, heat transfer between the gases and the surface of the structural elements can be modelled together with heat conduction within the members. With an appropriate mathematical model of these processes, the rise in temperature and the consequent reduction in strength of the steel over a given time can be found. Within the members the temperature depends on its shape factor (a function of its shape, the ratio of its surface area to its cross-section, etc.) and the degree of insulation provided to the surface. The effect of the temperature rise is included in a structural model of the space grid which describes the modified material properties, structural behaviour and stability of elements. Finally, a series of structural analyses are carried out (with increasing time and temperature) using the modified properties to determine the stability of the space grid as a whole at each stage. After each step, if collapse does not occur, the procedure is repeated for an incremental increase in time and temperature. Using this procedure it is possible to predict the order of failure of members and the behaviour of the structure over the duration of a fire. Depending on the specified period of fire resistance, it may be necessary to upgrade member sizes or insulate the steelwork to provide the protection required. Using the Natural Fire Model it may be necessary to carry out several discrete analyses to consider the effect of fires centred in different parts of the compartment.

Corner-supported space grids are most vulnerable in fire, due to the potentially catastrophic failure of the diagonal web members immediately adjacent to the supports or to bending failure due to the collapse of the chord members running perpendicular to a single section throughout the structure (as shown previously in Figure 4.1). Therefore, wherever possible, space trusses should be provided with full or intermittent edge supports. For improved performance of corner-supported space trusses critical members adjacent to the corners can be over-sized to reduce their working stresses (thus raising the temperature required to cause their failure).

Where fire protection of space grids is required, the only real practical (but expensive) solution for insulating the structure, whilst simultaneously preserving its aesthetic qualities, is to use intumescent coatings. Protection is afforded by the swelling and foaming of the coating at about 150 °C to form an insulating layer around the steel. It should be possible to coat only the critical members within a large space grid to reduce the cost of fire protection.

As with the thermal movements associated with normal changes in ambient temperature, it is desirable to provide appropriate sliding bearings to absorb the expansion of the space grid in a fire. Otherwise, the expansion may induce potentially damaging high compressive forces in the space grid due to the rigid restraint. In the case of a small fire beneath a large grid, the space grid itself will provide a relatively unyielding restraint around the localized expansion zone. Thus members not directly heated by the fire may experience increased stresses.

Space grids in seismic zones

Space grid structures form structurally rigid plates but are generally constructed of steel or aluminium using many joints. The combination of this rigidity with the ductility of the construction material and the energy-absorbing potential of the connections provides excellent resistance to seismic loading. However, there are situations in which space grids may exhibit 'brittle' behaviour where the failure of a few or even one critical element may lead to sudden collapse of the whole structure. In seismic design it is essential to identify the potential 'brittle' modes of failure and to provide ade-

quate resistance so that ductility is maintained. The common use of tubular members in space grids is beneficial due to their superior behaviour under the cyclic loading of earthquakes.

Seismic loading results from motion of the ground during an earthquake combined with the inertia of the structure. Rather than a direct loading the structure is actually forced to deform and this deformation induces internal forces. However, for design purposes, the seismic action is normally represented by an analogous system of external forces applied to the space grid. It is a potentially intense loading with a generally low probability of occurrence and its effect depends on factors that are different for each earthquake (such as maximum ground acceleration, frequency profile and duration).

Modern seismic design codes are based on a Design Response Spectrum together with the structure's location, importance, vibration period and ductility. In certain circumstances, and where the double-layer space grid has normal dimensions, regular shape and geometry, a straightforward Equivalent Static Force Analysis can be carried out. A simple elastic analysis ignores other characteristics of space grids, such as their potential for large inelastic deformation without collapse. Ductility of the structure dissipates seismic energy and can be used to achieve a more economical solution. However, there is always the possibility of 'brittle' behaviour, involving a progressive collapse initiated by the redistribution of load from buckled members overloaded in compression.

The behaviour of a space grid depends on the rigidity of the supporting structure with which it inevitably interacts. When it is supported on slender columns, the space grid can be considered to be a rigid diaphragm connecting the tops of flexible columns. Lateral restraint of the grid may be provided by the columns acting as vertical cantilevers or through diagonal bracing between columns. Where bracing is used, care must be taken to ensure that thermal expansion of the grid will not be unduly restricted. This is usually achieved by locating bracing midway along each side of a rectangular plan. Horizontal seismic forces are transmitted to the columns in proportion to their relative stiffness.

Alternatively, where a space grid is supported on a massive substructure, such as the inclined seating of a stadium, the roof is relatively flexible in comparison with the supports. It does not contribute to the general earthquake resistance of the whole building, solely transmitting seismic forces to the substructure. Detailing of connections between the grid and the supports in this case influences the behaviour of the grid under seismic loading. Horizontal seismic forces must be transmitted whilst allowing free thermal expansion of the space grid. It is essential that sufficient allowance is made at the sliding bearings for the differential horizontal movement of the substructure. Vertical support must be maintained to prevent the space grid from slipping off the bearings during an earthquake. The connections must also be sufficiently strong that the resistance of the substructure to seismic action is mobilized before the connections fail. A redundant strength factor of 1.2 to 1.5 is generally recommended.[4]

Notes

1 Makowski, Z. S. (ed.) (1981). *Analysis, Design and Construction of Double-Layer Grids.* Applied Science.
2 Motro, R. (1994). Structure and space structures. In *Application of Structural Morphology to Architecture* (R. Höller, J. Hennicke and F. Klenk, eds), p. 119, University of Stuttgart.
3 Yarza, A., Pavia, P. and Parke, G. A. R. (1993). An introduction to the fire analysis of double-layer grids. In *Space Structures 4* (G. A. R. Parke and C. M. Howard, eds), vol. 1, pp. 683–92, Thomas Telford.
4 Karamanos, A. S. and Karamanos, S. A. (1993). Seismic design of double-layer space grids and their supports. In *Space Structures 4* (G. A. R. Parke and C. M. Howard, eds), vol. 1, pp. 476–84, Thomas Telford.

5 Case studies

Perhaps the best way to illustrate the huge potential for the use of space grid structures is to show the many ways in which they can be used to produce aesthetically pleasing and efficient buildings. To this end, this chapter contains a series of case studies, presented in chronological order, to show how the technology has developed over approximately the last quarter of the twentieth century. The studies encompass different building types and sizes, in a variety of geometrical forms, ranging from small canopies to a stadium spanning over 200 m. Most of the examples feature one of the multitude of available proprietary space grid systems, although some purpose designed and fabricated grids are also represented. Significant aspects of their fabrication, construction and erection are described.

Space frame for the 'Symbol Zone', Expo '70, Osaka, Japan

The World Exposition in Osaka, in 1970, had as its theme 'Progress and Harmony for Humanity' and at its centre the Festival Square, masterminded by Kenzo Tange,[1] was to symbolize the expression of '... a festival where human beings can meet, shake hands, accord minds and exchange wisdoms'. A huge, translucent, space truss roof 291.6 m by 108 m, supported on only six lattice columns at a height of 30 m above the ground, covered the Festival Square and dominated the site (Figure 5.1). Based on a 10.8 m by 10.8 m square on square offset grid 7.637 m deep, the roof spanned 75.6 m between column centres across its width, with cantilevers of 16.2 m at each side. In the longitudinal direction, there were two 108 m spans and 37.8 m cantilevers at each end. As can be seen in the plan and east elevation of the pavilion shown in Figure 5.2, one main span of the space grid was pierced by a circular opening approximately 54 m in diameter to allow the symbolic Helios Tower or Tower of the Sun, rising from the Concourse of Humanity, to soar above the roof (see centre of Figure 5.1). The depth of the space truss was sufficient to allow exhibition spaces to be located within the roof structure.

This was space truss construction on a huge scale and the length of the compression members required the use of large-diameter steel tubes, 500 mm for chords and 350 mm for diagonals. The tubes, of similar external dimension, varied in thickness from 7.9 to 30 mm, depending on the forces to be resisted, and were welded to conical cast steel end pieces. These were then connected by 70 to 188 mm diameter high-tensile steel bolts to giant hollow cast steel spherical nodes 800 to 1000 mm in diameter (see Figures 5.3 and 5.4). The

5.1
Aerial view of the space truss 291.6 m × 108 m for the 'Symbol Zone', Festival Plaza Expo '70, Osaka, Japan (Photograph courtesy Mamoru Kawaguchi)

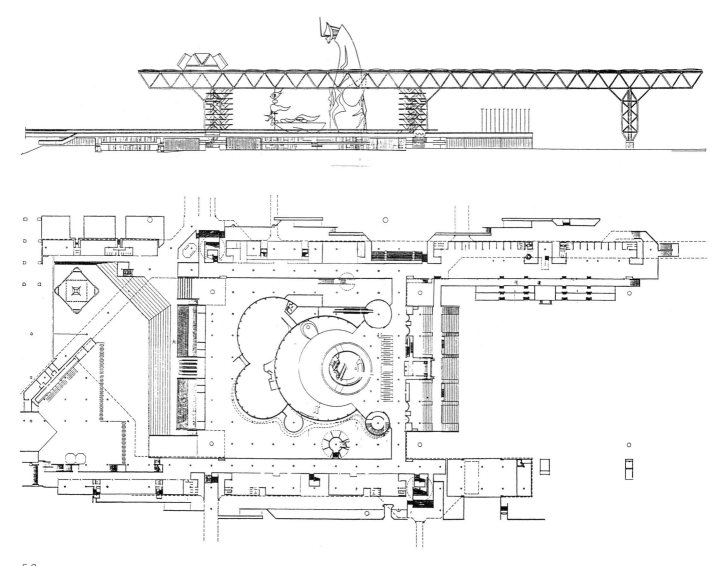

5.2
Plan and east elevation of the space truss for the 'Symbol Zone', Festival Plaza Expo '70, Osaka, Japan (Courtesy Mamoru Kawaguchi)

aesthetic of the roof structure was continued in the supporting columns which were constructed from similar elements, surrounding a central 1.8 m diameter tubular post. A total of 2272 tube members were used, connected at 639 nodes.[2]

It is interesting to note the philosophy that was adopted for this structure in terms of accuracy of fabrication. For space grids it is essential that the position of the nodes conforms with the proposed geometry. This is usually achieved by fabricating individual members and nodes to a high degree of accuracy, so that when they are assembled accumulated errors or tolerances do not affect the overall geometry, but this is expensive. The alternative solution, adopted here, was to fabricate the elements of the space grid to less rigorous dimensional accuracies and to accurately fix the position of the nodes

in space whilst allowing for small adjustments of member lengths in the connection details. Such a solution is not reasonable when there is a large number of nodes or when the grid is assembled in the air. However, in this case, where there are widely spaced nodes and assembly was at ground level it was a feasible and efficient solution. Here the adjustment in member length (up to ± 25 mm) was achieved using several steel shims (see Figure 5.4) inserted between the ends of the member cones and the spherical node. Angular discrepancies were catered for by the use of spherical contact faces between the fixing bolts and the inside of the node casting and by oversizing bolt holes by 12 mm to permit some degree of rotation. The bolts were introduced into the casting through an access hole that was later sealed by a cover plate.

5.3
Typical ball joint of space truss for the 'Symbol Zone', Festival Plaza Expo '70, Osaka, Japan (Photograph courtesy Mamoru Kawaguchi)

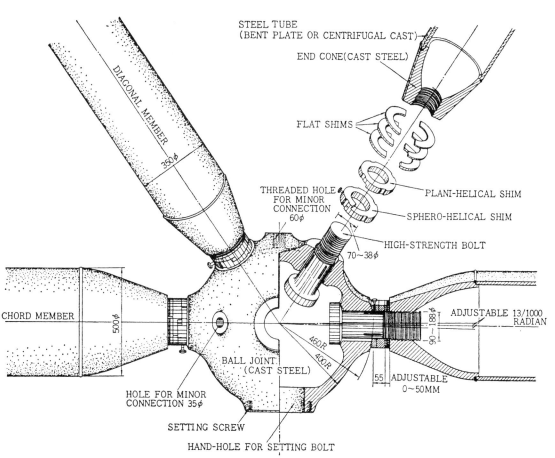

5.4
Diagram of typical ball joint, space truss for the 'Symbol Zone', Festival Plaza Expo '70, Osaka, Japan, showing method of connection with large high-strength bolts and shims to accommodate adjustments of the member length (Courtesy Mamoru Kawaguchi)

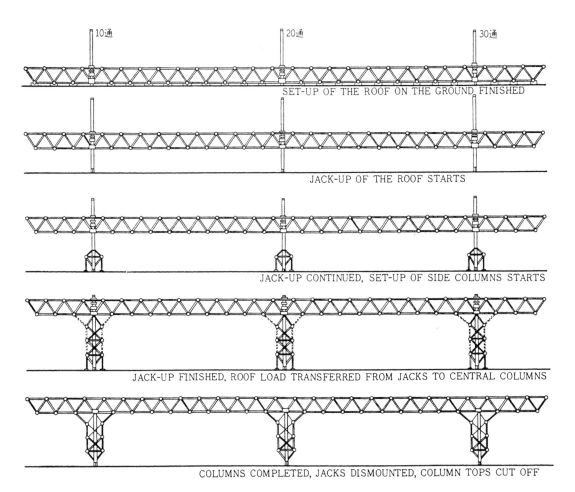

SET-UP OF THE ROOF ON THE GROUND FINISHED

JACK-UP OF THE ROOF STARTS

JACK-UP CONTINUED, SET-UP OF SIDE COLUMNS STARTS

JACK-UP FINISHED, ROOF LOAD TRANSFERRED FROM JACKS TO CENTRAL COLUMNS

COLUMNS COMPLETED, JACKS DISMOUNTED, COLUMN TOPS CUT OFF

5.5
Lifting sequence, for the space truss of the 'Symbol Zone', Festival Plaza Expo '70, Osaka, Japan (Courtesy Mamoru Kawaguchi)

Assembly of the space grid was carried out on the ground around the 1803 mm diameter central posts of the permanent columns. Subsequently, the roof was lifted in 80 mm steps, at the average rate of 2 m per day, using climbing pneumatic jacks of 450-tonne capacity. As the roof was lifted, erection of the outer framework of the columns was commenced and temporary struts were set in place at the base to provide rigidity against lateral seismic and wind forces, as can be seen in the erection sequence shown in Figure 5.5. When the lifting operation was completed, the load was transferred from the jacks to the permanent column structure by installation of the capital joints and removal of the temporary struts at the base. Lateral restraint was then provided by rigid frame action between the columns and roof structure, with 'pinned' column bases, thus reversing the previous temporary condition. To avoid 'locking-in' forces due to temperature differences during this transfer, it was carried out during one night.

An innovative solution, at the time, was the translucent roof which was made from inflated pillows introduced into each square of the top layer grid of the space truss. Two hundred and forty-three polyester film membrane cushions 9.9 m × 9.9 m were made from 1.1 m wide strips 250 microns thick. The upper skin was formed from six layers and the lower from five layers of polyester, with each layer running perpendicularly to those adjacent. Inflation was with dry air normally at 50 mm water pressure, or 100 mm in strong wind conditions. A special ultra-violet-resistant film was used for the outer layers of each pillow.[3] The use of inflated pillows within roof structures is currently finding favour with the use of highly translucent ethyltetrafluorethylene (ETFE) membranes.

Completed: 1969
Architects: Kenzo Tange
Space frame and theme space architects: Tomoo Fukuda and Koji Kamiya
Engineer: Yoshikatsu Tsuboi

Nusatsum House, Bella Coola Valley, British Columbia, Canada

The dwelling house is a building type where, in industrialized nations, there is little variation from the rigid adherence to cellular construction using orthogonal, load-bearing wall planes. This domination of the right angle was challenged by Randall G. Satterwhite in his design

5.6
Nusatsum House,
constructed in 1978
showing an uncanny
resemblance to the
surrounding mountain
peaks (Photograph
courtesy R. G.
Satterwhite)

for Nusatsum House, Bella Coola Valley, British Columbia, constructed in 1978. Tetrahedral and octahedral geometry was used in the design of a multi-layer space truss which initially splays outwards above the base before tapering inwards again towards the peaked roof. In fact, the steep-sided load-bearing three-dimensional structure, clad in timber shingles, is nearly all roof. The cladding colour and general form of the house make it highly reminiscent of the surrounding mountain peaks as can be seen in Figure 5.6.

Within the building, space truss nodes occur in horizontal planes at ten different levels. Nodes and bars are omitted from the multi-layer grid, as required, to form a series of interlinked irregular polyhedral cells, the living spaces, inside the space truss (see Figure 5.7). The layout of the triangulated grids at each horizontal level and a three-dimensional view of the structural configuration are shown in Figure 5.8. Architect, Randall Satterwhite, has commented that, rather than constructing the space truss to the pre-defined floor configurations with bars and nodes omitted, it might have been simpler to assemble the full dense grid and then subsequently to remove the unwanted structure, at each level, to form the required voids.

The space truss structure was composed of square section members, with a distance of approximately 1.5 m between node centres. Horizontal grid layers were thus spaced at approximately 1.06 m centres. The jointing system, illustrated in Figure 5.9, used prefabricated steel plate connectors with single bolts through the notched ends of the timber members.

5.7
Nusatsum House, internal view of irregular polyhedral living space
(Photograph courtesy R. G. Satterwhite)

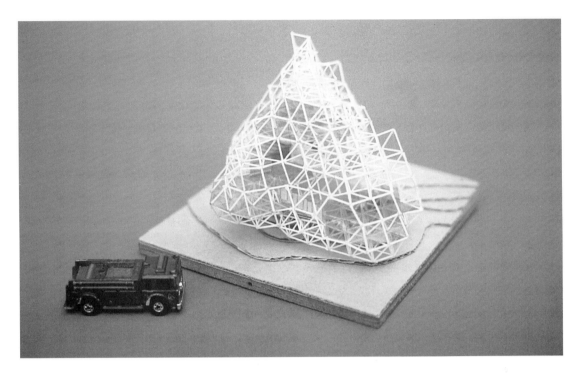

5.8
*Nusatsum House,
scale model of the
multi-layer space grid
(Photograph courtesy
R. G. Satterwhite)*

5.9
*Nusatsum House,
space truss node joint
(Photograph courtesy
R. G. Satterwhite)*

Noting the problems encountered in constructing this house, the architect Randall Satterwhite, proposed modifications to the system[4] as follows:

1 A revised jointing system that leaves flush surfaces for cladding, using a stronger member/node connector with improved geometric flexibility.

2 Improved provision for movement of the timber structure.

3 Increased member lengths to produce heights suitable for habitable spaces between the horizontal grids.

4 Computerized check on topography and member forces.

5   Prefabrication of wall and floor components using panels that can be joined at the angles that occur between planes in the truss (180°,125°, 54°, 70° and 109°).
6   A change to circular member cross-section.

A second research structure was later designed using 3.0 m long roundwood poles, 150 mm in diameter, connected at one-piece aluminium nodes cast from 356 T6 alloy.

Nusatsum House and the modified system demonstrate that it is possible to design and construct innovative housing forms using the efficient structural geometry of space trusses and the environmentally friendly material, timber. In particular, the second research structure used roundwood poles (usually considered low-grade timber suitable only for items such as fence posts) for the main elements. Problems of acceptance occur, however, due to the general public's reluctance to accommodate to a planning grid based on the triangle and polygonal living spaces with inclined wall planes. Inhabitable space grids (large and small) are discussed in more detail in Chapter 7.

The Crystal Cathedral, Garden Grove Community Church, California, USA

Space grid structures are primarily used for supporting horizontal and inclined roofs or, less commonly, floors. However, they are equally adaptable for use as vertical walls. Although not common, there are some interesting examples of buildings where almost all of the structure above ground is a space grid. The Crystal Cathedral, Garden Grove Community Church, in California is one such; a building almost totally enclosed in a fully glazed space structure (Figure 5.10). In fact the structure is not a true double-layer space grid as the inner chords run in only one direction, strictly making it a series of linked planar truss frames spanning in one direction. The architects dictated that there should be no transverse inner chords to interrupt the visual flow of the structure. Nevertheless, the building is included here as it is generally assumed to be a space grid or space frame structure (and could easily have been) and because the close connection of the frames does allow loads to be shared between them to some extent.

To those brought up in the European tradition of magnificent Gothic cathedrals constructed in masonry, the concept of a church or cathedral comprising a space structure fully clad in silver-coated reflective glass is anathema. However, the masons constructing the great cathedrals of medieval Europe were using their structural skills to admit ever more light to the interior. The Reverend Dr Robert Schuller, who commissioned the

building, had previously preached for many years in the open and would ideally have liked a building without roof or walls. With the benefits of modern materials and technology the architects and engineers achieved the next best thing – what has been described in an article by R. E. Fischer in the *Architectural Record*[5] as 'a glass tent of meaningful and breathtaking scale' (p. 78).

With a modified diamond plan, the cathedral has major and minor axes 126.5 m and 63.1 m long respectively (see Figure 5.11) and rises to 39 m above floor level. The space trusses are fabricated from tubular steel members, generally of 50.8, 63.5 and 76.2 mm diameter. Diagonals are mostly connected by welding or bolting to gusset plates welded to the chords that run parallel to the shorter axis of the diamond, as can be seen in the foreground of Figure 5.12. At the corners of the truss frames (the wall to roof junction) cast nodes are used to accommodate the high stresses and complex member configurations. Vertical as well as horizontal seismic forces, in accordance with the 1976 Uniform Building

5.10
Exterior view of the Crystal Cathedral, Garden Grove Community Church, California (Photograph courtesy N. M. T. Jackson)

Code, were considered owing to the slenderness of the roof in comparison with the much stiffer wall construction.

To minimize the visual intrusion of framing in the curtain wall glazing, the panes are flush-glazed using a low-modulus silicone sealant. Fixing to the space truss structure is by clips that allow six-way adjustment. A silver-coloured coating suppresses the heat of the solar radiation and the glazing admits just 8 per cent of incident light.

This is an example in which the use of a 'true', two-way spanning, space truss was rejected for architectural reasons, to maintain the visual flow of the structure. This tends to reinforce one of the common arguments against space grids in general, and space trusses in particular, that the clarity of the geometry displayed in plans and elevations is lost in the building as constructed. In the Crystal Cathedral, the purity of the efficient structural form was sacrificed to lighten the structure visually. Even then, the impression from within the space grid is of a dense white filigree overlying the transparent envelope.

Completed: 1979/80
Owner: Garden Grove Community Church, California
Architect: Johnson/Burgee Architects (Philip Johnson and John Burgee)
Engineer: Severud-Perrone-Szegezdy-Sturm
Structural steel fabricator: Pittsburgh-Des Moines Steel Co.

5.11
Interior view along the 126.5 m long major axis of the Crystal Cathedral, Garden Grove, California (Photograph courtesy N. M. T. Jackson)

5.12
Typical node connections in the Crystal Cathedral, Garden Grove, California (Photograph courtesy N. M. T. Jackson)

The National Exhibition Centre and Birmingham International Arena, Birmingham, UK

Phase 1 of the National Exhibition Centre on the outskirts of Birmingham represents one of the most extensive uses of the Nodus system developed by British Steel, Tubes

Division (now British Steel Tubes & Pipes). Constructed in the late 1970s, the exhibition halls are on a regular 30 m by 30 m column grid, which ideally lends itself to the modular nature of the Nodus space grid. Roof areas are supported by ninety-three identical square on square offset assemblies of Nodus space truss, each 27.9 m by 27.9 m (Figure 5.13). The repetitive nature of the standard

5.13
National Exhibition Centre Birmingham, UK, standard structural bay (Photograph courtesy British Steel, Tubes & Pipes)

5.14
National Exhibition Centre, Birmingham, UK, completed exhibition hall (Photograph courtesy British Steel, Tubes & Pipes)

5.15
The Birmingham
International Arena
(Photograph courtesy
British Steel, Tubes &
Pipes)

5.16
The Birmingham
International Arena
showing system of
Vierendeel masts and
CHS ties supporting
the planar beam grid.
Note the raised
section of roof at the
centre with clerestory
glazing around
(Photograph courtesy
British Steel, Tubes &
Pipes)

structural bay allowed efficient design and fabrication of the space grid. The completed exhibition area is shown in Figure 5.14.

Hall 7 of the National Exhibition Centre, (Figure 5.15) also known as The Birmingham International Arena, provides a column free area of 108 × 90 m and is used for concerts as well as exhibitions. The building received a Structural Steel Design Award in 1981.[6]

A system of eight 32 m high Vierendeel masts (each comprising four 450 mm × 250 mm RHS columns) and 273 mm diameter CHS ties support the intersection points of a planar grid of square hollow section box-

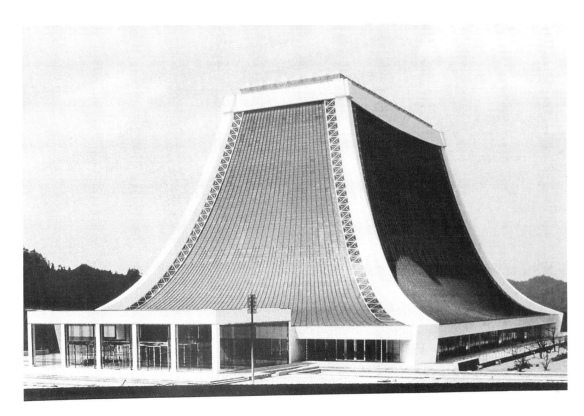

5.17
Meishusama Hall, Shiga Sacred Garden, Shigaraki, Shiga, Japan (Photograph courtesy Mamoru Kawaguchi)

trussed beams. The main trusses span at approximately the third points of each side and divide the plan into nine bays that are infilled with Nodus space trusses, similar to those used in the other exhibition halls. The space grid of the central zone is slightly raised to provide clerestory glazing to admit daylight when required. Each area of Nodus space truss was assembled on the ground, (including lighting, services and sprinklers) before being lifted and installed in the primary grid, as can be seen in Figure 5.16.

Owner: The National Exhibition Centre Ltd
Architect: Edward D. Mills & Partners
Engineer: Ove Arup & Partners
Steelwork contractor: Redpath Engineering Ltd
Main contractor: R. M. Douglas
Space frame fabricators (Nodus): Pipework Engineering Developments and Tubeworkers Ltd

Meishusama Hall, Shiga Sacred Garden, Shigaraki, Shiga, Japan

Completed in 1983, the Meishusama Hall of the Shiga Sacred Garden (Figure 5.17) is an example of the use of both a planar single-layer grid and curved double-layer space grids. This monumental building is a contemporary interpretation of the Japanese temple, which retains the traditional curved roof form whilst using the modern technology of steel structure and space grids to create

a vast enclosure of great presence, elegance and beauty in the mountain landscape. The hall, which is on an imposing podium approximately 150 m by 75 m, rectangular in plan (Figure 5.18) is located near to Kyoto in Japan and was constructed as a place of assembly and worship for Shinji-Shumei-kai.[7]

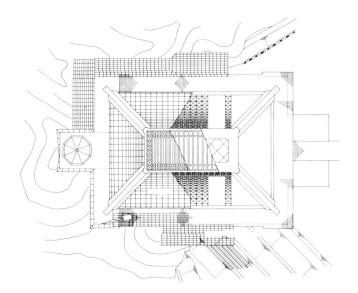

5.18
Plan of the Meishusama Hall, Shiga Sacred Garden, Shigaraki, Shiga, Japan

5.19
Interior of Meishusama Hall, Shiga Sacred Garden, Shigaraki, Shiga, Japan (Photograph courtesy Mamoru Kawaguchi)

5.20
The Jacob K. Javits, New York Exhibition and Convention Center (Photograph courtesy Alastair Gardner)

Four huge corner 'tusks', supported on massive concrete bases, rise above the reinforced concrete podium. The tusks, fabricated in sections from steel plates 23 to 32 mm in thickness, joined on site by high-strength bolts, support a rectangular steel box girder frame 49.4 m by 21.6 m. This in turn, is spanned by a planar diagonal grid roof. On each of the four sides of the hall, a curved double-layer space truss hangs in a shallow catenary curve. The space grids span 18.3 m horizontally between the high-level rectangular frame and girders at the perimeter walls, and have a vertical drop of around 34 m. Grid dimensions are 2.88 m by 2.88 m for both the top and bottom layers of the space truss, which is 1 m deep and constructed from 216.3 mm diameter steel tube chord members.

Together, these structural elements enclose the vast imposing space of the hall, 58.2 m wide, 86 m long, soaring 43 m above the podium and having a seating capacity of 5670. Externally, the enclosing catenary space grids are clad in 0.55 mm thick copper sheets supported on a 5 mm thick plywood deck. Beneath this, board insulation sits between timber rafters that are bolted to ribbed precast concrete panels (900 mm × 2.88 m × 60 mm

thick) fixed to the space grid. On the inside (Figure 5.19) there is a smooth, apparently jointless, pastel finish to reflect the light entering around the fully glazed perimeter walls, from the skylights and from glazed slots adjacent to each corner tusk.

Completed: 1983
Architect: Minoru Yamasaki & Associates
Engineer: Yoshikatsu Tsuboi
Contractor: Shimizu Construction Co.

Jacob K. Javits Center, New York, USA

The Jacob K. Javits, New York Exhibition and Convention Center (Figure 5.20), built in the early 1980s, is the biggest single area of space grid in the world.[8] Practically the whole envelope of the enormous building is constructed from space trusses on a standard grid module of 3.05 m. The gigantic pavilion, reminiscent of the Crystal Palace built in London in 1851, is sandwiched between Eleventh and Twelfth Avenues and Thirty-Fourth and Thirty-Ninth Streets in Manhattan, overlooking the Hudson River. The space grid has a plan area

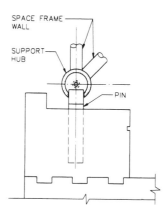

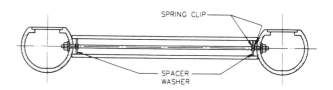

5.21
Typical bay of the space truss, Jacob K. Javits, New York Convention Center (Photograph courtesy Alastair Gardner)

5.22
Tension rod/tubular member detail, Jacob K. Javits, New York Convention Center (Courtesy Matthys Levy, Weidlinger Associates)

of over 53 000 m², stretching over 300 m by 165 m with a maximum width of 220 m in the section through the entrance hall, where it rises to a maximum height of 47 m above the floor. The architectural decision to clad the space grid mainly in semi-reflective glass, means that the giant structure all but disappears during the day as it reflects the sky, whilst at night the regular geometry of the delicate space grid web is revealed by the internal lighting.

A square 27 m × 27 m structural bay (Figure 5.21) is adopted for the Javits Center.[9] This is directly related to the normal stand size and layout for trade exhibitions. The structural bay dimensions, in turn, generate the 3 m × 3 m grid spacing of the space truss. At 1.5 m deep, the double-layer grid has a span/depth ratio of 18. This was adopted for reasons of geometry and aesthetics, to maintain the 45° inclination of the diagonals when viewed in section and to ease the transition from horizontal to vertical at the vertical corners of the walls. The

span/depth ratio appears to be rather conservative but this can be explained by the presence of heavy loads from ventilation equipment which, in some cases, can be up to 30 000 kg in one bay. To emphasize the way in which roof loads are channelled to the foundations, the space grid is supported on 'tree'-type columns, the 'trunks' consisting of four separate 400 mm diameter tubes. Fire resistance is provided by columns filled with reinforced concrete. Along the perimeter of each square bay an additional lower chord, connected by diagonal web bracing, is provided to form a diamond shaped truss 3 m deep overall. Each bay of the grid is therefore supported on all edges by an integral downstand beam which produces a partial triple layer grid.

In the patented PG System space grid, there are steel tubes running between hollow truncated spherical nodes, linked by a system of tension rods that pass through the centre of the tubes (see Figure 5.22). Individual tubes range from 75 mm to 215 mm in diameter, with the larger diameters being tapered at the ends to avoid contact with neighbouring tubes at the joints.

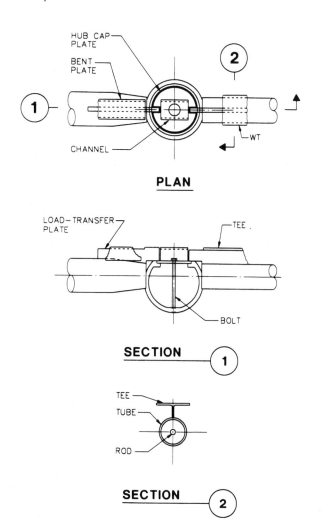

5.23
Decking support detail, New York Convention Center (Courtesy Matthys Levy, Weidlinger Associates)

5.24
Special glazing panels at angles, corners and the mansard roof (Photograph courtesy Alastair Gardner)

The tubes are considered to carry any compressive member forces whilst the 75 000 high-tensile steel rods, located inside the tubes, carry any tensile member forces. Rods range from 13 mm to 83 mm in diameter, and the hollow nodes have diameters of 215 mm to 240 mm with several different wall thicknesses. Assembly of the system induces a small pre-stress in the space grid. The upper chord tubes in the roof have a small 'T' section welded to the top to allow profiled steel decking to be fixed directly to the space grid without using secondary purlins (Figure 5.23).

To accommodate the thermal movement of the immense structure, the space truss is divided into several large areas bounded by diamond trusses with paired chords, so that each area acts as an independent structure. Expansion joints are provided in the cladding envelope and bearings of three types (fixed in position, sliding in one direction and free to slide in any horizontal direction, as appropriate) are installed at the top of the branched columns. Generally, the areas between expansion joints are fixed at the centre, thus minimizing the restraint to thermal movement and, consequently, the forces induced in the space grid by temperature changes. Almost exclusively the walls are not used to support the roof, which is supported by the internal columns. Predominantly the walls reaching down to the ground are restrained laterally at their bases but are free to move vertically.

A common problem with large flat roofs is that of disposal of rainwater. Usually, this is dealt with in space grid structures by providing a camber using slightly different member lengths for upper and lower chords. However, in the Javits Center the difficulty was overcome in a different manner. A minimum deflection was specified for the roof bays (as well as the more usual maximum deflection limit) and rainwater is assumed to pond at the low points where it is collected and discharged to the drainage system. This obviates the need for roof camber but might lead to problems if the drainage system is not adequately maintained. Although the glazed envelope of the building is 0.38 m from the outer layer of the space truss, panels were generally on the

5.25
Interior of New York Convention Center (Photograph courtesy Alastair Gardner)

same 3 m by 3 m grid but subdivided into 1.5 m by 1.5 m segments for reasons of economy and aesthetics. This means that special panels had to be used for re-entrant angles, corners and the mansard edge of the roof (Figure 5.24).

The Javits Center demonstrates the use of a proprietary space grid system to enclose a huge light and airy volume (Figure 5.25), creating this architectural space from a simple square on square offset structural configuration.

Owner: Convention Center Development Corp.
Architect: Pei, Cobb Freed
Engineer: Weidlinger Associates, Salmon Associates
Space frame: PG System (PG Structures Inc.)

Oguni Dome, Oguni-machi, Kumamoto Prefecture, Japan

Timber space grid structures are rare in comparison with their steel or aluminium counterparts. However, in Japan, there is a tradition of building large-scale structures, such as temples, castles and pagodas, from timber, and the Oguni Dome in the Kumamoto Prefecture of Kyushu follows this tradition. Located in the south island of Japan, this large gymnasium, built in 1988, is a fine example of the use of timber in a modern double-curved, double-layer space truss roof (Figure 5.26). Preservative-treated cedar, *sugi* in Japanese, is used throughout the roof which covers approximately 2835 m² with an organic domed form, clad in stainless steel. Plan dimensions are

5.26
Interior view of the Oguni Dome, Kumamoto Prefecture, Kyushu, Japan – a timber double-layer grid (Photograph courtesy Yoh Architects)

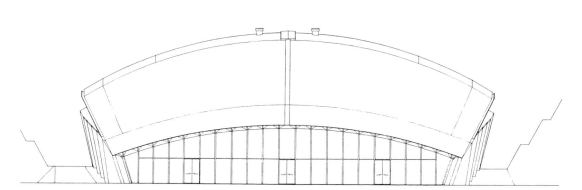

5.27(a)
North elevation, Oguni
Dome (Courtesy Yoh
Architects)

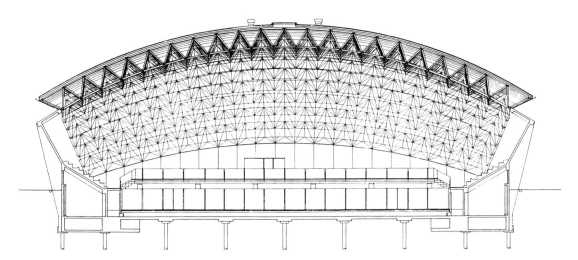

5.27(b)
Cross-section, Oguni
Dome (Courtesy Yoh
Architects)

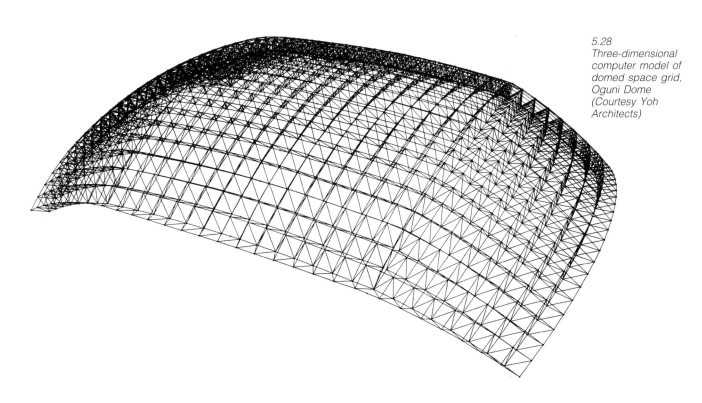

5.28
Three-dimensional
computer model of
domed space grid,
Oguni Dome
(Courtesy Yoh
Architects)

5.29
*Solid cedar members
of the Oguni Dome
(Courtesy Yoh
Architects)*

63 m by 47 m with a grid depth of only 2 m (a span to depth ratio of 23.5). Additional structural rigidity is derived from the three-dimensional curved form of the roof, seen in the elevations and sections Figures 5.27(a) and 5.27(b) and the three-dimensional view of Figure 5.28. This form allows a more slender space grid to be used.

The details of the space grid system used for the domed roof of the gymnasium were refined through a series of buildings by the same architect, Shoei Yoh.[10,11] A standard steel space grid system, TM truss, was adapted for use with timber members. As seen in Figure 5.29, solid cedar members, up to 110 by 150 mm, are used for the top chords and up to 110 by 170 mm for the bottom chords, with web bracing of 90 by 125 mm. At each end of the timber members there is a steel connector composed of a 42.7 mm diameter sleeve and bolt which is welded to an end cap and plate insert. These are fixed to the timber using two 16 mm bolts and pressure grouting with epoxy resin. The members are then ready for connection to the standard TM truss nodes, see Figures 5.29 and 5.30. A secondary system of purlins and rafters supports the stainless steel covered, insulated plywood roof deck and precast ceiling panels.

An important consideration in the use of timber for the space truss is its performance in case of fire. Timber burns or chars at a predictable rate and usually members can be oversized so that structural integrity is maintained for a prescribed period. In the Oguni Dome the space grid was raised, as can be seen in the detailed section Figure 5.31, to a minimum height of 6.2 m above

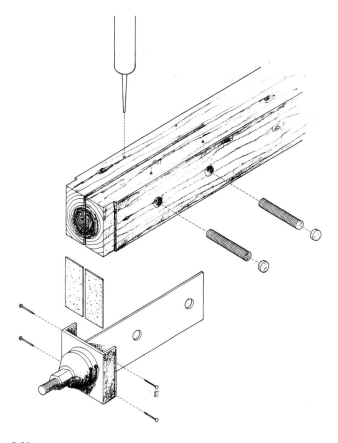

5.30
Oguni Dome, steel connector inserts for timber members for connection to standard TM truss ball nodes (Courtesy Yoh Architects)

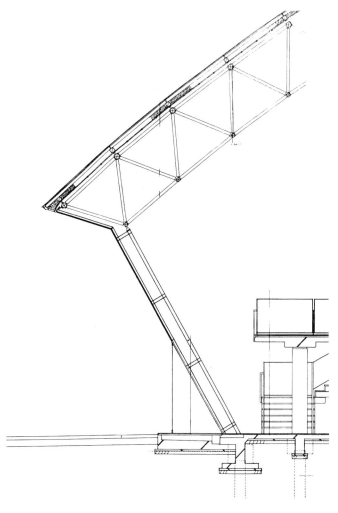

5.31
*Detailed section of perimeter wall and space grid, Oguni Dome
(Courtesy Yoh Architects)*

the gymnasium floor, to provide adequate distance between the structure and any possible fire at floor level. Some automatic sprinklers were also installed.

Considering the simplicity, elegance and aesthetic appeal of this space grid dome made from a warm natural, renewable structural material, it is perhaps surprising that more roofs of a similar nature are not constructed. Maybe this has something to do with a certain resistance, in many countries, to using timber for long-span structures as designers feel uncomfortable with its less predictable material properties.

Architects: Yoh Design Office
Engineers: Gengo Matsui and Atelier Furai
Contractor: Hashimoto Construction Co. Ltd

FFV Aerotech Hangar, Stansted Airport, UK

The FFV Aerotech Maintenance Hangar at Stansted Airport in the UK (Figure 5.32) is notable in that it is diamond shaped in plan and it is also the longest spanning CUBIC Space Frame to have been constructed to date.[12] Formed from two isosceles triangles with side lengths of 98 m, placed side by side, the long axis of the diamond is 170 m and the short axis is 98 m. With two door openings 72 m wide and 21 m high set in adjacent sides on the long axis of the hangar, it accommodates two Boeing 747-400 series aircraft (as shown in Figure 5.33). The space frame is supported on four major columns at the corners of the diamond, two 5.9 m deep lattice girders over the door openings and secondary columns at approximately 6.1 m centres around the remainder of the perimeter. Wind forces are predominantly transmitted to the ground by the four corner columns, which act as

5.32
*FFV Aerotech
Maintenance Hangar
at Stansted Airport,
UK (Photograph: John
Chilton)*

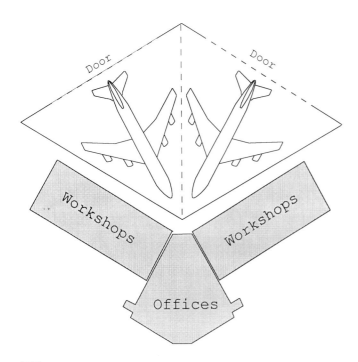

5.33
Sketch plan of hangar FFV Aerotech Maintenance Hangar at
Stansted Airport (Drawing: Carlos Márquez)

vertical cantilevers for this loading, whilst the remaining columns mainly resist vertical loads.

During the early development of the CUBIC Space Frame, there was some scepticism from engineers experienced in the design of space grids as to the economy of a true space-frame structure, that relies heavily on bending resistance to carry load, when compared to more conventional systems where the loads are resisted primarily by truss action (members in axial tension and compression only). However, the CUBIC Space Frame roof for the Stansted hangar was chosen on grounds of reduced cost over an alternative solution using a grid of deep lattice trusses infilled with space truss panels. Although the structural efficiency of the space frame may be lower (i.e the ratio of the live load carried by the structure when compared to its dead load) so that the structure is heavier than an equivalent space truss, the use of simple, cheap, fabrication techniques in its manufacture can make the system cost-effective.

An orthogonal double-layer grid, with an overall depth of 4.0 m, was used, with upper and lower chords running parallel to the principal axes of the diamond form (i.e. at an angle of 30° or 60° to the sides of the hangar). The main axes were divided into 48 equal bays in each direction, to give space grid modules approximately 3.5 m by 2.0 m (Figures 5.34(a) and (b)). In total, 1201 modules were used, the majority being 'X' shaped in plan, whilst the edge modules were generally 'L' shaped

in plan. All modules were fabricated in purpose-made jigs from standard Universal Beam and Column sections of seven different sizes, all nominally 200 or 400 mm deep, and the seven different size vertical web elements were all square or rectangular hollow sections varying from 200 by 200 mm to 300 by 300 mm. The resulting modules weighed between 0.5 and 1.0 tonnes. Rigid moment connections between the chords and verticals were reinforced with collar or flange plates and the ends of the tubular vertical posts were also capped with plates fully welded to the chord members. Connection between the modules used high-tensile steel, bolted, lap joints with plates welded to the webs at the ends of the chords. The maximum number of 24 mm diameter bolts in a lap was twenty, reducing to a minimum of two in the most lightly loaded lap joints. For rainwater run-off, the roof structure was cambered in both directions by shortening the chord module lengths in the lower grid.

Several methods of assembly were used at different stages of construction. Initially a temporary scaffolding tower was erected at the middle of the hangar. Three sections of space frame, with a total length equal to the short 98 m axis of the hangar and three modules in width, were then assembled on the ground. Using two mobile cranes the first section of space frame was then lifted and connected to one permanent column, whilst the other end was held in the air by one crane. The other crane then lifted the second preassembled section which was then bolted to the first section, using the standard chord lap joints, and rested on the temporary tower support. Subsequently, the remaining section of space frame was lifted and connected between the second section and the other permanent column. This formed a space grid bridge across the minor axis of the hangar so that erection could proceed on both sides if required. Modules were erected, individually or in small groups, on both sides of the bridge until it was seven modules wide, at which point the temporary tower was removed. Erection then proceeded on both sides of the bridge towards the acute corners of the diamond plan. During assembly of the grid some lack of fit problems were encountered due to the deformation of the grid under its own weight but these were overcome by use of purpose-designed frames and jacking devices to stress the new line of roof modules. Figure 5.35 shows the part-assembled grid under construction.

Compared to the original roof design, the CUBIC Space Frame saved approximately 2 m in the overall height of the hangar, reducing it to a little over 27 m. For the nearby Terminal Building, under construction at the same time, there had been a planning restriction that the height should not exceed that of the tallest tree on the site (approximately 15 m above ground level). A similar restriction would have been unreasonable for a hangar designed to house aircraft that themselves are around

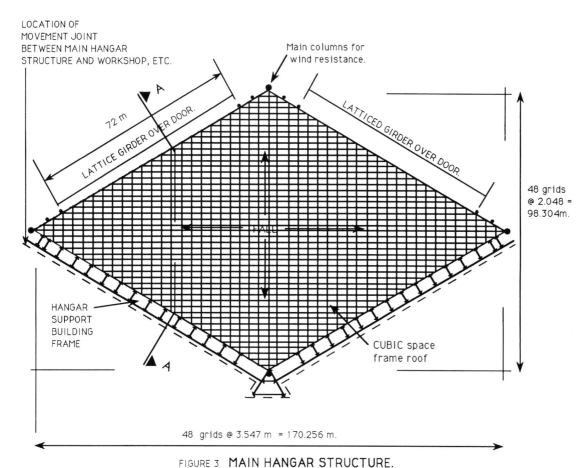

LOCATION OF
MOVEMENT JOINT
BETWEEN MAIN HANGAR
STRUCTURE AND WORKSHOP, ETC.

Main columns for
wind resistance.

▼ A

72 m

LATTICE GIRDER OVER DOOR.

LATTICED GIRDER OVER DOOR.

48 grids
@ 2.048 =
98.304m.

HANGAR
SUPPORT
BUILDING
FRAME

HALL

CUBIC space
frame roof

▲ A

48 grids @ 3.547 m = 170.256 m.

FIGURE 3 MAIN HANGAR STRUCTURE.

5.34(a)
Plan of FFV Aerotech
Maintenance Hangar
at Stansted Airport
(Drawing: Carlos
Márquez)

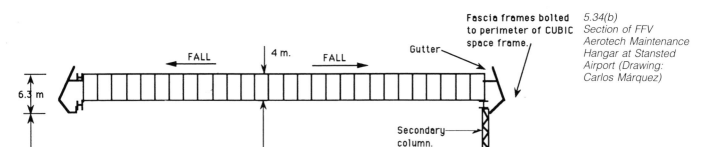

Fascia frames bolted
to perimeter of CUBIC
space frame.

Gutter

FALL   4 m.   FALL

6.3 m

21 m.

22.75 m + camber.

Secondary
column.

3.0 m

2.7 m

2.6 m

finished floor level.

1.2 m.

5.3 m.

TYPICAL SECTION A-A
(enlarged).

Hangar support building

5.34(b)
Section of FFV
Aerotech Maintenance
Hangar at Stansted
Airport (Drawing:
Carlos Márquez)

5.35
Part assembled roof
grid of FFV Aerotech
Maintenance Hangar
at Stansted Airport
(Photograph courtesy
L. A. Kubik)

20 m above ground at their highest point, however, keeping the overall height to a minimum was a major architectural design consideration.

In recognition of the innovative design of the hangar and its use of the CUBIC Space Frame, the project was honoured with the Supreme Award of the British Construction Industry Awards 1989 and also gained a Steel Design Award in 1990.

Completed: 1988
Architect: Faulks, Perry, Culley and Rech
Engineer: Sir Frederick Snow and Partners and Burks
Green and Partners (hangar steelwork and CUBIC
Space Frame)
Consultant: M. Leszek Kubik
Main contractor: Costain Construction Ltd
Steelwork and space frame fabricator: A. R. Hunt
Erector: Butler & George

Sant Jordi Sports Palace, Barcelona, Spain

One of the most frequent criticisms that is levelled at space grids, is that they are suitable for flat roofs covering rectilinear floor plans but that they become uneconomic when used for more complicated roof forms or building plans. This argument is powerfully and elegantly refuted by the Palau Sant Jordi, or Sant Jordi Sports Palace, in Barcelona (Figure 5.36). Following an international design competition held in 1983, Arata Isozaki (architect) and Mamoru Kawaguchi (engineer) were commissioned to design the 15 000-seat Sports Palace which was to be constructed as the main indoor arena for the 1992 Barcelona Olympiad. Conceptually, the designers wanted to capture the technology of the age and for this reason chose a 'mass-produced' system but in the modern sense where robotics, CAD, computer-aided manufacture (CAM) and NC techniques allow 'mass-production' of small quantities with many variants. Hence, a 'mass-produced' space truss was adopted but for a reasonably complex form that required the modern technology for its economic fabrication and erection.[13,14]

All four sides of the stadium are curved in plan and the cross-section is arched along both major axes (see Figures 5.37 and 5.38(a) and (b)). There is a central zone that is built to a slightly different curvature and also tapers slightly in the direction of the long axis of the arena. This area is surrounded by a continuous skylight and is also perforated with smaller domed skylights on a pattern conforming to the space grid upper chord configuration. In contrast to the profiled-metal decking that is more commonly used to clad space grids, the roof is finished with two alternative materials – black ceramic tiles and zinc metal sheeting.[15] The impression generated is that of a protective shell, shielding the athletes and spectators from the heat of the Barcelona summer sun.

The space grid roof has maximum plan dimensions of 128 by 106 m within which the central zone, of different curvature, is approximately 80 by 60 metres. In both the

5.36
Sant Jordi Sports
Palace, Barcelona,
Spain (Photograph:
John Chilton)

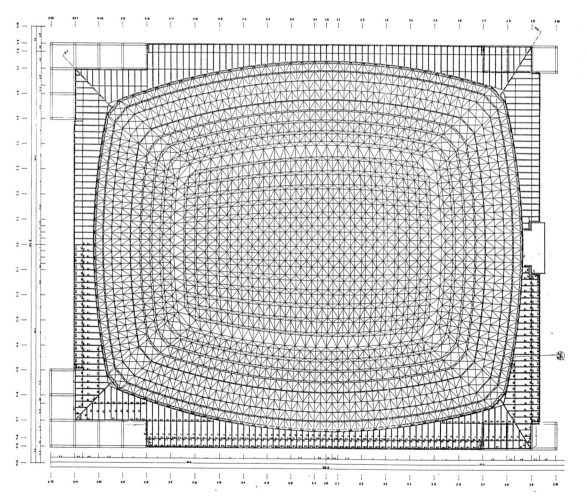

5.37
Plan of the roof
structure, Sant Jordi
Sports Palace
(Courtesy Mamoru
Kawaguchi)

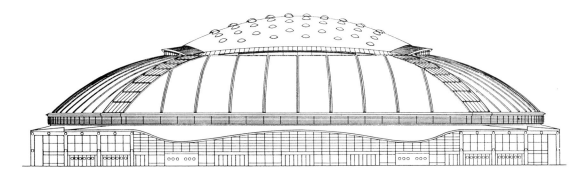

5.38(a)
North elevation of the
Sant Jordi Sports
Palace (Courtesy
Mamoru Kawaguchi)

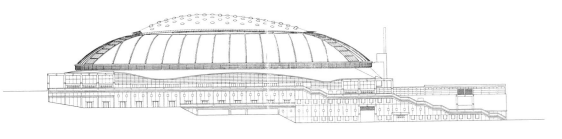

5.38(b)
West elevation and
longitudinal section of
the Sant Jordi Sports
Palace (Courtesy
Mamoru Kawaguchi)

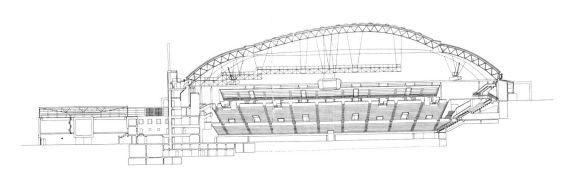

central and perimeter sections of the roof the space truss has a depth of only 2.50 metres (1/42 of the shorter span of the arena). However, the domed nature of the roof (see elevations in Figures 5.38(a) and (b)) clearly offers the development of significant arch (membrane) action so that normal flat roof span/depth ratios are not really applicable. From the top of the column supports to the high point of the roof the maximum rise is 21 m with a maximum final height above the arena floor of approximately 45 m.

The roof structure was assembled from 9190 members mainly ranging from 76 mm to 267 mm in diameter, although some 406 mm and 508 mm tubes were used at the periphery. Members are connected using 2403 cast steel spherical nodes varying from 100 to 250 mm in diameter. The whole space grid roof structure stands on just sixty perimeter tubular steel columns 508 mm or 609.6 mm in diameter, depending on their location. The SEO system space truss (described in Chapter 3) was manufactured by Orona using steel

tubes, fabricated to an accuracy of 0.3 mm in their length, and 'ball type' forged node joints drilled, using computerized numerical control (CNC) drilling equipment, to receive the connecting bolts. Modern computer-controlled cutting and drilling techniques allowed practical fabrication of dissimilar elements making the generation of the dome form more economic.

Notable though the form may be, perhaps the most innovative aspect of the space grid roof is its method of erection, which was developed by the Japanese engineer Mamoru Kawaguchi and is known as the 'Pantadome' System. This technique, first used for the erection of the roof of the World Memorial Hall in Kobe, Japan, is described in detail in Chapter 6. It involves the assembly of the space grid in a partially folded form that is subsequently unfolded into the final shape. Here, this allowed efficient erection of the central portion of this complex roof at low level near the arena floor before it was raised to its final location.

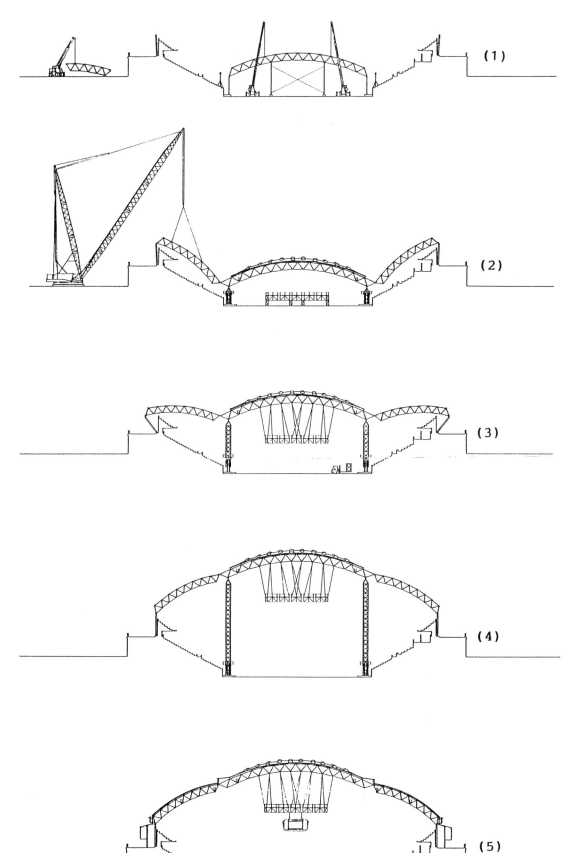

(1)

(2)

(3)

(4)

(5)

5.39
Erection sequence of
Sant Jordi Sports
Palace using the
'Pantadome' system
(1) erection of central
dome, (2)
erection/connection of
side frames, placed
by Orona, and
construction of lifting
towers and secondary
structure, (3) partial
lift, (4) completed lift,
(5) jacking towers
removed (Courtesy
Mamoru Kawaguchi)

A = Support frame for lifting unit
B = Lifting unit
C = Standard Acrow tower
D = Lifting frame

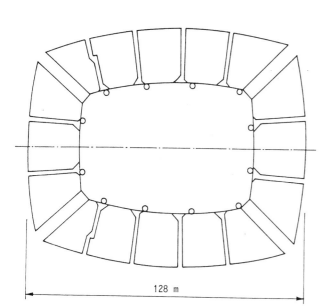

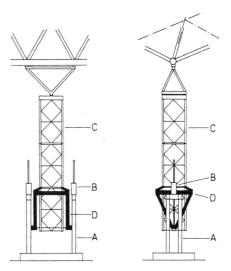

5.40
Plan layout of roof segments and location of jacking towers indicated by the small circles (Courtesy Mamoru Kawaguchi)

The erection sequence shown in Figure 5.39, commenced with the assembly of the centre portion of the roof on temporary supports, approximately 6 m above the floor of the arena, and directly beneath its final location in plan. Sixteen perimeter sections of space frame were then constructed and connected, by hinged joints, both to the perimeter columns and to the central roof section. The perimeter columns were also hinged at their bases (tangentially to the curve connecting the bases). It is interesting to note that the hinges were on the central axis of the 609.6 mm columns but offset towards the perimeter of the arena on the 508 mm columns. The consequent eccentricity of the vertical roof load aided the stability of the mechanism, as it 'encouraged' the hinges to fold in only one way (with the roof to the inside of the columns). At the corners of the arena, wide gaps were left between the perimeter space grid sections. Narrower gaps were left between the space grid sections along the arena sides. The plan view of the roof (Figure 5.40) shows the disposition of the space grid segments before lifting and small circles indicate the positions of lifting towers. At this stage, the whole structure was mechanically very flexible.

By a careful computer-controlled jacking operation, the central roof section was moved vertically to its final position between 22 November and 3 December 1988. Twelve jacking towers were used, with a tetrahedral frame at the top of each, to spread the jacking force into two nodes of the lower layer roof grid and to guarantee full horizontal articulation. The jacking process caused the perimeter space grid sections to be raised from their initial orientation, pointing down into the bowl of the arena, to their final position pointing upwards to support the central dome section. During this operation the tops of the perimeter columns were first forced outwards, to allow the perimeter space grid sections to change their alignment, before returning to the vertical when the central roof section achieved its final position. Subsequently, additional space grid members were inserted into the gaps between the perimeter sections to complete the three-dimensional dome form and lock the mechanism. The jacking towers were then removed leaving the floor of the arena free. Maximum vertical displacement of the roof during removal of the jacking force and props was 140 mm, in close agreement with the computer analysis of the roof. A secondary structure, 60 × 22 m in plan and weighing 83 tonnes, which carries electronic scoreboards, video screens and sound equipment, is suspended at the centre of the arena from the domed space truss. This assembly was erected on the floor of the arena beneath the space truss dome and lifted to its final position during the same operation, being raised from the arena floor on the second day of the lift. Four stages of the actual erection process are shown in the sequence of photographs in Figure 5.41.

On the principal hinge lines, those connecting the central dome to the side grids, and at the four corners of the arena, the roof has glazed strips that leave a permanent reminder of the method of erection.

5.41
Aerial views of roof
lifting sequence
(Photograph courtesy
Mamoru Kawaguchi)

(a)

(b)

To accommodate thermal expansion and contraction of the large roof structure without inducing stresses in the space truss, all of the perimeter columns are hinged at both top and bottom to allow free movement in a direction perpendicular to the roof perimeter. To resist lateral forces on the roof such as wind forces, pairs of adjacent columns are linked at the top to form rigid portal frames (twenty-two in total: fourteen longitudinally and

eight transversely). Due to the method of support on a limited number of columns, to the spectator inside the Sant Jordi Sports Palace, the space truss roof appears to float above the mass of the concrete stands.

There are several advantages to this system of construction and erection. First, the assembly of the complex roof form is accomplished at a convenient level above the ground, where exposure to strong winds is

(c)

(d)

reduced and the dangers associated with working at height are minimized. Second, it is possible to partially complete the roof covering and install services without using expensive secondary access structures. The same method of erection was also previously used for the National Indoor Stadium in Singapore, where Mamoru Kawaguchi worked with the architect Kenzo Tange. It has been used subsequently for the Kadoma Sports Hall

and a stepped-surfaced dome with a 116 m diameter circular plan, the Sun-Dome, Sabae, in Fukui Prefecture, Japan. Detailed studies of these further examples are presented in Chapter 6.

Completed: 1990
Architect: Arata Isozaki
Engineer: Mamoru Kawaguchi
Space frame: Orona SEO system

Biosphere 2, Sonoran Desert, Arizona, USA

Biosphere 2 was an exciting experiment in controlling the natural environment within an airtight envelope and it was fitting that such a project was housed within a giant space grid.[16] Constructed in 1990 in the harsh environment of the Arizona desert, near Tucson, the complex comprised five major pavilions; the Wilderness Biome; the Intensive Agriculture Biome; the Habitat and two Lung Domes (so called because the membranes within them controlled the

*5.42
Biosphere 2, Wilderness Biome, 55 m span stepped pyramid (Photograph courtesy Peter Trebilcock)*

*5.43
Biosphere 2, Intensive Agriculture Biome with the Lung Dome in the background (Photograph courtesy Peter Trebilcock)*

5.44
Multi-hinge System 'nodeless' joint (Photograph courtesy Peter Trebilcock)

Domes. Instead of a separate node, each tubular member is closed by welded end caps and has pre-drilled fin plates welded on to the tube in predetermined positions adjacent to the ends.[17] Assembly of the grid is achieved by bolting the members together directly, by means of the fins, in predetermined configurations. Transfer of forces within the joints is solely by shear resistance of the connecting bolts. A benefit of this method of 'nodeless' connection is the stiffness of the joint which improves the overall performance of the space truss.

An essential part of the Biosphere 2 project was the maintenance of an environment separate from that of Biosphere 1 (i.e. Earth itself). Therefore, it was of paramount importance that there was, as near as possible, an airtight seal between the structure and glazing or cladding panels. Pearce Systems developed an airtight version of their Integral Glazing System using materials compatible with those of the space grid, steel glazing frames with glass bonded to them in the factory, with silicone structural sealants. Pre-glazed frames were mechanically fixed to the space truss and a silicone caulking was applied between adjoining units. The structural geometry was designed to reduce movements due to thermal effects to a minimum and the use of steel glazing frames practically eliminated any differential thermal movement between the primary structure and its cladding. Therefore, no expansion joints were needed in the structure and the small movements between the glazing panels and the space truss could be accommodated easily by the sealant. However, as Biosphere 2 is designed for a life of over 100 years, there is the possibility that the sealing compounds may deteriorate with time and affect the airtightness.

In the Biosphere 2 project the flexibility in use of space grid structures is abundantly demonstrated as the Pearce Multi-hinge System is used for a wide range of structural forms and for both single- and double-layer space grids.

Architects: Margaret Augustine,
Phil Hawes, John Allen
Space frame contractor: Pearce Systems
International, USA

National Indoor Arena for Sport, Birmingham, UK

The Birmingham National Indoor Arena for Sport (NIAS)[18] is of similar size to the Sant Jordi Sports Palace in Barcelona (described above) and was built, under a design and build contract, at about the same time. However, the configuration chosen for its space grid roof and the method of erection were completely different. Although the Birmingham Arena, seen under construction in Figure 5.45, has the familiar stadium plan form

variations in internal pressure in the Biomes, due to changes in ambient temperature). The Wilderness Biome was constructed from 40 000 members forming two stepped pyramids linked by a galleria stepped in section. Overall the building is 168 m long and spans up to 55 m in the largest pyramid (Figure 5.42). The structure is totally glazed, as is the 15 000 member multi-vaulted structure of the Intensive Agriculture Biome, seen in Figure 5.43. A mixture of steel and glass cladding was used on the space grid shell structure of the Habitat and almost exclusively steel cladding on the 55 m diameter Lung Domes, seen in the background of Figure 5.43.

The space grid adopted for this project is a 'nodeless' form, the Multi-hinge System developed by Peter Pearce (Figure 5.44). It was used in a double-layer for the two Biomes and in a single layer for the Habitat and Lung

*5.45
Birmingham National
Indoor Arena for
Sport (NIAS) under
construction
(Photograph courtesy
Mero UK)*

of a quadrilateral with curved sides, the space grid roof in this case is a three-layer space truss with horizontal soffit, inclined top chords and mansard edges, constructed using the Mero KK system (described in Chapter 3). As the geometrical form (a flat plate rather than the domed profile of the Sant Jordi Sports Palace) is not as structurally efficient, the 128 m by 90 m space truss is 10 m deep at the centre, reducing to approximately 8 m deep at the top of the mansard edges (see the plan in Figure 5.46 and section in Figure 5.47). The span to depth ratio is, therefore, approximately 9:1 in this case.

With this depth of space grid it becomes more economical to use a triple-layer system, as this reduces the length of compression members (e.g. top chord and web bracing elements) which have to be designed to resist buckling under axial compressive forces, where the length of the member has a considerable influence on its load carrying capacity. Consequently, by the adoption of a triple-layer grid, the cross-sectional dimensions, and therefore the weight, of the compression members is reduced. This more than compensates for the increase in weight due to the additional horizontal middle grid layer and extra node joints. On the other hand, it adds to the number of node joints required and increases the complexity of the roof structure, thus tending to extend the time and cost of erection. In the Birmingham NIAS roof, the middle-layer nodes are situated 4.0 m above the lower layer at the perimeter and 4.7 m at the centre of the span.

The roof uses 4934 tubular members varying from 76.1 mm diameter with 2.9 mm wall thickness up to 219.1 mm diameter, 22.2 mm thick. Over half the members are 127 mm diameter or bigger. Diameters of the Mero KK nodes range from 110 mm to 350 mm with those of 155 and 228 mm diameter being the most common sizes. Self-weight of the space truss is 0.42 kN/m^2 which is approximately 20 per cent of the total design dead and imposed load for the roof.[19] The grid is supported at thirty-six nodes on sliding bearings that permit thermal movement to take place radially from the centre of the roof (see above, Figure 4.3).

One of the advantages of space grid construction is that large structures can be assembled from small elements on site with limited disruption to other site activities. At the Birmingham Arena the site had very restricted access, with a main railway line running through its centre and a canal to one side. In fact, the arena had to be built straddling the railway line, which was enclosed in a new tunnel. Multistorey car parks on each side of the tunnel completed the podium on which the stadium was built. Initially, the 145 m long tunnel was constructed by the main contractor to cover and protect the railway and provide a working platform at what would eventually become the arena floor level. At each side of this tunnel, the reinforced concrete framed car parks were erected and above these, the raked seating for the spectators. A concrete ring beam support for the space grid was cast in situ to the rear of the seating. Ring beam

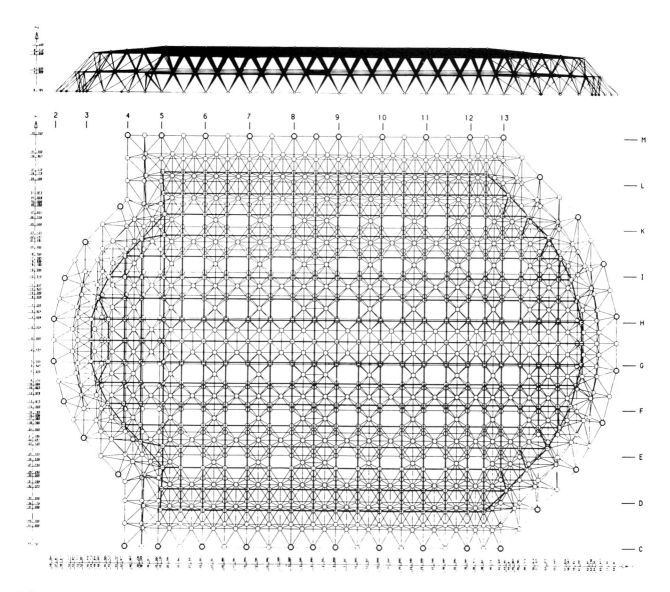

5.46
Plan of the space grid layout for the roof of the Birmingham National Indoor Arena for Sport (Courtesy Mero UK)

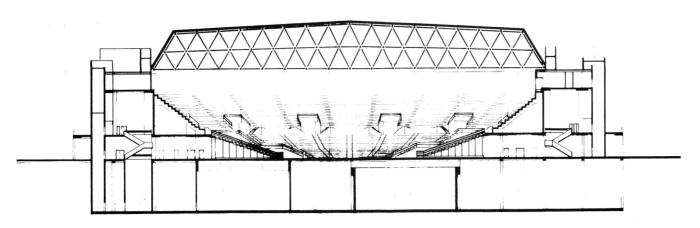

5.47
Cross-section of the Birmingham National Indoor Arena for Sport (Courtesy Mero UK)

5.48
Assembly at arena level of a 'spider' of several space grid members connected to a single node, NIAS, Birmingham (Photograph: John Chilton)

construction progressed from one end of the arena, thus allowing erection of the space frame to commence before the concrete substructure was complete. Installation of cladding and services then followed closely behind the erection of the space grid.

Two distinct methods of assembly were used for the space grid. The first section of roof to be installed was above the raked seating at one end of the arena and, to establish a structurally stable section of space grid, temporary falsework was constructed from standard Mero parts to provide a working platform and to sustain the grid until it became self-supporting. Subsequently, small 'spiders' of a few tubular members connected to one node were assembled at arena level (Figure 5.48) and lifted into position, using a gantry crane running along the top of the railway tunnel. The 'spider' sections were then connected, in the air, to the previously erected section of space grid (Figure 5.49).

As construction progressed along the principal axis of the arena, temporary props were installed at predetermined levels and locations to limit the deformation of the incomplete space grid under the dead loads. Once the roof structure was completed the temporary props were removed in order to fully transfer loads to the permanent supports and allow the roof to take up its natural deformed shape. During the process of load transfer, the measured vertical deflection at the centre of the roof (131 mm) was about 10 mm less than that predicted by the computer analysis of the structure.

5.49
Connection of 'spider' to previously erected section of space grid (Photograph: John Chilton)

The space grid roof of the Birmingham Arena is covered with a perforated steel deck supported on cold-formed steel purlins attached to the space truss by brackets screwed into the Mero KK ball joints in the top layer. Above the decking there are acoustic insulation and a further 130 mm of mineral wool thermal insulation separated by a vapour check membrane. A site heat-welded Trocal membrane, fixed mechanically through the insulation to the metal deck, provides the weatherproof envelope.

It was simple to install access ways and apparatus throughout the roof structure due to the regular supports provided by the grid chords. Given the building's use, an allowance of 0.72 kN/m^2 was included for roof service loading, plus 700 m of walkways with a load of 1.35 kN/m^2. At its centre, the space truss carries a large suspended electronic scoreboard and a large quantity of lighting, sound and ventilation equipment. The complete roof, including the built-up roofing system and all walkway gantries, was programmed to be completed in twenty-nine weeks. This tight schedule was achieved with two days to spare.

Completed: 1990
Architect: Hellmuth Obata Kassabaum (HOK)/
Percy Thomas Partnership
Space frame contractor: Mero UK
Main contractor: Laing Midlands

Lan Chile, Maintenance Hangar, Aeropuerto Comodoro Arturo Merino Benítez, Santiago, Chile

Aeropuerto Comodoro Arturo Merino Benítez, Santiago, is the main international airport for Chile, which has one of the fastest growing economies in Latin America. To cater for the increased number of national and international flights generated by the high level of economic activity, a maintenance hangar was constructed for Lan Chile, one of the national airlines.[20] As well as being used to maintain its own fleet, the facilities are also available to other carriers. The hangar (Figure 5.50) which is 5300 m^2 in area can accommodate simultaneously one Boeing B-747 and two B-737s. It also houses a mezzanine floor for stores, offices and specialist workshops. A steel structure was chosen because of the necessity for a long clear span to provide a flexible space and because it was predicted that the poor ground conditions would lead to differential settlement incompatible with other types of structure. Chile, being at the rim of the Pacific tectonic plate, is a zone of relatively high seismic activity. The well-known resistance of space grids to seismic loading pointed towards the adoption of this type of high-strength, lightweight steel structure for the large clear span.

The 75 m × 75 m hangar roof has four main trussed steel corner columns, 'L' shaped in plan, with columns of square hollow section 400 mm × 400 mm wall thickness 12.5 mm. These are designed to resist the lateral

5.50
Lan Chile hangar,
Aeropuerto Comodoro
Arturo Merino Benítez,
Santiago, Chile
(Photograph: John
Chilton)

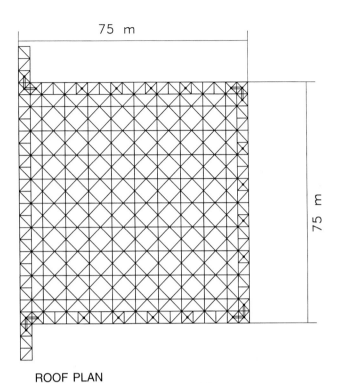

75 m

75 m

ROOF PLAN
LAN CHILE HANGAR SANTIAGO

5.51
Plan of space grid roof, Lan Chile hangar, Aeropuerto Comodoro Arturo Merino Benítez, Santiago, Chile (Drawing: John Chilton)

wind and seismic forces. Smaller intermediate columns carry only vertical load. Perimeter beams link the corner columns. The space grid is composed of eighty-one square inverted pyramidal modules set on a chequered pattern grid (i.e. as can be seen in Figure 5.51, alternate squares in the diagonal grid do not contain diagonal bracing members). Top chords of the grid run at an angle of 45° to the sides of the hangar whilst the bottom chords, which connect the vertices of the pyramids, run parallel to the sides at 7.5 m centres, thus forming a rotated square on square offset space truss. Each pyramid module is 5.3 m by 5.3 m (or 7.5 m by 7.5 m on the diagonal) and 3.87 m deep. They were fabricated on site in two purpose-made jigs to maintain the precise dimensional accuracy required. Although the space grid weighs only 20 kg/m² on average, it is able to sustain a concentrated load of 10 tonnes at any of its nodes, to allow for the installation of an overhead crane in future. This demonstrates one of the advantages of space grids, their ability to easily accommodate point loads at almost any location.

With a simple square roof supported on corner columns, it would have been relatively straightforward to assemble the space grid on the floor of the hangar and then to lift it to its final location by jacking using the per-

manent columns. However, the construction programme did not permit this and, in fact, the modules were assembled in the air, each being supported temporarily on a prop so that the correct unloaded roof profile was obtained.

To reduce the possibility of condensation on the steelwork, the aluminium-clad roof has mineral wool insulation. Roof drainage is into gutters running parallel to the door opening, at 15 m centres. Secondary steelwork supported on stools at the upper nodes support a purlin system to carry the roof decking. Overall, the building is an excellent example of the use of space grid structures to obtain large clear span volumes of great flexibility in using technology easily exploitable in developing countries.

Year: 1988–91
Architects: Cayo César Riquelme V., Rodrigo Riquelme A., Rafael Videla B., Arquitectos Asociados
Structural engineers: Fluor Daniel Chile S.A., Pablo Weithhofer, Reinaldo González (Chile), Ronald Taylor (England)
Project director engineer: Carlos Jouanne B.
Contractors: Tecsa, Socometal, Construtora B.D.S., Vapor Indutrial S.A., Emanor, Ingevec

Palafolls Sports Hall, Spain

Situated between the city of Barcelona and Spain's Costa Brava, Palafolls is a small town where a sports hall, constructed in 1991, has a space grid roof of striking form. This roof structure is an example that contradicts the commonly held perception that space grids are appropriate only for planar roofs of simple rectangular plan form. Its shape was derived from a simple scale working model (Figure 5.52) proposed by the project's architect Arata Isozaki, who also designed the Sant Jordi Sports Palace for the 1992 Olympics in Barcelona. In fact, the roof in Palafolls bears some resemblance to Isozaki's original proposal for the larger Barcelona roof.

The scheme as a whole is based on a 70 m diameter circular plan. Half of this is an open-air sports facility, whilst the remainder is a multi-use pavilion, semicircular in plan, covered by a double-layer, three-way space truss. To provide good natural illumination within the hall, the north elevation, which bisects the grand plan, comprises a vertical glazed façade incorporating deep triangulation (see Figure 5.53) down to a row of vertical columns. This dramatic aspect supports one edge of the space truss, whilst the remainder is supported at regular intervals along the circular perimeter (see Figure 5.54). Although symmetrical about an axis perpendicular to the glazed façade, the roof is an intricate three-dimensionally curved surface that is divided into three principal zones. The complexity is compounded by the introduction of a verti-

5.52
Concept model,
Palafolls Sports Hall,
near Barcelona
(Photograph courtesy
J. Martínez-Calzón)

5.53
Deep truss supports,
Palafolls Sports Hall,
near Barcelona
(Photograph courtesy
J. Martínez-Calzón)

5.54
Junction between the
toroidal and
spheroidal roof zones
also showing the
perimeter column
supports, Palafolls
Sports Hall, near
Barcelona
(Photograph courtesy
J. Martínez-Calzón)

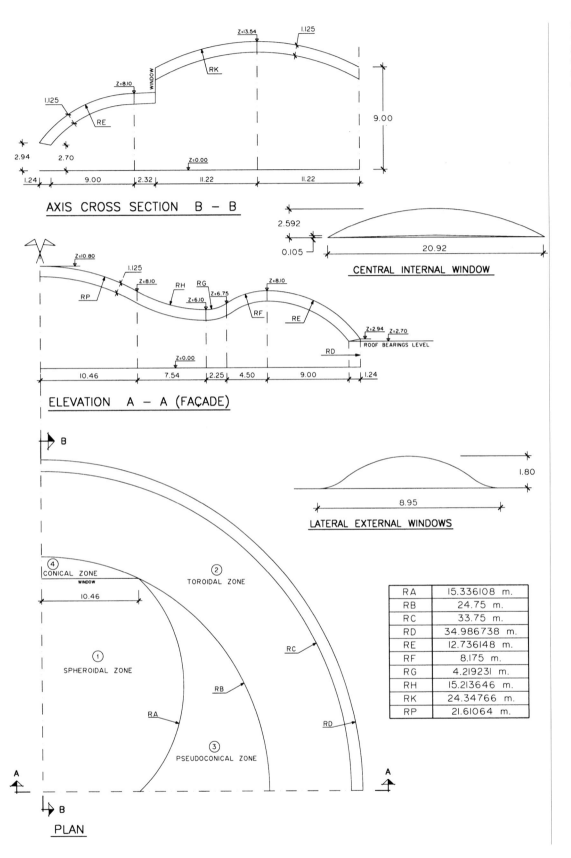

Z=13.54   1.125

RK

Z=8.10

WINDOW

1.125

RE

2.94   2.70

9.00

Z=0.00

1.24   9.00   2.32   11.22   11.22

AXIS CROSS SECTION B – B

2.592

0.105

20.92

CENTRAL INTERNAL WINDOW

Z=10.80

1.125

Z=8.10   RH   RG   Z=8.10

RP   Z=6.10   Z=6.75   RF   RE

Z=2.94 Z=2.70

ROOF BEARINGS LEVEL

RD

Z=0.00

10.46   7.54   2.25   4.50   9.00   1.24

ELEVATION A – A (FAÇADE)

B

1.80

8.95

LATERAL EXTERNAL WINDOWS

④ CONICAL ZONE

WINDOW

10.46

② TOROIDAL ZONE

① SPHEROIDAL ZONE

RC

RB

RA

③ PSEUDOCONICAL ZONE

RD

A   A

B

PLAN

RA	15.336108 m.
RB	24.75 m.
RC	33.75 m.
RD	34.986738 m.
RE	12.736148 m.
RF	8.175 m.
RG	4.219231 m.
RH	15.213646 m.
RK	24.34766 m.
RP	21.61064 m.

5.55
Detailed roof geometry, Palafolls Sports Hall, near Barcelona (Courtesy J. Martínez-Calzón)

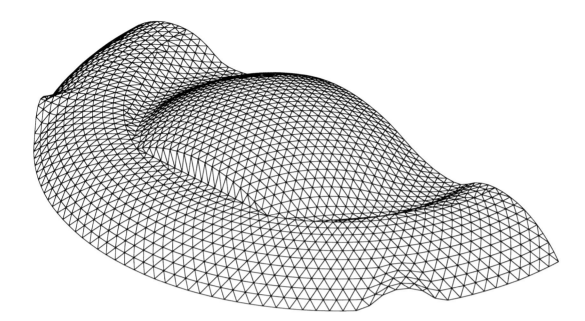

5.56
Three-dimensional
view of the outer layer
of the roof grid,
Palafolls Sports Hall,
near Barcelona
(Courtesy J. Martínez-
Calzón)

cal orange segment main rooflight window near the centre and two 'eyebrow' windows at the perimeter, to admit natural daylight to the areas remote from the north elevation. At the centre, covering the main sports hall area, there is a spheroidal dome area, external radius 24.35 m, bordered on two sides by the vertical faces of the façade and the main roof window parallel to it. The centre of rotation of this dome is offset from the centre of the overall circular plan. At a lower level a toroidal area, 24.75 m radius in plan and 12.74 m radius in section, surrounds

the central dome and covers the ancillary accommodation. A pseudo-conical area forms a transition between these two main parts, a small conical area joins the base of the roof window to the outer toroidal zone and two folds in the perimeter of the toroid form the secondary windows. The complex curved roof geometry is shown in detail in the part-plan and sections of Figure 5.55 and the three-dimensional view of Figure 5.56.

Both the upper and lower surfaces of the double-layer grid were generated from a triangular mesh. To achieve

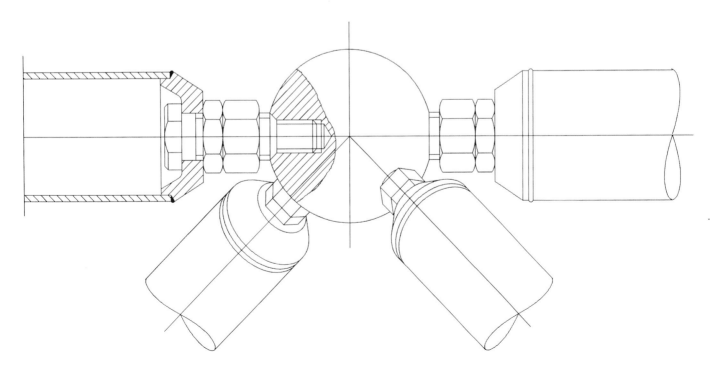

5.57
ORTZ joint detail, Palafolls Sports Hall, near Barcelona (Courtesy J. Martínez-Calzón)

5.58
Erection of pre-assembled roof sections, showing temporary propping of the space grid, Palafolls Sports Hall, near Barcelona (Photograph courtesy J. Martínez-Calzón)

a smooth surface and accommodate the defined roof geometry, with its rapid variation in shape, a relatively fine grid was required for the upper and lower layers. In turn, this necessitated a small distance between the top and bottom grids (only 1.125 m). For a roof of this size the grid, therefore, required an abnormally large number of spherical nodes joints (1691 in the top layer and 1607 in the bottom layer) and a total of 14 429 members.[21,22]

Construction of the roof used the ORTZ space truss system (Figure 5.57) formed from spherical nodes and tubular bars. The CAD-CAM computerized design and manufacturing system employed by LANIK S.A. of San Sebastián, Spain, ensured that site assembly was straightforward. Tubular steel bars varying between 40.2 and 115.7 mm in diameter were used to connect the spherical nodes of between 60 and 210 mm in diameter. In total the space truss weighs 64 tonnes, around 33 kg/m^2 overall, of which approximately 17 per cent results from the weight of the nodes. Erection was facilitated by using vertical props (Figure 5.58) at predetermined nodes to receive previously assembled roof segments. On completion of the space truss structure, load was transferred to the permanent supports by gradually lowering the props using the threaded spindles at their bases. During this procedure, the noted maximum vertical deflection at symmetrical points on the structure agreed closely with the predicted value of 21 mm.

Internally, the roof is lined with timber decking which is fixed to timber purlins spanning between the nodes of the space grid. As can be seen in Figure 5.59, the white

5.59
Interior view of the roof after cladding, Palafolls Sports Hall, near Barcelona (Photograph courtesy J. Martínez-Calzón)

dense, wave-form grid contrasts with the warm shades of timber roof lining, whilst the segment window introduces diffused light to the centre of the sports hall.[23] Externally, the roof is covered with standing seam metal decking (Figure 5.60).

Completed: November 1991
Client: Ayuntamiento de Palafolls (Barcelona)
Architect: Arata Isozaki
Structural engineer: Professor Dr J. Martínez-Calzón, Estudio de Ingenieria, Madrid
Contractor: LANIK S.A., Chofre 11 – 1, 20001 San Sebastian, Spain

Space grids at Expo '92, Seville, Spain

Although it is often thought that space grids were structures of the 1970s and 1980s and that architects now prefer to use individual 'one-off' solutions for their steel buildings rather than industrialized modular systems, there were many examples to be seen at Expo '92 held in Seville, Spain.[24,25] Space grids were, in fact, to be seen everywhere as over 50 000 m² of the site was covered by these structures planted with flowers and small shrubs in order to provide shading. The system developed by Félix Escrig and J. Valcarcel was based on the

5.61(a)
Concept sketch, Expo '92, Seville (Courtesy Félix Escrig)

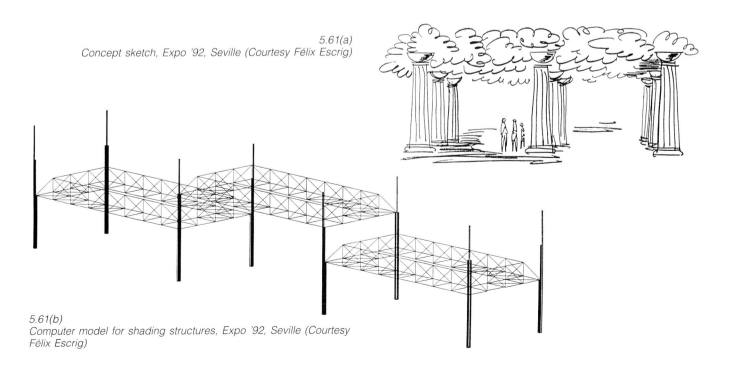

5.61(b)
Computer model for shading structures, Expo '92, Seville (Courtesy Félix Escrig)

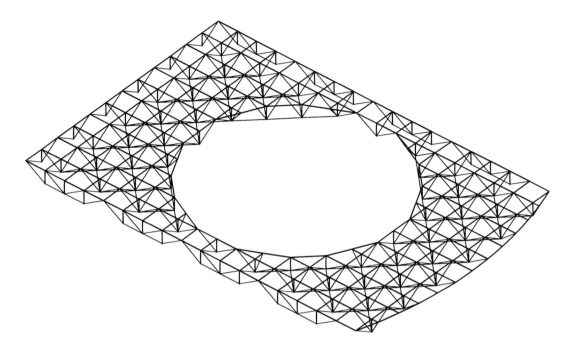

5.62
Floor grid layout for the Pavilion of Extremadura, Expo '92, Seville (Courtesy Félix Escrig)

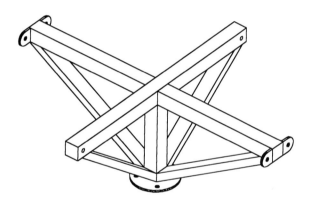

concept shown in Figure 5.61(a) realized in the structure shown in Figure 5.61(b). The grid, approximately 1.0 m deep and 1.5 m wide, had the web elements made from a continuous length of steel tube bent to the correct profile.

In the Pavilion of Extremadura, a glass floor with large central opening was supported by a space grid (Figure 5.62) assembled from the modules shown in Figure 5.63 connected by ties in the bottom layer. This structure was assembled in the air, with no temporary support, by gradually adding modules from the perimeter towards the centre (Figure 5.64).

ONCE Pavilion

Architecturally, the ONCE (Organización Nacional de Ciegos de España) pavilion at Expo '92 (Figure 5.65) had a simple rectangular plan form based on the combination of two cuboids. Main lateral and vertical supports for the pavilion were provided by eight, full-height, diagonal reinforced concrete walls clad in stone (one at each corner of the two cuboids). Figure 5.66 shows the plan of the pavilion.

In this pavilion constructed for the Spanish National Organisation for the Blind, the contrast between darkness and light, opacity and transparency, was emphasized by the insertion of six large, fully glazed curtain walls between these solid walls in order to admit natural light. The glazed walls were supported by double-layer grids assembled from Orona space trusses used vertically instead of the more usual horizontal orientation. The six space truss panels totalling 2533 m² consist of three walls of 436 m², one wall of 389 m² and two walls

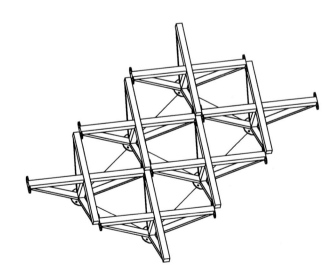

5.63
Individual module and method of assembly for floor construction of the Pavilion of Extremadura, Expo '92, Seville (Courtesy Félix Escrig)

5.64
Pavilion of
Extremadura floor grid
during erection
(Photograph courtesy
Félix Escrig)

5.65
ONCE Pavilion Expo
'92, Seville
(Photograph courtesy
ORONA S. Coop.
Ltda.)

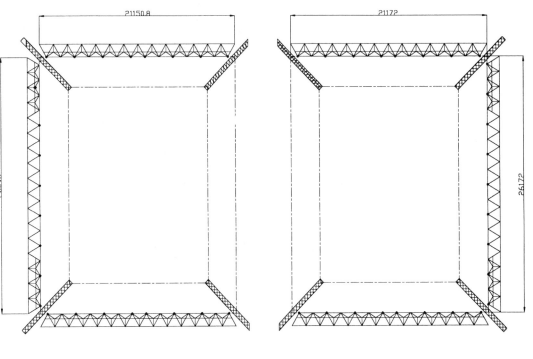

5.66
Plan of ONCE Pavilion
Expo '92, Seville,
showing layout of
solid diagonal walls
and vertical space
grids (Courtesy
ORONA S. Coop.
Ltda.)

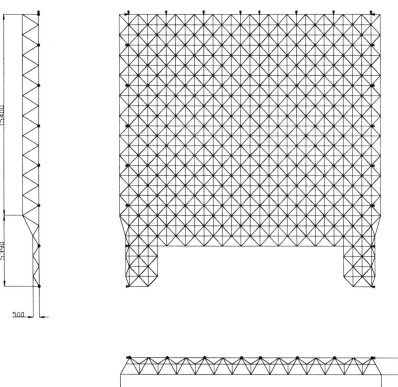

5.67
Elevation and section of typical vertical
space grid wall panel for ONCE Pavilion
Expo '92, Seville (Courtesy ORONA S.
Coop. Ltda.)

of 418 m², all of square on square offset configuration. Module size was standardized at 1.51 by 1.54 m with a grid depth of 1.3 m for the upper 15.4 m of the walls reducing to 0.5 m for 5.4 m at the base, as can be seen in the wall elevation and section shown in Figure 5.67. The main supports for the space grids, which have main-

ly to resist lateral wind forces, were located at the roof and down the two abutting concrete side walls.

To moderate the hot summer climate of Seville, there was a ventilated space between the two layers of glazing that were fixed to the opposite faces of the space truss (Figure 5.68). The single-glazed outer skin of grey

5.68
ONCE Pavilion Expo
'92, Seville, lower wall
construction
(Photograph: John
Chilton)

reflective glass was designed to reject a high proportion of the solar radiation and the double-glazed inner skin formed the weatherproof building envelope. Special fixings (Figures 5.69(a) and (b)) designed and fabricated by Orona were used to secure the glazing panels to the standard spherical nodes of the space trusses.

*Client: ONCE
Architect: M & B Arquitectos, S.A. (Gilbert Barbany and Sebastián Mateu)
Contractor: Construcción y Gestión de Servicios S.A.
Space frame contractor: Orona S. Coop. Ltda., San Sebastián, Spain*

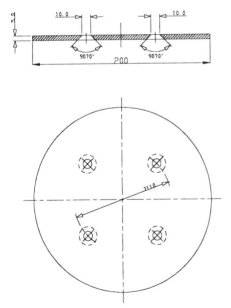

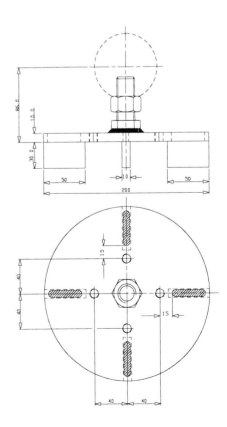

*5.69(a)
Details of special glazing fixings, for the ONCE Pavilion interior (Courtesy Orona S. Coop. Ltda.)*

*5.69(b)
Details of special glazing fixings, for the ONCE Pavilion exterior (Courtesy Orona S. Coop. Ltda.)*

United Nations Pavilion

One of the more striking structures at the Expo was the sculptural half-dome, double-layer space grid of the United Nations Pavilion. The white finish of the tubular metal structure contrasted magnificently with the deep blue of the Seville sky (Figure 5.70) and the massing of the pavilion.

Slightly more than a quarter segment of a sphere, the structure had an outer radius of 18 m, an overall height of 22 m and a grid thickness of 1 m. The total developed surface of 1244 m² was supported at thirteen points (at alternate perimeter nodes) around the semicircular base, radius 17.55 m (see Figure 5.71). Design loadings included the grid self-weight of 10 kg/m², point loads of 38 kg/node at the joints supporting ornamental features and an allowance of ± 30 °C for change of ambient temperature.

Architects: José Ramón Rodriguez Gautier, Javier Morales and Luis Uruñuela (Expo '92)
Space frame contractor: Orona S. Coop. Ltda., San Sebastián, Spain

Markethall, Eagle Centre, Derby, UK

As part of the refurbishment programme of the Eagle Centre Market in Derby, UK (Figure 5.72), a Conder Harley System 80, space grid roof of about 9000 m² was erected in ten weeks from October 1991 to January 1992.[26,27] The original market, constructed in the 1970s, had hexagonal stalls on a honeycomb grid but was considered below standard for modern fire regulations due to the distances to fire exits and their poor visibility. There was also limited provision for the evacuation of smoke in the event of a fire. Alternative solutions within the several design constraints were sought by Derby City Council. These included that the new roof and market structures had to be within the load capacity of the existing market floor and substructure and that the amenities and access to the adjacent Derby Playhouse and basement car park had to be maintained during construction.

Fire escape routes were improved and the visibility problem overcome by changing to a rectangular grid layout for the stalls. To combat the smoke evacuation problem the roof was raised over the whole market and additional ventilation provided. The Conder Harley System 80 space truss, which employs cold-rolled steel members, was selected for the roof as it provided a lightweight structure that could be easily installed within the site access constraints. Along two sides the roof abuts the main structure of the Eagle Centre, whilst on the other sides a proprietary glazed curtain wall system admits light into Markethall.

Existing columns were on a 8.1 m by 7.5 m grid but these dimensions were doubled for the new column grid

5.70
Quarter sphere space grid for the United Nations Pavilion, Expo '92, Seville (Photograph: John Chilton)

used to support the rectangle on rectangle offset space truss. Tubular steel four-branched 'trees' were provided on a regular 16.2 m by 15 m grid at approximately 6 m above the market floor. Despite being supported on alternate columns of the original grid, the roof load per foundation pile was still within the original capacity. As the exact perimeter of the new space grid roof was difficult to ascertain before demolition of the old structure, the edges were cantilevered close to the sides and over existing buildings and then a weather-tight infill was provided later.

Cold-rolled 'C' section steel profiles were used for the upper and lower chords which were continuous across several bays of the 2.7 × 2.5 m grid. Diagonal web bracing was of lightweight steel tubes crimped and bent at the required angle for bolting. The chords were spliced between nodes to simplify the connection of the bracing

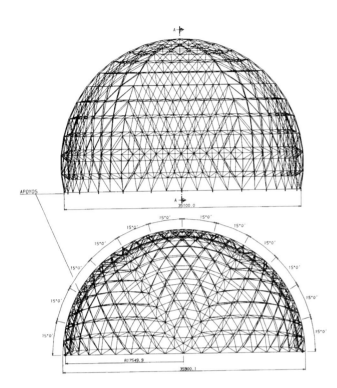

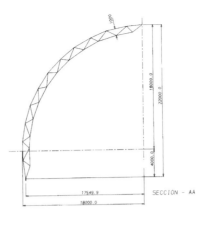

5.71
Plan, section and three-dimensional view of quarter sphere space grid, United Nations Pavilion, Expo '92, Seville (Courtesy Orona S. Coop. Ltda.)

at the chord intersections. A typical chord splice is shown in Figure 5.73. Given the access problems at the site, the small, lightweight components of the Conder Harley System 80 made delivery, handling and erection of the roof structure much easier.

Three alternative methods of erection were used for this project. Parts of the space grid were erected over areas where public access had to be maintained (e.g. the Derby Playhouse entrance) and these were assembled on temporary scaffolding. Other sectors at the perimeter were assembled in small sections and lifted into place by mobile crane. However, the majority of the space grid, in areas of up to 1000 m², was preassembled on the existing concrete slab of the market floor and raised into its final position by a proprietary hydraulic lifting process over a system of temporary columns (Figure 5.74). Rooflights were installed on top of the space truss before it was lifted.

Although this may be considered a rather mundane and simple project from the architectural point of view, the new Eagle Centre Markethall roof demonstrates the suitability of space grid structures for refurbishment projects, especially where lightness is paramount (as in this case where the new structure had to be carried by the existing foundation piles).

Owner: CIN Properties
Architect: Building Design Partnership and Progressive Design Associates
Engineer: Kenchington Ford plc
General and space frame contractor: Conder Projects

5.72
Eagle Centre Market, Derby, UK (Photograph: John Chilton)

5.73
Eagle Centre Market,
Conder Harley,
System 80 chord
splice with reinforcing
section bolted inside
the channel section
(Photograph: John
Chilton)

5.74
Eagle Centre Market, preassembled grid ready for lifting over
temporary columns. A further area of space grid assembled
previously on temporary scaffolding can be seen in the
background (Photograph: John Chilton)

Barrel Vault Atrium, The Bentall Centre, Kingston upon Thames, UK

The fully glazed atrium roof at The Bentall Centre, Kingston upon Thames (Figure 5.75) is a relatively small span, space truss, barrel vault that stretches for 120 m and reaches 31 m above the floor of the shopping mall. Within this length, the barrel vault incorporates a 15.4 m span semicircular three-pinned arch section, a similar smaller arch supported on vertical space grid walls 3.75 m high and 10.01 m between bearings, and an apse in the form of a quarter sphere.[28,29] Figure 5.76 (a) shows the part roof plan and side elevation and Figure 5.76 (b) shows the junction between the barrel vaults of different radius. The main vaults are constructed from a modified version of the standard Space Deck welded pyramidal modular system. In order to incorporate a fibre optic light for decorative illumination at night, a variation of the standard module was developed with a flat circular boss (120 mm diameter, 50 mm thick and with a central hole) at the vertex of the inverted pyramids.

Twenty-four modules, each 495 mm deep overall, form the 15.4 m span barrel vault. These are not square, being 937.5 mm wide along the axis of the vault and forming chords of 1010 mm around the arch. To accommodate the 7.5° angle between each module, the steel angles of the upper grid frame parallel to the main axis of the vault, use specially produced sections with an angle of 93.75° between the legs. In the smaller vault the same number of modules, of the same 495 mm depth, were used around the curve of the vault, thus maintaining the same angle between modules. Here, the modules were 625 mm along the main roof axis and 698 mm around the arch; 625 mm by 625 mm in the vertical walls. Figure 5.77 shows the cross-section through the 10.1 m barrel vault and Figure 5.78 shows support, glazing fixing and coffered panel fixing details.

It is generally necessary to consider the potential thermal movement of space grids, and this structure was no exception. Due to its overall length, expansion joints had to be incorporated along the barrel vault by breaking down the structure into smaller lengths and leaving a gap between these bays. The possibility of differential movement between the buildings supporting the barrel vault also had to be considered. Following computer analysis of alternative structural mechanisms it was decided to construct the barrel vault as a three-pinned arch (with pin joints at the supports and crown as seen in the section in Figure 5.77) to minimize adverse effects on the glazing and cladding panels. The predicted maximum temperature for the roof structure was 50 °C and the adoption of the three-pinned arch avoided the generation of excessive forces due to thermal expansion that could have otherwise occurred in this case.

Erection of the space grid was expedited by the construction of a temporary working platform, made from standard Space Deck modules, positioned just below the

5.75
Barrel-vault atrium at The Bentall Centre, Kingston upon Thames (Photograph courtesy Space Decks Ltd)

(a)

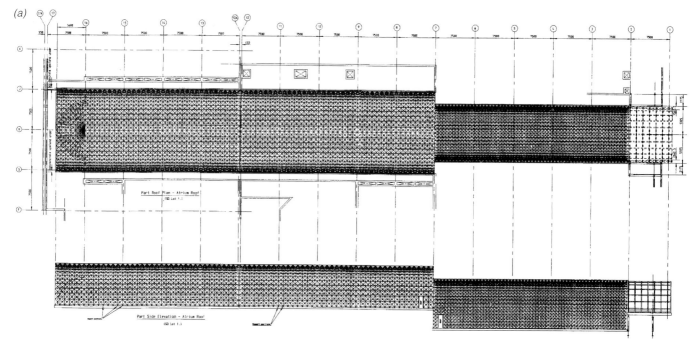

Part Roof Plan - Atrium Roof

Part Side Elevation - Atrium Roof

(b)

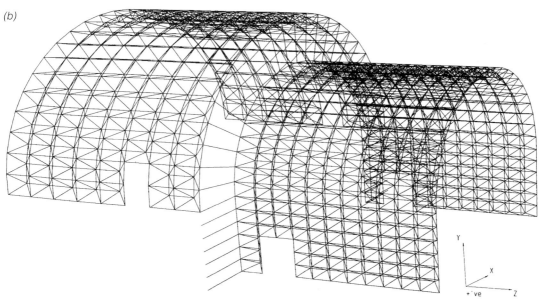

5.76
(a) Part roof plan and side elevation of the atrium roof, Bentall Centre, Kingston upon Thames (courtesy Space Decks Ltd). (b) The Bentall Centre, Kingston upon Thames, three-dimensional view of junction between 15.4 and 10.l m barrel vaults (Courtesy Space Decks Ltd)

springing point of the vaults and spanning the width of the atrium. This solution allowed other work to proceed beneath the temporary deck and was cheaper than erecting scaffolding from the atrium floor level. To erect the barrel vaults, half-arch sections were assembled on the working platform. Then, following the erection procedure shown in Figure 5.79, one half section was positioned and held in place by tower crane, whilst the other half was lifted into position and joined to it at the ridge to form the stable three-pinned arch. The new bay was then connected to the adjacent completed space truss. Tower crane lifting capacity dictated the size of the preassembled sections.

Overall, the space grid provided a lightweight modu-lar solution to the architectural problem of controlling the illumination within the extensive atrium of the Bentall Centre. Perforated metal coffered ceiling panels, designed to curtail direct sunlight by 50 per cent, are supported easily on the regular grid, and the bosses of the inner nodes house the fibre optic lighting that produces a star-spangled array against the dark night sky. Primary and secondary structures are combined to produce an efficient system.

Client: Norwich Union
Architect and engineer: Building Design Partnership
Main contractor: Mowlem
Space frame contractor: Space Decks Ltd

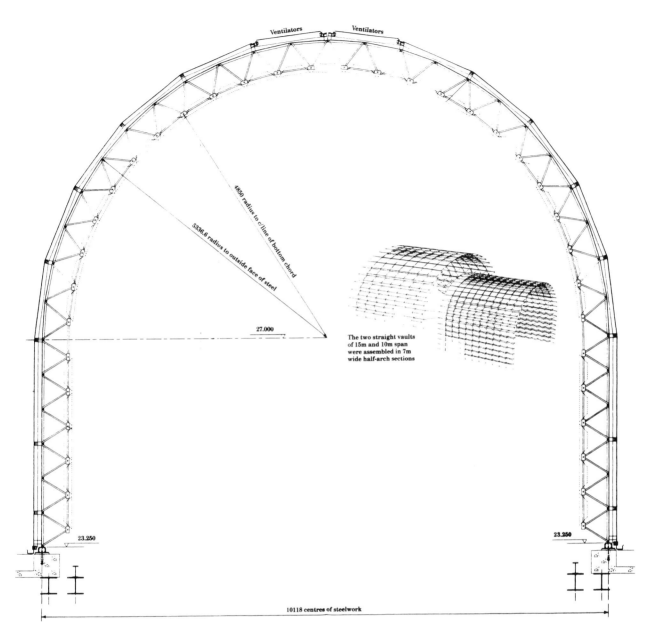

Ventilators   Ventilators

4850 radius to c/line of bottom chord

5336.6 radius to outside face of steel

27.000

The two straight vaults
of 15m and 10m span
were assembled in 7m
wide half-arch sections

23.250   23.250

10118 centres of steelwork

5.77
The Bentall Centre, Kingston upon Thames, cross-section through 10.1 m span three-pinned barrel-vault (Courtesy Space Decks Ltd)

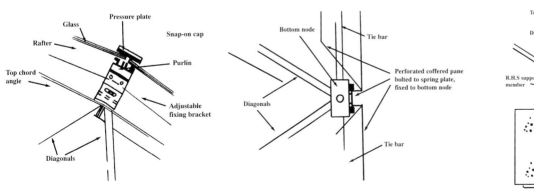

Glass   Pressure plate

Rafter   Snap-on cap

Top chord angle   Purlin

Adjustable
fixing bracket

Diagonals

Bottom node   Tie bar

Diagonals   Perforated coffered pane
bolted to spring plate,
fixed to bottom node

Tie bar

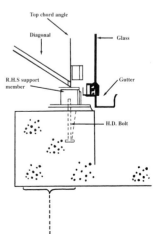

Top chord angle

Diagonal   Glass

R.H.S support
member   Gutter

H.D. Bolt

5.78
*The Bentall Centre, Kingston upon Thames, construction details for supports, glazing fixing
and coffered panel fixing (Courtesy Space Decks Ltd)*

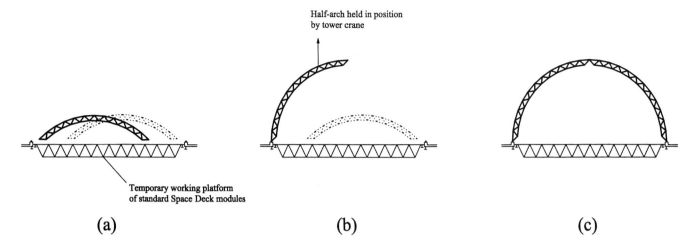

Half-arch held in position
by tower crane

Temporary working platform
of standard Space Deck modules

(a)   (b)   (c)

5.79
The Bentall Centre, Kingston upon Thames, diagram of erection procedure; (a) half-arches assembled on temporary Space Deck working platform (b) one half lifted on to permanent support and held up by tower crane and (c) second half lifted placed and connected to form full arch (Courtesy Space Decks Ltd)

Terminal 2, Manchester Airport, UK

Pressure on the existing terminal facilities at Manchester Airport, UK, required a new terminal building, which was opened in 1993.[30] The new facility incorporates 6000 m² of space grid roof. Powder polyester-coated Nodus space truss, is used to form three glazed atria and an entrance concourse 115 m long. This comprises approximately 180 tonnes of steel, in excess of 2500 joints and 10 000 tubular members. The square on square off-

5.80
Aerial view of Nodus space grid roof under construction, Terminal 2, Manchester Airport, UK (Photograph courtesy Space Decks Ltd)

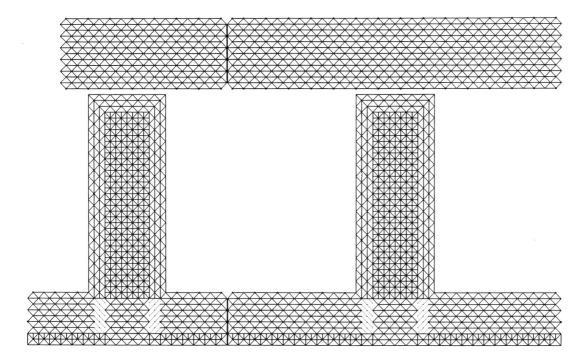

5.81
Roof plan, Terminal 2,
Manchester Airport,
UK (Courtesy Space
Decks Ltd)

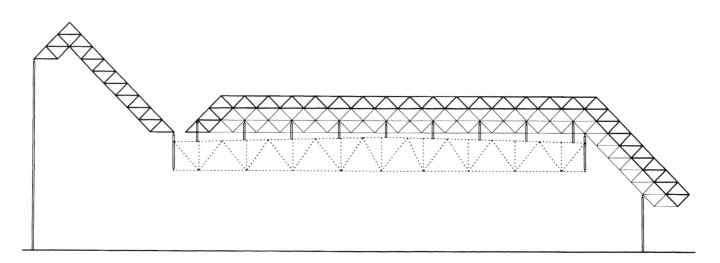

5.82
Roof section, Terminal 2 , Manchester Airport, UK (Courtesy Space Decks Ltd)

set grid includes inclined and flat planar sections on a total of sixteen levels, as can be seen in the aerial view of the space grid under construction (Figure 5.80). In such a visually prominent situation, the space grid requires a high level of consistent detailing. Therefore, throughout the space truss, hot-finished British Steel 60.3 mm diameter circular hollow section top and bottom chords and 48.3 mm diameter bracing members are used. For economy, the tube wall thicknesses are var-ied depending on the member forces but the size of the Nodus joints is standardized to maintain a consistent aesthetic.

The three atria are perimeter-supported every two grid bays along their length, whilst the entrance concourse is generally supported every two bays at the rear and at three bay intervals at the front, where there is also a 4.8 m, two bay, cantilevered section (as shown in the roof plan and section in Figures 5.81 and 5.82).

*5.83
Lifting a pre-assembled section of Nodus space grid at Terminal 2, Manchester Airport (Photograph courtesy Space Decks Ltd)*

Assembly of the space truss was carried out on the ground away from the terminal building to avoid interference with other construction work. After assembly, the roof was lifted in eleven separate sections by a 500 tonne mobile crane (Figure 5.83). The heaviest roof assembly weighed 25 tonnes and the longest reach required to place a space truss section was over 75 metres.

A separate entrance canopy was also constructed using 30 tonnes of Nodus space truss. The double-layer grids of the canopy provide a homogeneous structural theme although space grids are not usually considered economical when used to span primarily in one direction, as a beam, as they do here. In this roof structure, supported on ten tubular lattice columns, there were 885 joints. Some cantilevered sections of the canopy were suspended from tubular ties/struts attached to masts. The canopy was covered with single-skin profiled metal decking on the horizontal surfaces and tinted laminated glass on the inclined faces of the mansard edges.

Overall, the Manchester Airport Terminal 2 project demonstrates the versatility of the Nodus space truss which allows coherent structural detailing throughout the exposed and glazed sections of the roof despite the many different forms.

*Client: Manchester International Airport PLC
Project Management: T2 Project Management Team, Manchester Airport Directorate of Development and Planning. City Architect, City Engineer, Audit Team, Taylor Woodrow Construction*

*Management contractor: AMEC Projects Ltd
Design co-ordinator, architect and interior designer: Scott, Brownrigg & Turner
Structural engineer: Scott, Wilson Kirkpatrick
Steelwork contractor: William Hare Ltd
Steelwork contractor (space frame): Space Decks Ltd*

Fantasy Island, Pyramid, Skegness, UK

This project illustrates the use of lightweight sections (the Space Decks Ltd Multiframe System) to form a large pyramidal structure, but perhaps the most interesting aspect of this project is that the whole space grid was assembled in an adjacent car park before being lifted and transported 100 m to its final location.

The pyramid 50 m by 50 m in plan and 20 m high (see the plan and elevation in Figure 5.84) was assembled from four similar triangular segments of rectangle on rectangle space grid, having a 2.94 m by 3.84 m module, 1.9 m deep. To erect the structure several cranes were required. Initially, one segment was lifted on to temporary supports and the apex of the triangle was held aloft, to maintain the segment in its correct inclined position. A second segment was then lifted and connected to its temporary supports on the opposite side of the square based pyramid and to the first segment at the apex.

Thus a stable 'A' frame (Figure 5.85) was created to which the remaining two segments were then fixed. Once

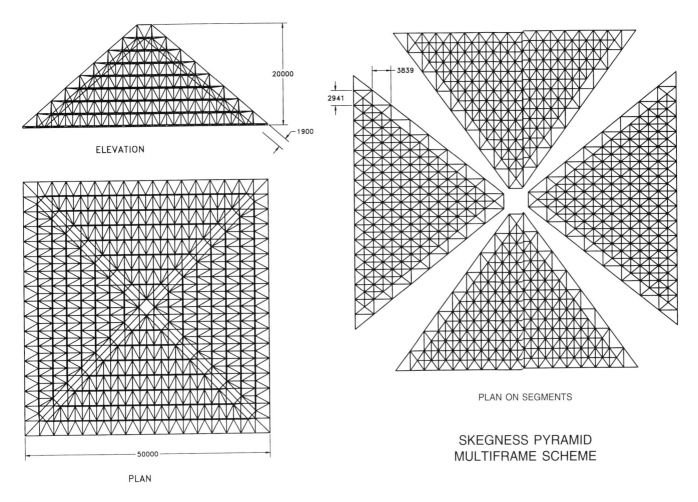

ELEVATION

20000

1900

50000

PLAN

3839

2941

PLAN ON SEGMENTS

SKEGNESS PYRAMID
MULTIFRAME SCHEME

5.84
Plan and elevation, pyramidal Multiframe space grid for Fantasy Island, Skegness, UK (Courtesy Space Decks Ltd)

5.85
Part erected pyramid in the car park adjacent to its final location; two segments are already connected to form a stable 'A' frame (Courtesy Space Decks Ltd)

5.86
Complete 50 m by 50 m pyramid being lifted into its final location by a single large mobile crane (Courtesy Space Decks Ltd)

the complete pyramid had been assembled, it was lifted at its apex by a single large mobile crane and swung into its final position (Figure 5.86). The strength and lightness of the Multiframe grid enabled this delicate lifting operation to be accomplished without difficulty.

Client: Blue Anchor Leisure Ltd
Architect: IDS Studios
Engineer and space frame contractor: Space Decks Ltd

Roundwood timber space trusses

Timber is a material that is not commonly used for the construction of space grid structures. However, some examples have been constructed using what is rarely considered a suitable material for long-span buildings, roundwood poles. In well-managed timber plantations trees are initially planted close together to encourage them to grow fast and straight. As their size increases it is necessary to thin out the plantation to provide more light and nutrition to each tree. During this thinning process many trees between 150 and 200 mm in diameter are felled, a size too small to be of much practical use as structural sawn timber. However, after debarking, suitably straight specimens can be used structurally, as roundwood poles, and these are eminently suitable for use in cheap timber space truss structures.

The fibres in the section of a tree trunk run only approximately longitudinally. Thus, when the cross-section is sawn into smaller rectangular sections, the strength of the timber is reduced as some of the fibres are now no longer continuous along the piece of wood. Typically, the basic permissible stresses in bending, tension and compression of sawn structural timber are respectively about one-third, one-quarter and two-thirds of those of round debarked timber. Machine-rounded timber is slightly weaker than debarked timber. Equally important, much of the original cross-section is simply cut off and wasted. By trimming four sides of a circular trunk to form a square section the usable cross-sectional area is reduced by 36 per cent, the elastic section modulus (directly related to the bending resistance of the beam) is reduced by 40 per cent and the second moment of area (related to buckling of struts under axial compression and deflection of beams) by 57 per cent (Figure 5.87). The members in space trusses carry mainly axial forces and the solid circular cross-section of the roundwood poles is ideal for resisting axial compression (just as circular tubes of steel and aluminium are used in metal space trusses). As with all timber structures the main problem to be overcome is the design of a strong connection between the individual elements, particularly in tension, and this is further exacerbated when the sections are circular. The difficulty of joining timber is especially pertinent to space trusses where there will typically be eight members radiating from a node in a square on square offset grid. Metal connectors of some form are therefore necessary.

The basic material for the members – roundwood poles – is relatively cheap. Therefore, it is logical to derive a jointing system that is also cheap and simple. Dr Pieter Huybers at the Technical University in Delft, the Netherlands, has developed a simple wire lacing method (using an appropriate lacing tool) for clamping galvanized steel connector plates in the pre-slotted ends of round-wood poles (Figure 5.88). The procedure for installation of connector plates is as follows. After cutting the slot and drilling transverse holes, the pre-drilled, plate connector is inserted. Then tubular liners are installed in the holes and the wire lacing is passed through. The lacing tool is then used to tension the wire to a preset value; the ends of the wires are trimmed and hammered into the face of the timber.

Several different plate connectors have been developed, some of which require a separate node and others that can be connected together directly (nodeless construction). Experimental and agricultural space grid projects have been constructed from roundwood poles in the Netherlands and in the UK.[31] For example, a small single-layer, lattice dome exhibition pavilion 5.8 m diameter and 5.5 m high was built in 1984 and reconstructed in Delft in 1987. An equipment storage shed, 16.2 m by 10.8 m, constructed at Lelystad, in the Netherlands (Figure 5.89) had a space truss roof made of 100 mm diameter larch poles, supported on eleven timber columns. The four by six bay square on square offset grid was built in 1986 using the galvanized steel 6 mm thick circular node and 6 × 90 × 260 mm connector plates shown in Figure 5.90. For durability, the timber was impregnated with CCA (copper cyanide arsenic) preservative. In the UK, also in 1986, an 8.1 m × 18.9 m prototype agricultural building was constructed at Bridget's Farm, near Winchester (a Ministry of Agriculture experimental farm). Supported on twelve columns, the roundwood timber space truss was 1.9 m deep and comprised of 168 roundwood members of 100 mm diameter and 2.5 m in length. All members were prepared off site and only bolted connections were necessary to assemble the grid before it was lifted by crane on to the 200 mm diameter timber columns. More recently, in 1995, an observation tower 27 m in height was erected, at Apeldoorn in the Netherlands, using roundwood poles up to 200 mm in diameter.

The tower (Figure 5.91) can be considered a vertical set of rectangular on rectangular offset grids (Figure 5.92) in which the connecting nodes (Figure 5.93) are assembled from four identical components fabricated from standard steel angle. Once assembled the nodes allow up to eighteen bars to be connected, depending on the configuration.

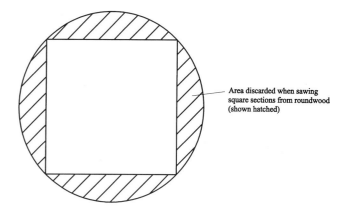

Area discarded when sawing square sections from roundwood (shown hatched)

5.87
Reduction in section of a piece of timber from roundwood to square. (This reduces the area by 36 per cent, the elastic section modulus by 40 per cent and the second moment of area by 57 per cent) (Drawing: John Chilton)

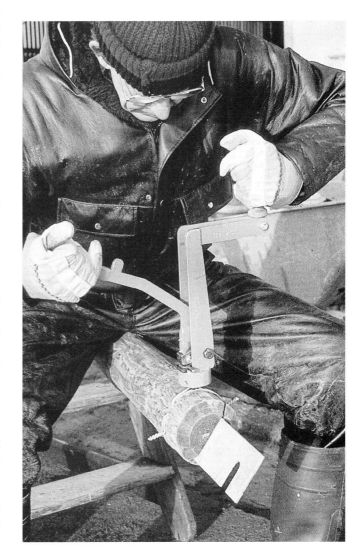

5.88
Lacing tool being used to secure a metal connector plate into a roundwood pole (Photograph courtesy Pieter Huybers)

5.89
Equipment storage shed, 16.2 m by 10.8 m, constructed at Lelystad, in the Netherlands (Photograph courtesy Pieter Huybers)

5.90
Galvanized steel 6 mm thick circular node and 6 × 90 × 260 mm connector plates used at Lelystad, in the Netherlands (Photograph courtesy Pieter Huybers)

5.91
Roundwood pole tower at Apeldoorn, the Netherlands, assembled from timber components 120 to 200 mm diameter (Photograph courtesy Pieter Huybers)

The projects described above, although generally small in nature, demonstrate that efficient three-dimensional structures can be constructed from what is often considered to be, at best, low-grade timber and in many cases material only fit for being reduced to wood chips or pulp. There is, of course, no reason why this form of construction should not be used for more prestigious architectural projects, for instance, visitor centres, museums or low-energy designs. As the material is cheap and plentifully available in countries with forests, and the assembly technique is relatively simple, roundwood pole space grids have high potential for exploitation in the construction of factory, storage and agricultural buildings in developing countries.

Architect: Pieter Huybers
Engineer: Pieter Huybers/De Bondt
Construction: Mulder b.v., Apeldoorn

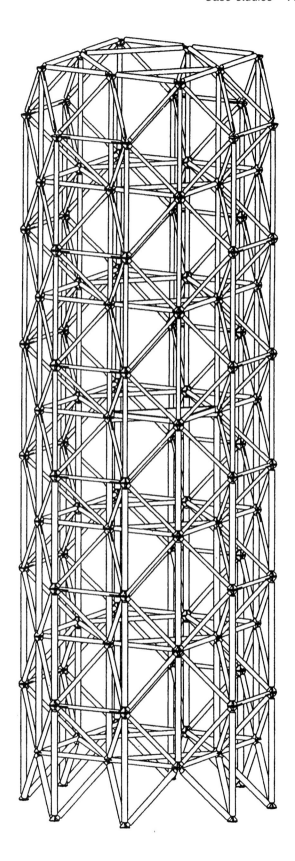

5.92
Three-dimensional view of the structure for the roundwood pole tower at Apeldoorn, the Netherlands (Courtesy Pieter Huybers/H. Hendriks, De Bondt)

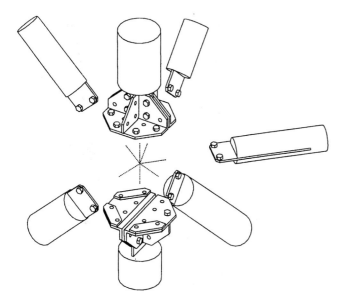

5.93
Typical node for tower at Apeldoorn, the Netherlands (a) unassembled and (b) assembled (Courtesy Pieter Huybers/H. Hendriks, de Bondt)

Atlanta Pavilion (unbuilt project)

As noted in the previous example, timber is used infrequently for space grids and in turn space grids are rarely used to support roofs having irregular geometry. However, timber was the material chosen for the proposed Atlanta Pavilion, which was to be built to house facilities for visitors to that city during the Olympic Games held there in July 1996. The pavilion would have included an exciting free-form, space grid with apparently random, roof geometry.

The original project brief given to the Atlanta-based architects, Scogin Elam and Bray by the Committee for the Olympic Development Atlanta (CODA), called for a ticket booth, a cafeteria and an audio visual experience – The Atlanta Experience – to provide information about the city and its environs. To generate a striking landmark for the prominent air-rights site, situated above the Peachtree MARTA station in central Atlanta, the architects proposed a large free-form shading canopy rising to approximately 33 m at its highest point.

The client, CODA, invited Ove Arup and Partners International Ltd to collaborate with the architects to investigate how the project might be accomplished. Timber products are manufactured by the owners of the air rights, Georgia Pacific, who have offices in a high-rise building adjacent to the site. This, together with the proposed short life for the building (two to three years) and restrictions on the load (an additional 250 lb/ft^2 or 1050 kg/m^2) that could be imposed on the existing con-

crete roof structure, suggested timber as the main material for the exhibition space, access ramps and roof canopy.

Initially, the free-form roof was rationalized in such a way that the random appearance could be maintained whilst the geometry could be defined and communicated to the contractor to permit economic construction. After measurement of the architects' model, a computer model (shown in elevation in Figure 5.94 (a)) was generated based on 2.4 m × 2.4 m (8 ft × 8 ft) grid, viewed in plan (see Figure 5.94(b)).

Individual nodes were displaced vertically until the surface obtained approximated to that of the physical model. Thus, each square in plan was covered by a warped surface. To produce a surface that could be clad using flat panels, each quadrilateral was divided into two triangular facets that could be supported by the timber space grid (Figure 5.95).

Three options were considered for the structure to support the roof surface: two alternative space grids, one with 2.4 m × 1.2 m (8 ft × 4 ft) triangular upper grid and the other with an 2.4 m × 2.4 m (8 ft × 8 ft) square upper grid, and a tree-like structure on a 3.05 m × 3.05 m (10 ft × 10 ft) grid. Models were constructed by the architects to assess the structural alternatives from the aesthetic viewpoint and the 2.4 m by 2.4 m (8 ft by 8 ft) square grid was subsequently selected. The space grid and enclosure model are shown in Figure 5.96.

Because of the irregular geometry of the space grid, steel spherical nodes were considered most appropriate to connect the glulam timber members in a manner similar to the Mero Holz system described in Chapter 3. Supports for the grid were arranged in an apparently random pattern with inclined columns of glulam timber up to 30.5 m (100 ft) in length. This configuration of cruciform glulam columns, fabricated from two square sections fixed to a rectangular section, one on each side, provided overall lateral stability to the canopy when linked to the bending stiff space grid. Sizes for the spherical nodes and the minimum angle that could be accommodated between the grid members were determined by Ingenieurbüro Peter Bertsche in Germany.

Client: Committee for the Olympic Development Atlanta
Architect: Scogin Elam and Bray, Atlanta
Engineer: Ove Arup and Partners/
Ingenieurbüro Bertsche

Milan Fair, New Exhibition Facilities, Milan, Italy

The new buildings for the Milan Fair, situated in a restricted location near the centre of the city and adjacent to a

5.94(a)
Elevation of the
rationalized computer
model of the Atlanta
Pavilion (Courtesy
Scogin Elam and
Bray)

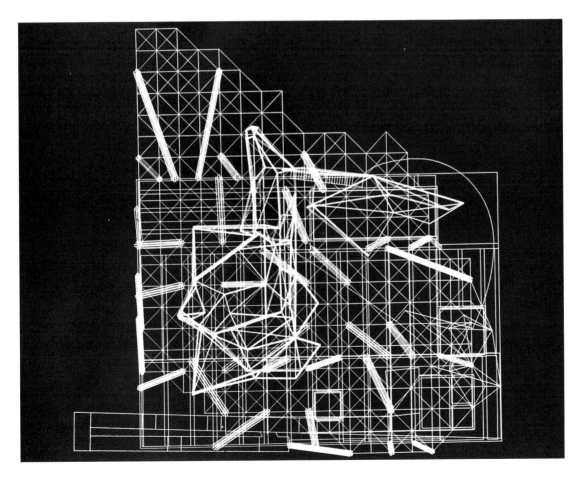

5.94(b)
Plan of the
rationalized computer
model of the Atlanta
Pavilion. (Courtesy
Scogin Elam and
Bray)

5.95
Cladding model for
the Atlanta Pavilion
showing the division
of warped square
planes into triangular
cladding sections
(Courtesy Scogin
Elam and Bray)

5.96
Space grid and
enclosure model
demonstrating the
geometrical
complexity of the
structure (Courtesy
Scogin Elam and
Bray)

principal road, feature three large pavilions accommodating two-storey exhibition areas and roof-top parking facilities (Figures 5.97). The pavilions, which cover an area approximately 650 × 100 m, incorporate many prefabricated elements, primarily precast concrete components, for speed of erection. However, the upper exhibition floor is of particular interest in this study as it

features a deep, double-layer composite space truss structure.[32,33]

The exhibition floor is suspended 15 m above ground level in square bays corner-supported by columns on a 20 m by 20 m grid. A live load of 15 kN/m² was specified for the exhibition area floor. When this heavy loading was considered together with the regular square plan

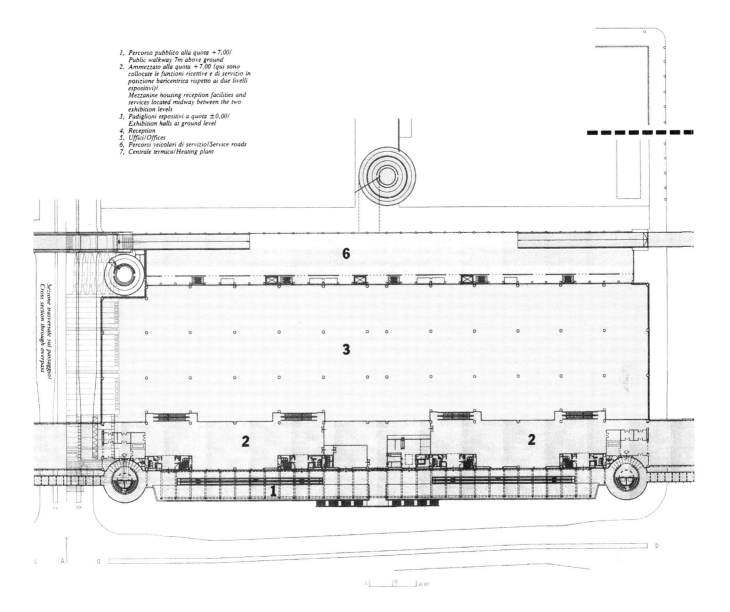

1. *Percorso pubblico alla quota +7,00/*
   Public walkway 7m above ground
2. *Ammezzato alla quota +7,00 (qui sono*
   collocate le funzioni ricettive e di servizio in
   posizione baricentrica rispetto ai due livelli
   espositivi)/
   Mezzanine housing reception facilities and
   services located midway between the two
   exhibition levels
3. *Padiglioni espositivi a quota ±0,00/*
   Exhibition halls at ground level
4. *Reception*
5. *Uffici/Offices*
6. *Percorsi veicolari di servizio/Service roads*
7. *Centrale termica/Heating plant*

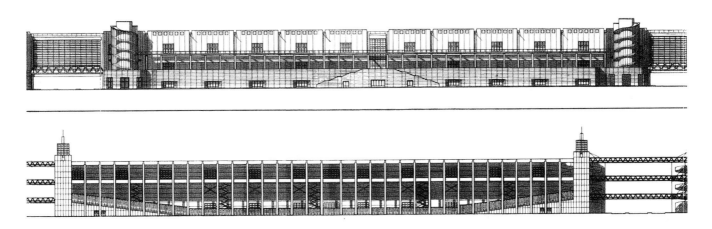

5.97
Milan Fair Exhibition Facilities floor plan and elevations of a typical pavilion (Courtesy G. C. Giuliani, Redesco srl.)

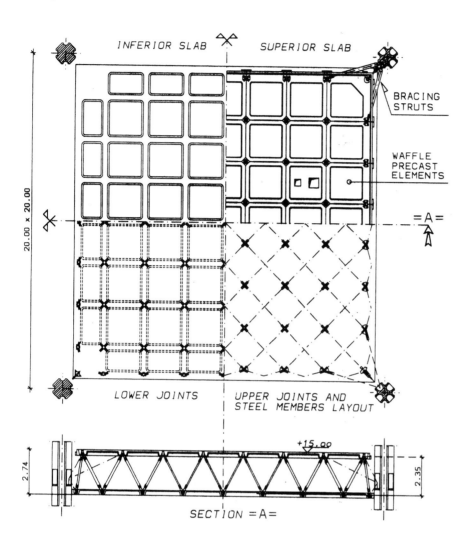

INFERIOR SLAB   SUPERIOR SLAB

BRACING STRUTS

WAFFLE PRECAST ELEMENTS

= A =

20.00 × 20.00

LOWER JOINTS   UPPER JOINTS AND STEEL MEMBERS LAYOUT

+15.00

2.74   2.35

SECTION = A =

5.98
Plan and section of typical floor bay, Milan Fair Exhibition Facilities (Courtesy G. C. Giuliani, Redesco srl.)

bays, the access required for mechanical and electrical services and adequate fire separation of the upper and lower exhibition areas, the adoption of a deep two-way spanning floor structure with concrete deck was deemed appropriate.

The solution employed utilizes upper and lower concrete decks separated by steel space truss diagonals to form a composite space grid structure 2.74 m deep overall. Figure 5.98 shows the plan and section of a typical floor bay, with the top left quadrant of the plan illustrating the waffle pattern of the lower concrete slab and the top right quadrant representing the disposition of the precast waffles and the corner bracing struts. The lower left and right quadrants depict the position and orientation of the cast nodes in the lower and upper layers respectively and the layout of the steel 'web' members. Lower deck concrete slabs were post-tensioned, cast in situ, waffle type. Generally only 60 mm thick, the slab had 0.3 m deep by 0.55 m wide ribs housing the pre-stressing cables on a 2.5 m by 2.5 m grid and ductile cast iron nodes embedded in the concrete at each

rib intersection. Between the upper and lower concrete slabs, each 20 m by 20 m floor bay contained internal half-octahedral/tetrahedral tubular steel bracing on a 2.5 m by 2.5 m grid and tetrahedral edge assemblies on a 1.25 m by 2.5 m grid. Grid depth between the upper and lower layers was 2.35 m. After installation of the reinforcement, pre-stressing cables and the steel truss components the lower deck concrete was cast on reusable metal formwork. Upper slabs were also cast in-situ, on permanent waffle-shaped precast concrete formwork only 50 mm thick. The permanent formwork was supported from the upper cast nodes again on a 2.5 m by 2.5 m grid. A three-dimensional view of a full floor bay is shown in Figure 5.99 and detailed views of the steel and prestressing components (before concreting) and the completed column/deck junction are shown in Figure 5.100. At the corners, additional steel bracing struts and cast iron elements link the adjacent floor nodes to bearings set in recesses in the precast concrete columns. These elements articulate so that they do not interfere with the raising of the floor between

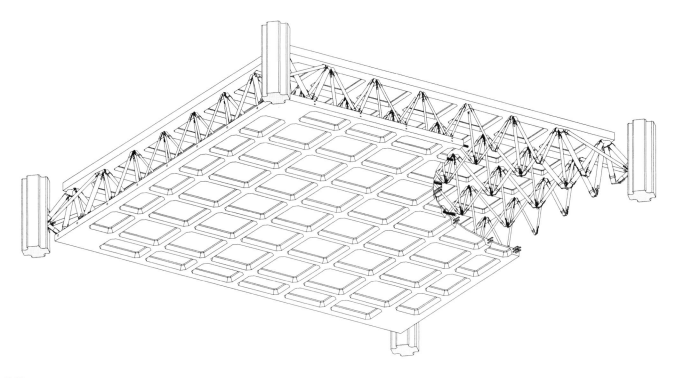

5.99
Three-dimensional view of typical floor bay 20 m by 20 m seen from below, Milan Fair Exhibition Facilities (Courtesy G. C. Giuliani, Redesco srl.)

the precast columns but can be subsequently deployed to provide support from the columns. The assembly procedure for the composite space truss structure is shown in Figure 5.101 and can be summarized in the following phases:

1 Preparation of the 20 × 20 m steel movable formwork between the four columns; preassembly of space truss segments complete with nodes attached.
2 Placing of preassembled space truss segments on formwork; placing of preassembled steel bar reinforcement and pre-stressing cables.
3 Concreting, curing and pre-stressing of the lower slab; installation of ducts, wiring equipment, etc.
4 Placing of precast waffles and reinforcement for upper slab.
5 Concreting of the upper slab.
6 Hoisting of the complete orthotropic slab using hydraulic jacks.
7 Final positioning, extension of retractable corner elements inside column recesses; connection to columns.

Phases 1 to 5 were carried out at ground level before raising each 480 tonne floor bay to its final location 15 m in the air. The placing of precast waffles on top of the preassembled space truss units (phase 4), is shown in Figure 5.102.

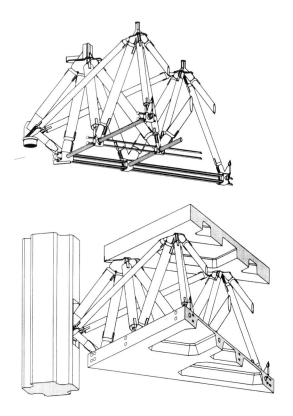

5.100
Detailed views of steel components and the completed floor assembly at the corners. Note the pre-stressing tendons passing through the cast nodes (Courtesy G. C. Giuliani, Redesco srl.)

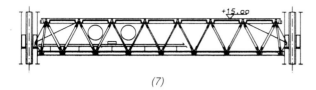

(7)

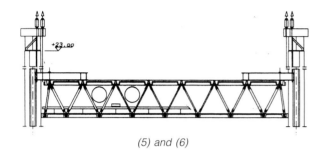

(5) and (6)

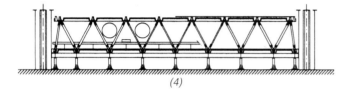

(4)

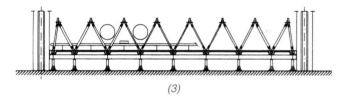

(3)

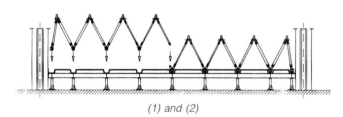

(1) and (2)

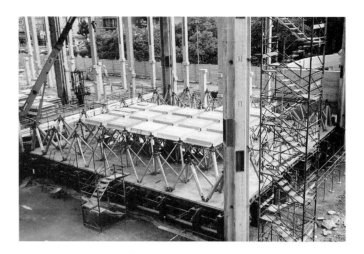

5.102
Phase 4 of assembly/erection of the floor bay, Milan Fair Exhibition Facilities, the precast waffles being installed prior to concreting of the upper floor (Courtesy G. C. Giuliani, Redesco srl.)

5.101
Phases for assembly and erection of a floor bay, Milan Fair Exhibition Facilities: (1) preparation of the movable steel formwork and preassembly of space truss elements; (2) placing of space truss, reinforcing bars and pre-stressing cables; (3) concreting of lower slab, installation of services; (4) placing of precast waffles and reinforcement of upper deck; (5 and 6) concreting of upper slab and lifting of completed floor section; (7) extension of retractable corners and connection to columns (Courtesy G. C. Giuliani, Redesco srl.)

An important feature of the floor construction is the cast node joints which act as shear connectors between the concrete slabs and the steel bracing. Of the three solutions considered for these joints, (fabrication from welded plates and machined billets, casting in steel or ductile cast iron) the latter was selected due to its economy and the possibility of monitoring defects using non-destructive ultrasonic testing. All of the cast nodes have a portion embedded in the concrete slab and lugs orientated to connect the steel tube diagonals. In the bottom layer the embedded cast section has holes to allow the pre-stressing tendons to pass through the casting and in the upper layer the embedded section is a more traditional shear stud. Different pin diameters for connection to the tubular diagonals and the different thicknesses required to cater for the design forces, resulted in twenty-eight types of node casting. Dimensions for the cast nodes were accurately controlled and the use of automated drilling and machining ensured that the holes to receive pins were correctly located relative to the centre of the joint with a tolerance of ± 0.5 mm. Fabrication details for a typical lower-layer node, where provision is made for the passing of pre-stressing strands and for a typical upper-layer node, with shear connection and supports for the precast floor formwork, are shown in Figure 5.103. Typical finished top-node castings are shown in Figure 5.104.

Steel tube sizes for the bracing members varied according to the forces to be resisted. Diameters ranged from 75 to 270 mm but those over 140 mm were only required near the corners to transfer the load to the bearings. With variations of section size and lug connector plate size, thirty different member-types were produced using automated CAM technology to ensure that the required tolerance for the distance between pin connector holes was achieved.

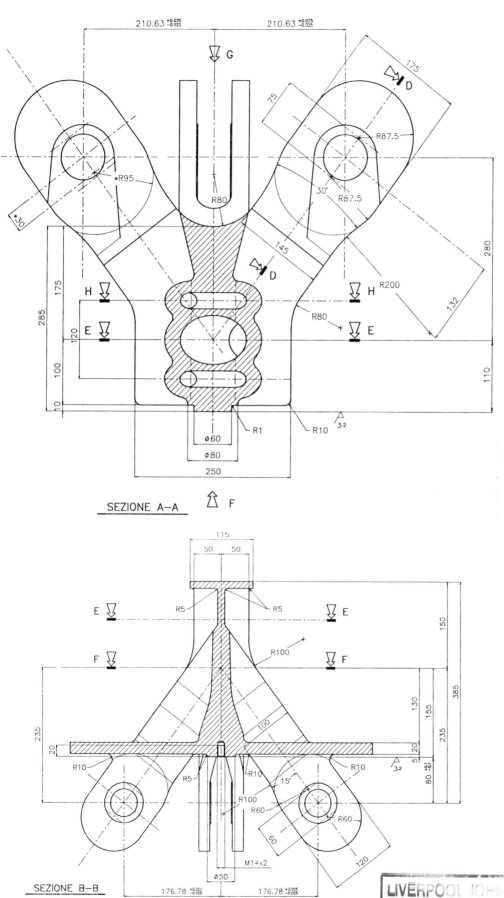

SEZIONE A—A

SEZIONE B—B

5.103
Fabrication details for
typical lower layer
cast node and typical
upper layer cast
node, Milan Fair
Exhibition Facilities
(Courtesy G. C.
Giuliani, Redesco srl.)

5.104
Typical upper layer
cast nodes awaiting
installation, Milan Fair
Exhibition Facilities.
Examples of the
tubular steel web
elements can be seen
in the foreground
(Photograph: John
Chilton)

This floor structure demonstrates the adaptability of space grids from their more common role as lightweight supports for long-span roofs to more heavily loaded applications. It shows how well tried technologies and materials can be used in combination to their best advantage, in an innovative way, to achieve an economical solution for long-span floors.

Client: Ente Autonomo Fiera Milano
Contract period: September 1994 – November 1996
Structural consultants: dr. eng. Gian Carlo Giuliani,
dr. eng. Mauro Eugenio Giuliani
Structural design: Redesco srl, Milan, Italy
Construction: Itaca Joint Venture (CMC/Recchi/G.
Maltauro/E. Frabboni/CGC/Italtel Telesis/Kone)

Stadium Australia, Sydney, Australia

At the time of writing, December 1998, Stadium Australia (Figure 5.105) is currently under construction[34] in preparation for the Olympic Games to be held in Sydney in the year 2000. The vast stadium, of 110 000 seated capacity for the duration of the Games, will eventually hold 80 000 spectators (after the removal of temporary stands at each end of the arena). Sight distances to the field of play dictate the form of the stadium which is approximately circular in plan around the rectangular playing field with covered seating along the longer sides of the arena.

The solution adopted for the roof over this seating is a diagrid steel space truss supported at the outer perimeter on the raked stand and at the other edge by a deep arch truss spanning 285.6 m (Figure 5.106). The space grid supports secondary members that, in turn, support the twin-wall polycarbonate sheet glazing. To minimize the overall height of the stadium the roof diagrid forms part of a hyperbolic paraboloid surface, arching along the major axis of the stadium and sagging along the minor axis. Placing the arch above the roof surface improves its structural efficiency and also maintains unobstructed views for the spectators high in the stands. The chords of the double-layer grid are set on the diagonal (i.e. at an angle of 45° to the stadium axis) in order to generate the double-curved surface using straight lines. A 10 m × 10 m grid (Figure 5.107) was adopted. This has a depth that varies from a maximum of 4 m down to zero at the perimeter, in line with the three-dimensional bending moment envelope for the surface. To accommodate differences in geometry between the positions of the diagrid perimeter nodes and the support beams of the raked seating, the two were linked by a prismatic truss (Figure 5.108).

In its eventual form the stadium will have additional areas of roof over the end stands. These will also utilize a 10 m × 10 m grid and taper towards the edges

5.105
*Stadium Australia,
Sydney, under
construction in
preparation for the
Olympic Games in
the year 2000
(Photograph: John
Chilton)*

5.106
*The 285.6 m span
arch supporting the
front edge of the
hyperbolic paraboloid
space grid roof
surface of Stadium
Australia. The
curvature of the roof
grid can clearly be
seen (Photograph:
John Chilton)*

from a maximum depth of 6 m at the centre. Before these end roof sections are installed the membrane action associated with the saddle surface is unable to develop. In the permanent roof configuration, the perimeter pris-matic beam is extended to form a complete undulating ring and the infill diagrids allow some significant mem-brane action to occur. Thus the structural efficiency of the infill sections is enhanced.

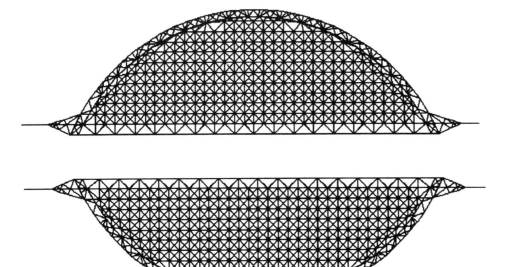

5.107
Roof plan of 10 m × 10 m diagrid,
Stadium Australia (Courtesy
MODUS Consulting)

5.108
Perimeter roof truss
between the diagrid
and the raked
seating. Installation
of the twin-wall
polycarbonate roof
panels is in progress
(Photograph: John
Chilton)

Anticipating future developments, the design of the roof and arch supports allows for the addition of a fully retractable infill roof weighing up to 6000 tonnes. An interesting feature of the space grid roof is that (at the suggestion of the fabricator, National Engineering) the elements are connected by vertical axis pins that pass through horizontal connector plates (Figure 5.109). In the top layer the chords follow straight lines but in the bot-tom layer the variations in chord direction are achieved by a fold in the node plates.

Although it was originally proposed to erect the dia-grid by connection of individual inverted pyramids, in the air, the eventual erection process commenced with the production, on the ground, of assemblies up to 90 m in length. These were then craned into position, connect-ed at each end to the arch and perimeter truss respec-

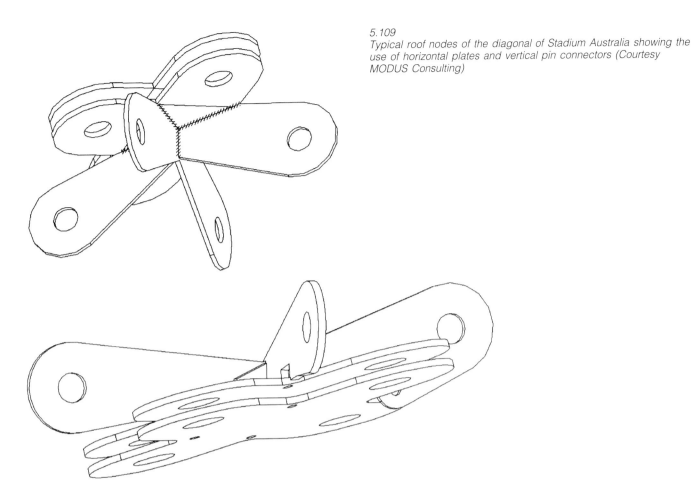

5.109
Typical roof nodes of the diagonal of Stadium Australia showing the use of horizontal plates and vertical pin connectors (Courtesy MODUS Consulting)

tively, before being gradually lowered and connected to the adjacent grid elements.

Despite its enormous span of almost 300 m, at a weight of 88 kg/m² the roof steelwork of Stadium Australia demonstrates the economy and efficiency of space grids. In this project the provision for the later addition of a retractable roof appropriately leads us into the following chapter where such structures are discussed along with foldable and deployable space grids.

Client: Olympic Coordination Authority
Architect: Bligh Lobb Sports Architects (Sydney)
Contractor: Multiplex Constructions (NSW) Pty Limited
Engineer: MODUS Consulting

Notes

1 Tange, K. (1970). Kenzo Tange 1946–69, *Architecture and Urban Design* (Udo Kultermann, ed.) p. 284, Pall Mall Press, London. © Verlag für Architektur Artemis Zürich, Switzerland.

2 Tsuboi, Y. and Kawaguchi, M. (1972). The space frame for the Symbol Zone of Expo 70. In *Proceedings 1971 IASS Pacific Symposium Part II on Tension Structures and Space Frames, Tokyo and Kyoto*, pp. 893–904, Architectural Institute of Japan.

3 Kawaguchi, M. (1992). On a few topics of membrane structures. In *Innovative Large Span Structures* (N. K. Srivastava, A. N. Sherbourne and J. Roorda, eds) vol. 1, pp. 28–48, The Canadian Society for Civil Engineering.

4 Satterwhite, R. G. (1984). Space frames as houses. In *Proceedings of the Third International Conference on Space Frames* (H. Nooshin, ed.) pp. 1031–4, Elsevier.

5 Fischer, R. E. (1980). The Crystal Cathedral: embodiment of light and nature. *Architectural Record*, November, **168** (7), 77–85.

6 Anon (1981). Structural Steel Design Award 1981. *Acier-Stahl-Steel*, **4**, p. 149.

7 Yamasaki, M. (1983) Shinji Shumei-kai Temple. *Japan Architect*, September 1983 (8309) **58** (317) 22–29.

8 Anon (1980). A vast space frame wraps New York's Convention Center like a taut fabric. *Architectural Record*, Mid-August **168** (3), 47–57.

9 Levy, M. (1997). Tetrahedral purity: the Javits Center. In *Beyond the Cube* (J.-F. Gabriel, ed.) pp. 189–209, Wiley.

10 Yoh, S. (1989). Oguni Dome. *The Japan Architect*, February **382**, 35–41.

11 Sakamoto, I. (1992). Wooden spatial structures in Japan. *Bulletin of IASS*, **33** (109), 111–13.

12 Kubik, L. A. and Chilton, J. C. (1991). Design and construction of the CUBIC Space Frame roof, Maintenance Hangar, Stansted Airport. In *Spatial Structures at the Turn of the Century*, (T. Wester, S. J. Medwadowski, and I. Mogensen, eds) vol. 1, pp. 135–42, Kunstakademiets Forlag Arkitektskolen.

13 Reina, P. (1990). Barcelona builds for the Olympics and beyond. *Engineering News Record*, 15 February, 34–6.

14 Kawaguchi, M. and Abe, M. (1992). Design and construction of Sant Jordi Sports Palace, a venue for Barcelona Olympics. *Bulletin of the International Association for Shell and Spatial Structures*, **33** (109), 69–88.

15 Delgado, R. (1990). *Palau D'Sports Sant Jordi*, Editorial Trazos SA de Arquitectura y Construccion, (in Spanish).

16 Allen, J. (1991). *Biosphere 2 – The Human Experiment* (Anthony Blake, ed.). Penguin Books.

17 Pearce, P. J. (1993). From snow crystals to space enclosure systems: implementing the future of architecture. In *Space Structures 4* (G. A. R. Parke and C. M. Howard, eds) vol. 2, pp. 2063–73, Thomas Telford.

18 Doyle, N. (1990). World class Birmingham. *New Builder*, **59** November, 20–1.

19 Roche, J. J. and Elliott, A. W. (1991). The Mero space frame roof to Birmingham's National Indoor Arena for Sport. *Steel Construction Today*, **5** (2) March, 64–7.

20 Anon (1992). *Obras Relevantes en Acero 1962–1992*. Compañia Siderurgica Huachipato S.A., Empresa CAP, pp. 81–4 (in Spanish).

21 Martínez-Calzón, J. (1995). Palafolls Sports Hall : a singular roof. In *Spatial Structures: Heritage, Present and Future* (G. C. Giuliani, ed.) vol. 1, pp. 629–38, IASS International Symposium.

22 Martínez-Calzón, J. (1995). Palafolls Sports Hall: a singular roof. *IASS Bulletin*, **36** (3), 157–66.

23 Arata Isozaki and Associates (1995). Multi-sports pavilion in Palafolls, Barcelona. *ON Diseño*, **179,** 68–85.

24 Rispa, R., Alonso de los Rios, C. and Aguaza, M.-J. (eds) (1992). *Expo '92 Sevilla, Arquitectura y Diseño*. Electa, pp. 290–1.

25 La Arquitectura de la Expo '92. *ON Diseño*, 224–8.

26 Codd, B. and White, S. H. (1992). Eagle Centre Market refurbishment, Derby. *The Structural Engineer*, **70** (5), March, 77–80.

27 Codd, B. (1991). Conder introduces Harley space frame to Europe. *Steel Construction Today*, **5** (2), March, 77–80.

28 Baird, S. C., James, N. L. and Shotton, J. E. (1993). Space deck barrel vault to the Bentall Centre, Kingston upon Thames. In *Space Structures 4* (G. A. R. Parke and C. M. Howard, eds) vol. 2, pp. 1392–9, Thomas Telford.

29 Peachey, D. H. and Dyer, D. J. (1994). Design and construction of the new Bentall Centre, Kingston-upon-Thames, Surrey. *Proceedings of the Institution of Civil Engineers, Structures and Buildings*, **104**, November, 369–76.

30 British Steel (Tubes and Pipes) (1994). *Case Study 8, Manchester Airport Building*, 12 August, pp. 34–36.

31 Huybers, P. (1990). Thin poles of roundwood for structural engineering applications in building. *Structural Engineering Review*, **2**, 169–82.

32 Guiliani, M. E. (1995). Innovative composite spatial structures for the New Milano Fair Exhibition facilities. In *Spatial Structures: Heritage, Present and Future* (G. C. Giuliani, ed.) vol. 1, pp. 451–66, IASS International Symposium.

33 Giuliani, M. E. (1995). Innovative composite spatial structures for the New Milano Fair Exhibition facilities. *IASS Bulletin*, **36** (3), 167–82.

34 Morley, S. and Whatmore, J. (1998). Stadium Australia. In *Lightweight Structures in Architecture, Engineering and Construction* (R. Hough and R. Melchers, eds) pp. 41–8, LSAA.

6 Deployable, foldable and retractable space grids

Deployable and foldable space grids

One area in which space grids are set to advance in the future is the field of deployable and foldable structures. The property of deployability in a space grid structure may be used just once or many times. For example, the deployability may be used to facilitate the erection of a permanent building or support structure. An obvious application is in outer space where large structures are required to support equipment such as arrays of photovoltaic panels. These space grids can be assembled in compact form, transported into outer space and then deployed in a 'one-off' operation. Alternatively, temporary transportable buildings can benefit from the use of rapidly deployable structures. In this case, the space grid is deployed each time the building is erected, later being collapsed down to a more compact form before being moved to store or another location. The process can be repeated any number of times.

Emilio Pérez Piñero

The concept of deployable structures is not new. Among his many studies of structures, the great Renaissance thinker and artist, Leonardo da Vinci (1452–1519) sketched a simple planar deployable mechanism in Volume 1 of his *Codex Madrid*.[1] We are also familiar with common deployable structures such as the folding lattices used for lift doors. Three-dimensional structures of this type were first developed by Spanish engineer Emilio Pérez Piñero (Figure 6.1), who was born in 1936 and died tragically in a car accident in 1972.[2] In the early 1960s he designed and patented reticulated foldable space grids. In such structures the basic folding unit is made of two members connected together at or near their mid-length to produce a 'scissor' mechanism (Figure 6.2(a)). The ends of the members of several scissor mechanisms may then be connected together in a predefined way, in order to form an expanding truss-like

6.1
Emilio Pérez Piñero seen with one of his experimental folding space grids (Photograph courtesy Fundación Piñero)

131

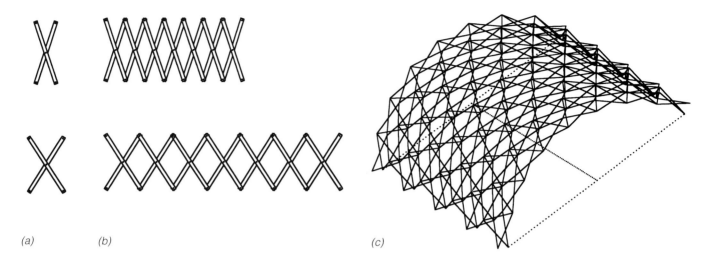

(a)   (b)   (c)

6.2
Deployable structures: (a) basic 'scissor' mechanism, (b) 'scissor' truss-like assembly and (c) three-dimensional folding barrel vault grid (Drawing: John Chilton)

arrangement, as seen in Figure 6.2(b). A series of these planar assemblies may be connected by similar scissor mechanisms running transversely, so forming a folding three-dimensional grid (Figure 6.2(c)). To limit the extension of the planar assemblies, some form of restraint, such as flexible or folding ties, may be inserted between adjacent member ends. To lock the mechanism fully the flexible ties may be replaced by bars. A similar process can be used to stabilize a three-dimensional deployable grid.

Pérez Piñero proposed single and double-layer domed and planar grids for mobile theatres, pavilions and exhi-

bition buildings. For example, in 1964 an 8000 m² exhibition pavilion, composed of many 12 × 9 m deployable space grid modules weighing only 500 kg each, was erected in Madrid for the summer. Folded for transport each module was only 0.8 × 0.7 m in plan (see Figures 6.3). Module deployment was carried out on the ground, using sets of wheels (Figure 6.4), then the foldable structure was made stable by introducing additional bars before the profiled metal roofing panels were fixed (Figure 6.5). Taken down in only seven days, the whole pavilion was subsequently moved to San Sebastián and later to Barcelona.

6.3
Travelling exhibition pavilion of 8000 m² with foldable space grid roof designed by Emilio Pérez Piñero – folded state (Photograph courtesy Fundación Piñero)

6.4
Foldable travelling exhibition pavilion during deployment (Photograph courtesy Fundación Piñero)

6.5
Foldable travelling exhibition pavilion – deployed state with some of the roof plates installed (Photograph courtesy Fundación Piñero)

The long section and plan of a similar demountable theatre project of 1971 is shown in Figures 6.6(a) and 6.6(b). Here the folding space grid is primarily supported at four locations each with four struts guyed to maintain lateral stability of the structure.

Pérez Piñero also worked with Salvador Dalí on a project to develop a foldable sculpture that was covered with eighty-four glass panes and had geometry based on the hypercube. Figure 6.7 shows Pérez Piñero presenting his third scale model of the structure to Dalí, in its completely folded state and Figure 6.8 shows the unfolded structure against the background of the Eiffel Tower in Paris. Félix Escrig has commented[2] that this was the first example of a foldable space grid (see Figure 6.9) in which the covering was attached to the structure during deployment, all previous examples having had the cladding fixed once they were fully open.

The work of Pérez Piñero was sadly curtailed due to his untimely death. However, in later years his ideas were taken up and further developed by (among others)

sección longitudinal

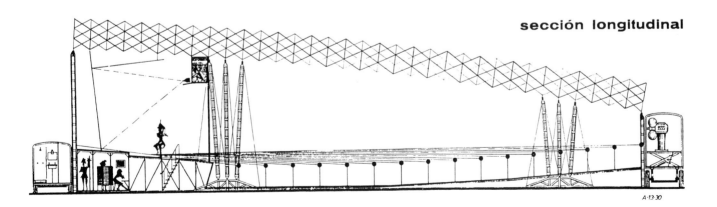

A·13·30

6.6 (a)
Long section through the demountable theatre, designed by Emilio Pérez Piñero 1971, showing the folding roof in its open position and the system of supports (Courtesy Fundación Piñero)

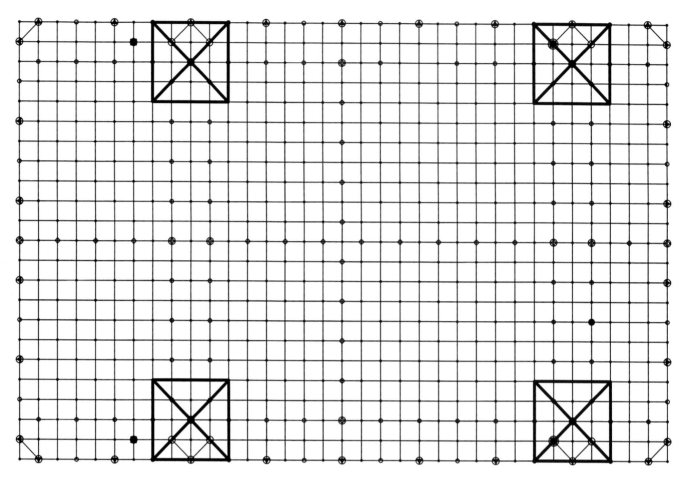

6.6 (b)
Plan of the demountable theatre, designed by Emilio Pérez Piñero 1971, showing the folding roof in its open position and the system of supports (Courtesy Fundación Piñero)

6.7
Third scale model of folding sculpture (in fully folded state) being shown by Emilio Pérez Piñero to Salvador Dalí at his home in Cadaqués, Spain (Photograph courtesy Fundación Piñero)

6.8
Glass-covered folding sculpture by Emilio Pérez Piñero and Salvador Dalí (in unfolded state) against the background of the Eiffel Tower in Paris (Photograph courtesy Fundación Piñero)

Ziegler, Calatrava, Valcárcel, Escrig and Hernandez. Examples of the work of some of these are described later in this chapter. The easy acceptance of foldable grids is demonstrated by the ubiquitous cylindrically curved foldable display panels developed by Ziegler and used at exhibitions worldwide.

Venezuela Pavilion, Expo '92, Seville, Spain

One of the grounds often stated for not using space grids is cost of erection. In recent times, the use of foldable or deployable structures has been explored as a means of countering this argument. A remarkable example of this is the Venezuela Pavilion constructed for Expo '92 in Seville, Spain, (see Figure 6.10). Due to the high cost of construction in Spain it was proposed to manufacture the pavilion in Venezuela and transport it to Seville.[3,4,5] Further, as it was to be a temporary building that would be transported back to Venezuela after the Exposition, a deployable space grid was an attractive alternative. The concept was also considered to accord well with the theme of the Exposition, 'The Era of the Discoveries'.

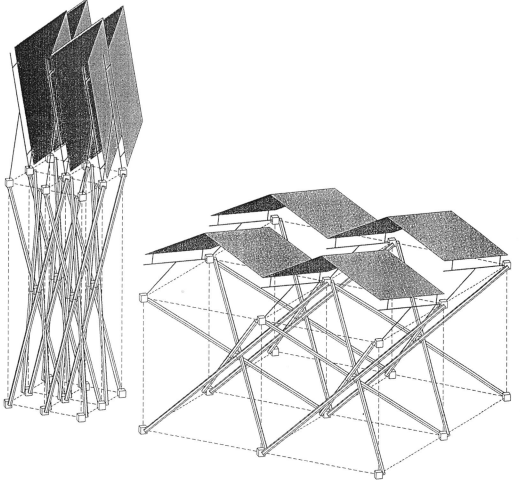

6.9
Detail drawing of the folding structure with folding glass covering plates that remain attached to it during deployment (Courtesy Fundación Piñero)

6.10
Venezuela Pavilion at
Expo '92, Seville
(Photograph: John
Chilton)

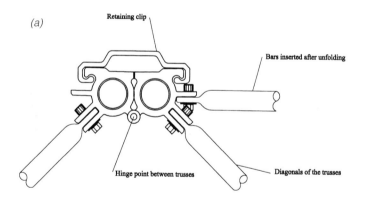

(a)

Retaining clip

Bars inserted after unfolding

Hinge point between trusses

Diagonals of the trusses

SECTION THROUGH TYPICAL HINGED NODE

Essentially a large audiovisual display room, the pavilion was conceived with a basic triangular cross-section that would permit the use of simple foldable planar space trusses. The longer of the two inclined planes of the section was divided into spans of 13 and 18 m by an intermediate support while the other plane (a slightly inclined,

6.11
(a) Section through a typical hinged node for the deployable space grid, (b) deployment sequence for the space grid of the Venezuela Pavilion at Expo '92, Seville. The grid changes from the tightly folded to fully open and restrained state from left to right (Courtesy C. H. Hernandez, and W. Zalewski; drawing: John Chilton)

(b)

Grid in folded state

Grid unfolding

Bars inserted after unfolding

Retaining clip

Grid in fully unfolded state

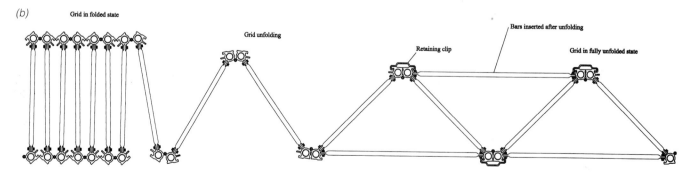

SECTION SHOWING SEQUENCE OF UNFOLDING THE GRID

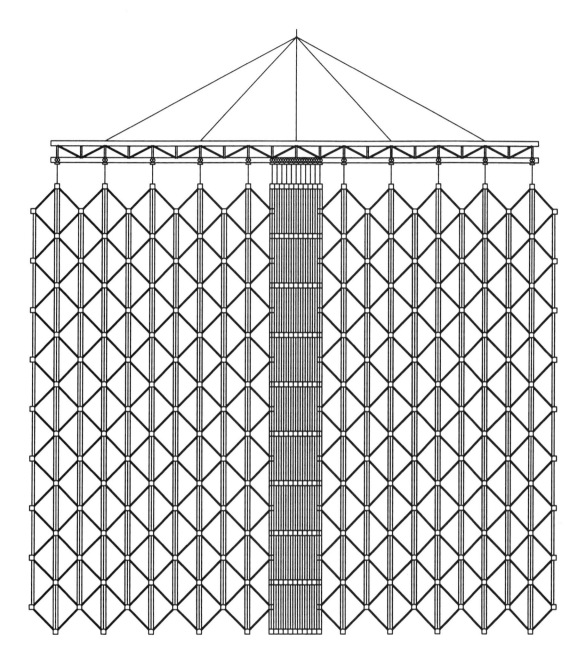

*6.12
Deployment of the
Venezuela Pavilion
space grid
(expanding from the
centre) whilst
suspended from a
stiff lifting beam
(Courtesy C. H.
Hernandez, and W.
Zalewski; drawing:
John Chilton)*

almost vertical, wall) was 18 m high. Although predominantly spanning in one direction, the addition of transverse elements between the unfolded trusses ensured load distribution in three dimensions.

Aluminium alloy 6261 (with a density of 2.71 kg/m^3) was selected for the structure to reduce the weight to be transported and handled. The aluminium industries of Venezuela combined to produce the material, the required moulds for extrusions, and to fabricate and paint the foldable space truss. To enable deployment, the space truss contains hinged nodes (Figure 6.11(a)) that permit a 'concertina'-type folding in one plane so that the trusses, initially parallel in the folded state, finally splay at 90° to each other in the unfolded state. The

hinges are locked after full deployment by 'staples' that also carry the cladding that is suspended from the lower chords of the space truss. In the main spanning direction the twin tubular upper and lower chord members are continuous, with the hinged nodes fixed to them at 2 m intervals. Diagonal bracing in the folded trusses and the transverse members used to fix the space grid after deployment are tubes with flattened ends to facilitate bolting to the nodes. Figure 6.11(b) shows in section the sequence of deployment from the fully folded state, through unfolding to the fully deployed state with stabilizing bars inserted.

Two separate sections of deployable space grid were preassembled. One section of twenty-two trusses 13 m

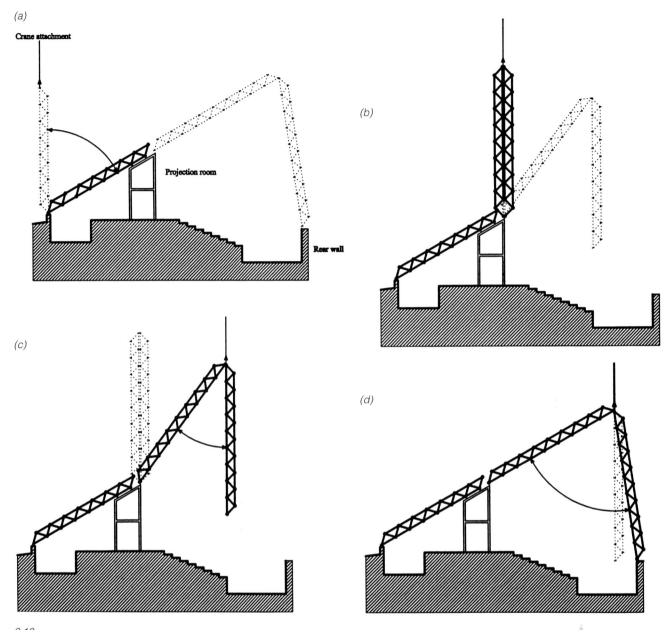

(a)

Crane attachment

Projection room

Rear wall

(b)

(c)

(d)

6.13
Unfolding of the fully deployed space grid of the Venezuela Pavilion at Expo '92, Seville. A short section spans from the ground to an intermediate support and the doubled section opens out leaving the hinge line at the apex of the pavilion (Courtesy C. H. Hernandez and W. Zalewski; drawing: John Chilton)

long and a second section that was made from two independent sets each of twenty-two trusses, 18 m long. One end of each of the two parts of this second, 18 m long, section were joined together by hinges to form a closed package for transportation. This package (including the packing material) weighed only 8000 kg and had overall dimensions of 18.8 m × 3 m × 2.8 m.

On site, each 2.8 m wide bundle was hung like a curtain from the centre of a special truss lifting beam, provided at the bottom chord with a rail and a set of bogies joined together by a steel cable. To deploy each space grid, the folded bundle was pulled out symmetrically from

the centre until it reached its full 22 m width, as shown in Figure 6.12. Temporary measures were taken to prevent re-folding then transverse elements were added to stabilize the structure and form a two-way grid. Finally, the unfolded grids were placed in their permanent positions in the building. The shorter section spanning between the ground and the intermediate support provided by the projection area and the doubled section opening out to be fixed at two supports leaving the hinge line at the apex of the pavilion section (see Figure 6.13).

Sandwich cladding panels were composed of a light grey glass reinforced polyester (GRP) exterior surface and dark-grey coated galvanized steel interior filled with rigid polyurethane foam insulation. The panels were fixed to secondary tubular elements suspended by adjustable bolts from the underside of the grid nodes. Joints between panels were weather-proofed with silicone sealant.

This simple but elegant Pavilion demonstrated the potential for deployable building structures in architecture as the 6475 piece, 1242 m², space grid was fabricated in Venezuela, over 5000 miles (8000 km), from the Expo '92 site. It was transported to Seville in compact form, and then unfolded and erected in just thirteen hours (including the installation of the members needed to make the grid rigid). By using continuous members in one direction, the number of grid components was smaller and assembly was therefore quicker. Fabrication took place in controlled conditions in a workshop but the size of grid was restricted by transportation and crane capacity. Nevertheless, the wider use of rapidly erected, deployable space grids is an exciting prospect for the future.

The 'Pantadome' erection system

Space grids are frequently used for long-span roof structures for sports stadiums or aircraft hangars, for example, and in these situations the method of erection may significantly affect the cost of construction. Considerable savings in time and cost can be made, if the roof can be erected with the minimum of interference with the rest of the construction process and as near to the ground as possible, to reduce cranage costs. For this reason, planar space grids are often erected on temporary supports a few metres above the ground at a level convenient for the installation of services and roof cladding, prior to hoisting or jacking into the final position. This works well for flat space grids but, when there is significant three-dimensional curvature in the roof, this method is more difficult to employ. R. Buckminster Fuller tried alternative methods of erection to facilitate the construction of his geodesic domes. For instance, in 1957, in Honolulu, he used a system suspending the partially completed dome with wire ropes from a central tower.[6,7] As concentric rings of structure were added at the perimeter the dome was raised further up the tower. Construction work was therefore always near to ground level. Two years later he constructed a 117 m dome at

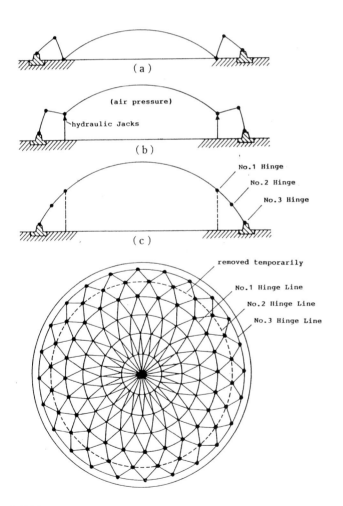

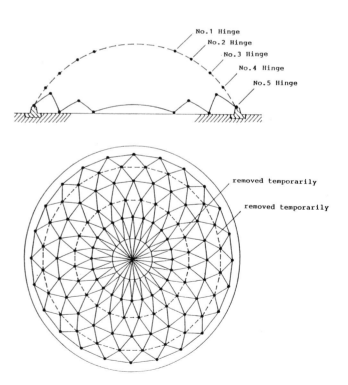

6.14(a)
Plans and cross-sections of the 'Pantadome' system for domes with three hinge lines (where bars are temporarily removed on hinge line No.2 to allow deployment and replaced later to stabilize the mechanism) (Courtesy Mamoru Kawaguchi)

6.14(b)
Plans and cross-sections of the 'Pantadome' system for doubly-folded domes with five hinge lines (in this case bars are temporarily removed on hinge lines No.2 and No.4, to allow deployment, and replaced later to stabilize the mechanism.) (Courtesy Mamoru Kawaguchi)

(a)

6.15
Model showing the erection procedure for the 'Pantadome' system for a single-layer grid dome with three hinge lines showing (a) the central dome at or near ground level with an intermediate ring of structure folded down to connect the dome and supports, (b) the dome partially lifted (note that the hinge points at the top of the supporting triangles have moved outwards to allow the central area to pass through), (c) the fully deployed mechanism and (d) the fully stable structure after insertion of additional bars between the intermediate hinge points (Photographs courtesy Mamoru Kawaguchi)

(b)

Wood River, USA, where part was lifted using air pressure on a balloon-like envelope.

A recent innovation in this area is the 'Pantadome' system developed by the Japanese engineer, Mamoru Kawaguchi.[8] The principle of this system depends on the fact that a structure having four or more hinged joints in one plane is a mechanism and can be moved freely. Most people are familiar with the hinged mechanisms, or pantographs, that are used to maintain electrical contact between the electric motors of railway locomotives and the overhead cables that provide the power to drive them or as a device for copying drawings either direct-

(c)

(d)

ly or with a change of scale. Similarly, we are familiar with the flexibility of hinged mechanisms (in the engineering sense) in general. Mamoru Kawaguchi has adapted this flexibility to allow efficient erection of nonplanar roof forms.

Complex building cross-sections to be constructed using space grids may be subdivided into sections that can be hinged to each other and to the supports at the perimeter. With an appropriate selection of the hinge locations, it may be possible to 'fold' the cross-section so that, in its folded form, the majority of the roof contour is near to the ground. Subsequently the space grid

6.16
*World Memorial Hall
in Kobe, Japan
(Photograph courtesy
Mamoru Kawaguchi)*

6.17
*Interior of the World
Memorial Hall in
Kobe, Japan
(Photograph courtesy
Mamoru Kawaguchi)*

may be unfolded into the desired profile and 'locked' into position, so that it is no longer a mechanism. The basic principle of the 'Pantadome' system is shown in Figures 6.14(a) and 6.14(b) for domes with a three-hinged or a five-hinged mechanism respectively. In order to stabilize the dome after lifting, additional bars must be introduced along hinge line No.2 in Figure 6.14(a) or along hinge lines No.2 and No.4 in Figure 6.14(b). Figure 6.15(a) to (d) shows photographs of a model demonstrating the procedure for the erection of a single layer grid dome with three hinge lines. Detailed studies of the use of the 'Pantadome' system for the erection of roof structures of

different configuration show the flexibility of the method. The Sant Jordi Sport Palace, Barcelona, Spain, constructed as the arena for the 1992 Olympic Games was described in detail in Chapter 5 and other roofs are described below.

World Memorial Hall, Kobe, Japan

The first realization of the 'Pantadome' system[8] was for the World Memorial Hall in Kobe, Japan, which was completed in 1984 ready for the Universiade held there in

1985 (see Figure 6.16 and 6.17) and subsequently as an all-purpose hall. Particular design requirements were that it should house a 160 m running track, seat 10 000 spectators and that there should be at least 24 m headroom internally to accommodate large yachts in exhibitions. The final solution was a building approximately 70 × 110 m with 34 m radius quarter spheres at each end connected by a 40.8 m long cylindrical vault. Centred 1 m above ground level the semicircular vault rises to almost 40 m.

Rigid frames were used to accommodate a large number of window openings in the lower part of the side walls, however, a 1.5 m deep space truss formed the rest of the building envelope. On a standard 2.5 × 2.5 m grid the space truss used more than 12 000 steel tubular members (respectively, 101.6 mm diameter for the chords and 76.3 mm diameter for the web members). All members were welded to the spherical nodes (216.3 mm and 267.4 mm in diameter) which were formed from pressed steel plates with welded diaphragms.

The erection procedure for the Kobe World Memorial Hall is shown in section in Figure 6.18. There was one hinge line at the base of the enclosure, a second at the interface between the rigid frames and the space truss and a third within the space truss itself. During assembly there were eighteen temporary supports 6.5 m high located under the hinge line in the space truss. These supports were subsequently used in the lifting operation. Some members were omitted from the structure at this stage to permit the mechanism to form and to allow it to move freely whilst the dome was being raised. Although there were several possible methods for lifting the assembled grid, the well tried 'push-up' system was preferred by the contractor Takenaka Komuten Co. Ltd. Parallel 50 tonne jacks at each temporary support were used to push up posts that were extendible at the base as lifting progressed. Temporary ties connected the hinges at the tops of the posts (under the central cylindrical vault) to take the horizontal thrust and maintain stability. Initially, the tops of the rigid side frames moved outwards as the space truss thrust upwards between them, subsequently they moved inwards to form part of dome cross-section as it reached its full height. After lifting, additional members were added to complete the dome, clamping the mechanism, and the props and ties were removed. The change in shape experienced by the roof structure during lifting can be seen in Figures 6.19 (a) and (b). During this process the 'push-up' points were raised by over 20 m and the structure almost tripled in height.

To prevent permanent damage due to over-stressing of the roof during the lifting operation, the process was carefully monitored and controlled. For the lifting frames, measurements were taken of horizontal and vertical displacement, loading and pressure of hydraulic units and,

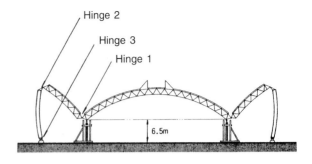

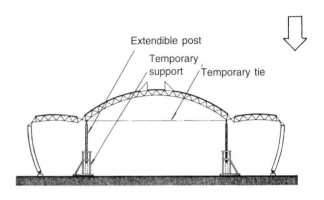

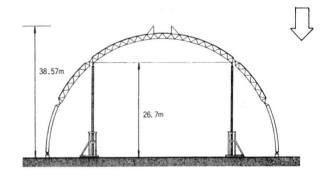

6.18
Sections showing three stages of erection for the World Memorial Hall, Kobe (top) before lifting, (middle) during lifting and (bottom) final position (Courtesy Mamoru Kawaguchi)

for the roof structure, stresses were monitored using strain gauges at 281 positions and deflections by means of automatic levelling at 33 locations.

In a preliminary report on the effects of the catastrophic 'Great Hanshin-Awaji' earthquake, magnitude 7.2 on the Richter scale, which struck the city of Kobe on 17 January 1995, it was reported that 'no major structural damage was found' in the space grid structure of the dome.[9] The performance of the dome, which was constructed on

6.19(a)
Raising of World Memorial Hall in Kobe, Japan, roof in folded position (Photograph courtesy Mamoru Kawaguchi)

6.19(b)
Raising of World Memorial Hall in Kobe, Japan, roof in final position (Photograph courtesy Mamoru Kawaguchi)

made ground, under the severe accelerations imposed by the earthquake demonstrates the suitability of space grids for structures in seismic zones.

Engineer: Mamoru Kawaguchi
Contractor: Takenaka Komuten Co. Ltd

Indoor Stadium, Singapore

The Singapore Indoor Stadium (Figure 6.20) completed in 1989, is a building of totally different form for which the same Pantadome system of erection was used. Reminiscent of the traditional roof form of an oriental

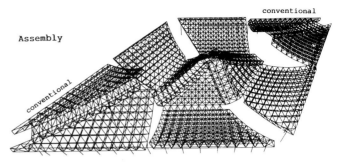

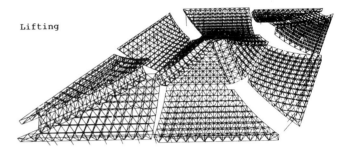

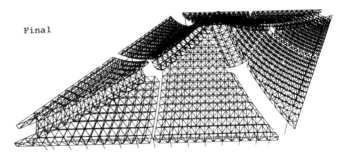

6.20
The Singapore Indoor Stadium (Photograph courtesy Mamoru Kawaguchi)

6.21
Computer-generated, three-dimensional view of the assembly, lifting and final phases of erection for the space grid roof, Singapore Indoor Stadium (Courtesy Mamoru Kawaguchi)

temple or pagoda the 14 000 m² roof is a diamond shape with maximum dimensions 219 m × 126 m. The completed multipurpose stadium houses almost 12 000 spectators around a playing area 65 × 45 m and accommodates 'either two basketball, five volleyball, four indoor tennis or 12 badminton courts'.[10,11]

The space grid structure is a combination of two major 'keel' trusses, spanning along the main axes of the diamond plan, and four double-layer curved space trusses, each part of a 65 m radius cylinder. Connecting the ends of the fully welded keel trusses there is a tension ring to resist their outward thrust. Sixty-four columns along the perimeter and two pairs of internal columns, set 121 m apart under the keel trusses running on the longer roof axis, provide permanent support for the structure. Nippon Steel Corporation's NS truss system was used on a 3.0 × 3.0 m grid, 2.5 m deep, for the space truss surfaces between the keel trusses. A total of 7700 tubular steel members 76.2 mm to 457.2 mm diameter were used in the space truss with nodes between 150 and 490 mm diameter.

At first glance, the form of this roof appears to be more complex than that of the Kobe Memorial Hall; however it was divided into only seven separate sections for construction, five of which were to be moved using the Pantadome System. Two sections of roof in the acute angles of the diamond shape were constructed by conventional methods. A central 'hat' section bounded by four hinge lines parallel to the sides of the building

(essentially a small version of the whole roof structure) was constructed on temporary supports and scaffolding 9 m above the arena floor. Four curved roof sections were constructed close to the profile of the arena stands, each connected at one end to a hinge line of the central hat section and at the other to hinge lines at the top of the perimeter columns. There was also a third hinge line at the base of the perimeter columns. Between these assembled sections, four small areas of roof were left to be filled in after the roof had been raised 20 m, over one week at the end of February 1989, to its final position · using a push-up system similar to that used at Kobe. Different stages of the erection process are shown diagrammatically in Figure 6.21.

A maximum allowance of 20 mm differential height between push-up points was considered in the structural analysis of the simulated erection sequence. Following computer analysis, it was found that horizontal tie bars between lifting points were not required in this instance to maintain stability. Reasons given for adopting this method of erection for the roof project were the improved safety of working at lower level, better quality control, the reduced construction period and a reduction of the need for scaffolding.

Architect: Kenzo Tange Associates, and RSP Architects, Planners and Engineers
Engineers : Mamoru Kawaguchi & Engineers (roof structure), Takumi Orimoto Structural Engineers & Associates, RSP Architects, Planners and Engineers
Contractors: Ssangyong-Guan Ho Construction J/V, and Nippon Steel Corporation

Sun-Dome, Sabae, Fukui Prefecture, Japan

In 1995, the 'Pantadome' system was used for the erection of the 116 m diameter Sun-Dome at Sabae, Fukui Prefecture, in Japan.[12] Designed for use as the main venue for the 1995 World Gymnastics Championships, the multi-use arena has fully retractable seating for 6000 and can also be used for exhibitions, fairs, concerts and other sporting events.

Because of the heavy snowfalls experienced in the region, the final roof surface of the space grid is stepped to control the possibility of snow sliding in avalanches from the spherical dome (see the aerial photograph, Figure 6.22). In fact, the roof was designed to retain all of the snow that falls on it, with a consequent design snow load of 600 kg/m^2. To cater for this high loading,

the double-layer space grid was designed with the intention of carrying the load in the most efficient manner. Consequently, the highest compression forces are in the bottom layer of the space truss, whilst the role of the upper layer and web bracing is primarily to preclude buckling of the lower chords. Special cast steel joints were developed to ensure high efficiency force transmission in the lower layer of the grid.

Initially, the roof grid was folded to form a 40 m diameter central dome, constructed on the arena floor, encompassed by sixteen radial segments of the lower dome, each supported on four perimeter columns. As in previous Pantadome applications, small slots of incomplete structure were left between each dome segment to be filled in after the lifting operation. Hinged connections were provided at the perimeter of the central raised dome and at the top and bottom of each perimeter column. To raise the roof structure, it was pushed up vertically at eight points around the perimeter of the central dome. Final locking of the structural mechanism was achieved by introducing the missing space truss members between the radial segments. A series of sections through the dome at various stages of the lifting process are shown in Figure 6.23. As can be seen from these, the short supporting perimeter columns are inclined at more than 50° to the vertical during deployment whilst returning to the vertical position in the final phase.

Architect: Professor S. Okazaki, Fukui University
Engineer: Mamoru Kawaguchi & Engineers
(roof structure)

6.22
Aerial view of the Sun-Dome, Sabae, Fukui Prefecture, Japan. The stepped profile adopted to prevent snow from slipping from the roof may clearly be seen (Photograph courtesy Mamoru Kawaguchi)

6.23
Sections showing the lifting sequence for the Sun-Dome, Sabae (Courtesy Mamoru Kawaguchi)

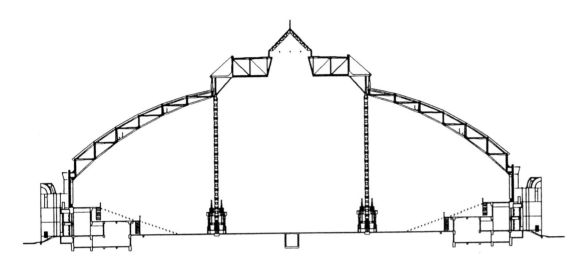

Final position

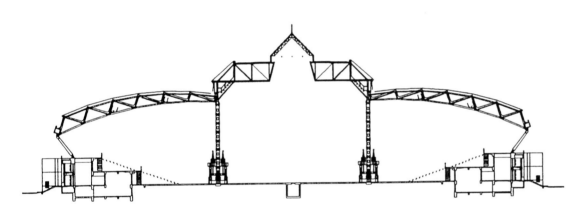

During lifting

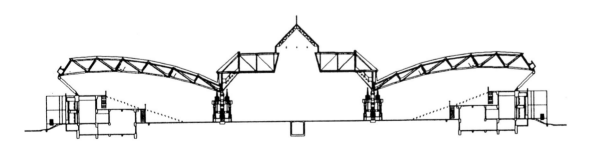

Initial position

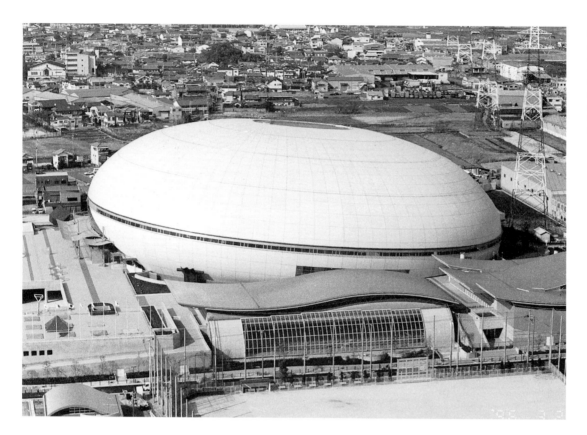

6.24
Namihaya Dome,
Kadoma Sports
Centre – exterior view
clearly showing the 5°
inclination of the roof
structure (Photograph
courtesy Mamoru
Kawaguchi)

Namihaya Dome, Kadoma Sports Centre, Mitsushima, Kadoma-City, Osaka Prefecture, Japan

Completed in March 1996, the Kadoma Sports Centre, Osaka, Japan (Figure 6.24), is a complex comprising a 6000-seat main arena with two swimming pools (a racing pool 50 × 25.5 m and a diving pool 25 × 25 m) and two ancillary facilities, a smaller arena and another pool (Figure 6.25). Of prime interest in this study of space grids, is the main arena, which has an oval plan enveloped by an oval double-layer space truss structure, the Namihaya Dome, 110 m × 127 m and rising to 42.65 m (Figure 6.26). However, the major architectural feature of the spectacular shallow-domed roof is the 5° inclination of its equator. The overall effect of the building's form is that of a gigantic discus half buried in the ground, as can be seen in Figure 6.24.

As the roof was to be raised using the Pantadome System,[8,12] the inclination introduced additional erection problems. The detailed longitudinal section illustrating the lifting sequence (Figure 6.27), shows that the posts used to push-up the roof are themselves inclined at 5° to the vertical. This section also shows the disposition of the hinges in the space truss, in both top and bottom chords. The central section of the dome comprised a complete oval panel 66 m by 86 m whilst the middle and lower sections were each divided radially into fourteen segments.

A special lifting system was devised for this structure so that the roof could be raised from its position near arena level to almost its full height in just one day. The partially lifted roof structure of the sports hall is shown in Figure 6.28, where it can be seen that some of the cladding has already been installed. Distinct areas of space grid are clearly visible, separated by zones that will be infilled after the structure has been fully lifted and the dome has achieved its prescribed geometry. The posts used to lift the roof can be seen contrasted against the underside of the central roof section.

Because of its inclined equator, the roof was analysed closely by computer at nine different steps in the Pantadome process. Following this analysis, it was discovered that some member stresses and dome deformations might be very large during the final stages of the push-up although they were within acceptable limits until then. The major lift, of just over 28 m, was achieved using temporary posts, hydraulic jacks and steel cables, and accomplished in just one day. It left the central section of the dome 0.6 m below its final location as there were fears that the dome could become unstable at that stage. As the roof was raised, forces in the posts gradually decreased as the roof load was transferred to the perimeter supports. However, the majority of load transfer took place during the last small push-up steps, which

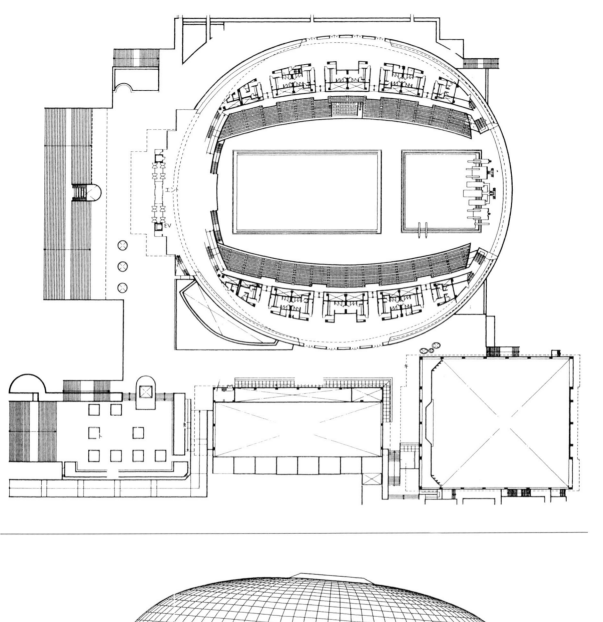

6.25
Namihaya Dome, Kadoma Sports Centre – floor plan and elevation (Courtesy Mamoru Kawaguchi)

took place over three months. During this slow raising through the last 0.6 m, a total of 1296 members were introduced into the slots between the segments of the middle and lower sections of the dome, according to a strict order of placement to maintain the stability of the structure.

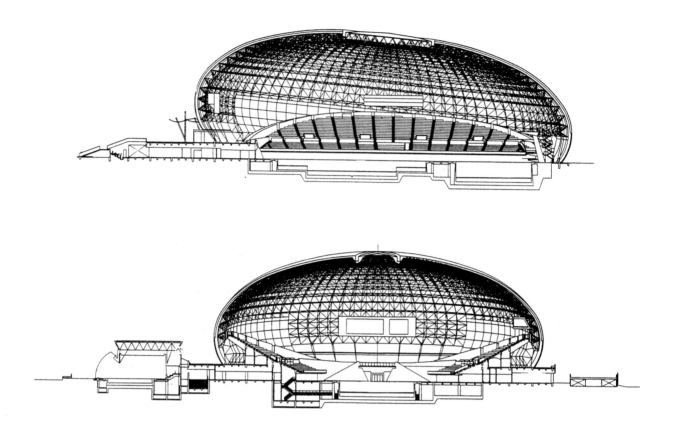

6.26
Namihaya Dome, Kadoma Sports Centre – longitudinal and transverse sections showing the complex geometry of the double curved space grid (Courtesy Mamoru Kawaguchi)

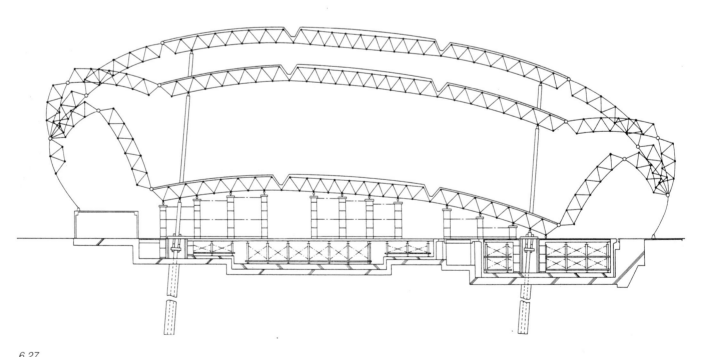

6.27
Namihaya Dome, Kadoma Sports Centre – section showing folding and lifting arrangements with hinge lines in the top and bottom chord layers (Courtesy Mamoru Kawaguchi)

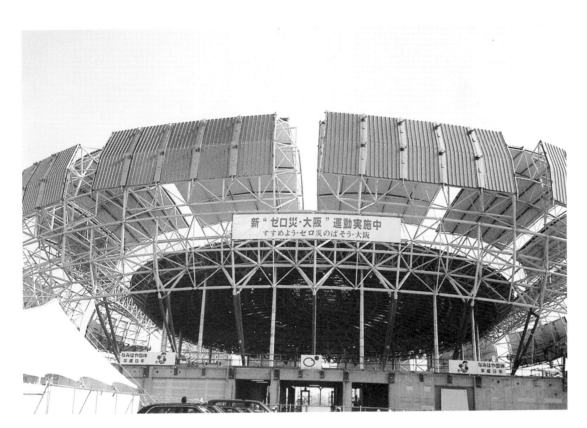

*6.28
Lower structure of the Kadoma Sports Centre showing the extent of pre-installation of cladding and services before lifting and the zones that will be infilled after lifting (Photograph courtesy Kyo Takenouchi)*

The successful conclusion of this project demonstrated the adaptability of the Pantadome system of erection to a complex structural form, an inclined oval space grid dome. At the same time, it showed that extreme care must be taken to ensure the stability of the structure at all times during the push-up process.

*Client: Osaka Prefecture
Architects: Showa Sekkei Co. Ltd
Engineer: Mamoru Kawaguchi & Engineers (roof structure)
Main contractor: Takenaka Corporation*

During 1997 the same system of erection was used for the Nara Convention Hall where the walls of the long, narrow lenticular plan building were hinged at their base, at the top and at a point a little above their mid-height.[12] This structure was raised between 1 and 6 December 1997. The wide variety of large scale projects so far completed using the 'Pantadome' System have demonstrated its eminent suitability for efficient and speedy construction of space grids of complex form. It will most certainly be widely used for similar projects in the future.

Folding roof for swimming pool, San Pablo, Seville, Spain

Following the early work of Pérez Piñero, Félix Escrig and his colleagues at the School of Architecture in Seville have experimented with lightweight folding grid structures.[13,14,15] A recent example was used for the cover of an Olympic-sized swimming pool in San Pablo, Seville, where curved grids of this form were used to suspend a membrane cover over the pool. Delivered to site as a tight bundle of connected tubular members, the expanding grid was placed in the bottom of the empty pool and partially deployed to allow attachment of the membrane to the lower nodes. Then the whole roof structure was lifted by crane from a single point at the centre of the grid, and stretched out over the empty pool, deploying the membrane at the same time. Subsequently, diagonals were added between the upper nodes to convert the mechanism into a stable form. The sequence of unfolding is shown in Figures 6.29. A typical central node detail is shown in Figure 6.30 where the method of connection of individual members around a central spindle can be seen as well as the method of suspending the membrane inside the folding grid.

The completed roofs provide a lightweight and demountable cover for the pool, offering enclosure from the elements in winter and an appealing glowing structural form at night (Figure 6.31).

Architects: Félix Escrig and José Sanchez.

Retractable roof structures

During the late 1980s and the 1990s it has become increasingly popular to provide large sports stadiums with

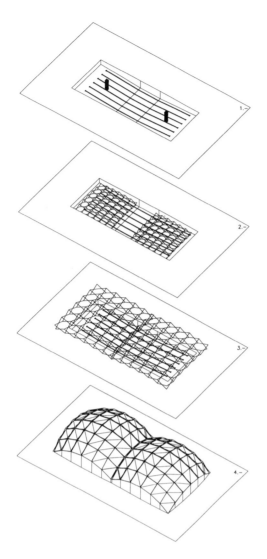

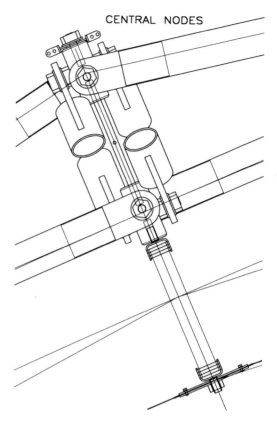

CENTRAL NODES

6.30
Typical central node of the pool cover showing the method of suspending the membrane inside the folding grid (Courtesy Félix Escrig)

6.29
Swimming pool cover, San Pablo, Seville, Spain: the sequence of unfolding the deployable roof grid (Courtesy Félix Escrig)

6.31
Exterior night view of the deployable three-dimensional space grid pool cover, San Pablo, Seville, Spain (Photograph courtesy Félix Escrig)

6.32
Roof of the Toronto Skydome in the closed position seen from the CN tower. The roof retracts from left to right as seen from this position (Photograph: John Chilton)

a retractable roof, especially in countries where the climate is such that adverse weather conditions may occur at almost any time of the year. Although such roofs are expensive and in purely financial terms it is difficult to justify their construction, municipal authorities are well aware of the prestige that they give their city.

Skydome, Toronto, Canada

The roof of the Skydome, besides being one of the longest clear-span space grid structures in the world, is also retractable, leaving 91 per cent of the seating open to the sky when fully open. This striking feature of the Skydome lends spectacle to the sporting events held within the arena, as well as permitting the facilities to be used to their best advantage in all weathers, all year round. Completed in 1989, the circular bowl of the stadium is the home of the Toronto Blue Jays baseball team. By moving some of the seating, the arena can also be adapted for football. Near Lake Ontario and close to the centre of the city, the Skydome is adjacent to the CN Tower, one of the tallest structures in the world. Thus two imposing architectural and engineering achievements stand side by side. From the start, the Skydome was envisaged as a symbol for the city of Toronto and the dominant roof form has been described by the architect Rod Robbie as 'an organic crustacean form with a clearly visible orientation towards the south and the noon sun'.[16]

The retractable roof, which can be opened in 20 minutes, is divided into four sections, one fixed and three moving (see Figure 6.32 in the closed state). There are two sliding arch sections, of 208 m and 202 m span respectively, one moving inside the other, and one retractable quarter dome sector, of 175 m maximum span, that moves along a circular track. A further static quarter dome forms the remaining section of the roof. The upper arch is 55 m wide, the lower 48 m wide whilst the fixed and moving dome segments have maximum widths of 44.4 and 48.4 m respectively. Although not built from a modular space grid system, the structure is included here as the structural configuration used effectively forms a double-layer space grid. The arch sections are generated from a series of parallel planar arch trusses, generally at 7.0 m centres, with transverse trusses and bracing in the planes of the top and bottom chords. Similarly, a space grid structure is produced for each of the quarter domes by four main arch trusses, with radial rib trusses and diagonal bracing.

During the retraction process, first the smaller 'inner' arch (segment B in Figure 6.33) moves along its 55 m track to rest over the fixed quarter dome (segment D), then the larger 'outer' arch (segment A) retracts 103 m to its final position over these two segments. Finally, the movable quarter dome (segment C) glides 309 m round the curved perimeter track and nests under segment A and B and above segment D (see the open and closed positions shown in Figure 6.33). The weights of the mov-

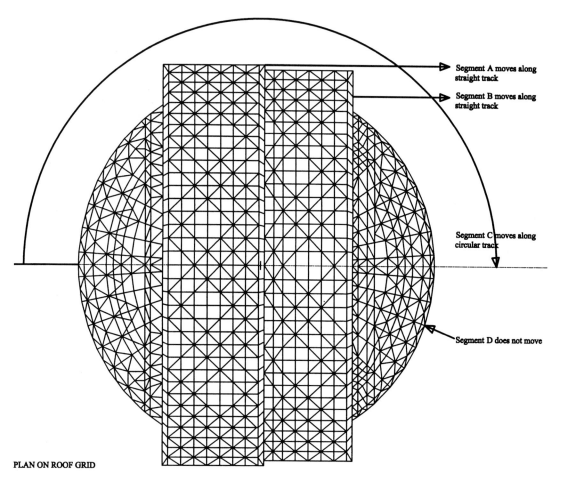

6.33
Diagram of roof
movements during
retraction. Segments
A, B and C retract to
positions above
segment D in the
order B, A, D
(Drawing: John
Chilton)

Segment A moves along
straight track

Segment B moves along
straight track

Segment C moves along
circular track

Segment D does not move

PLAN ON ROOF GRID

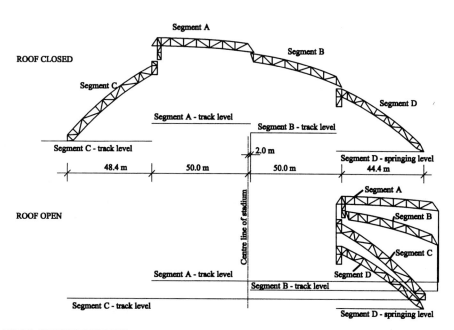

ROOF CLOSED

Segment A

Segment B

Segment C

Segment D

Segment A - track level

Segment B - track level

Segment C - track level

2.0 m

Segment D - springing level

48.4 m   50.0 m   50.0 m   44.4 m

Centre line of stadium

ROOF OPEN

Segment A

Segment B

Segment C

Segment D

Segment A - track level

Segment B - track level

Segment C - track level

Segment D - springing level

NORTH - SOUTH ROOF SECTION

able roof segments A, B and C are 2400, 2200 and 1800 tonnes respectively.[17,18]

Architect: Roderick G. Robbie
Engineer: Michael Allen, Adjeleian Allen Rubeli
Limited
Space frame contractor: Dominion Bridge Co.

In this chapter we have seen some innovative ideas and methods of using folding, deployable and retractable space grids. Single-layer folding grids are also being explored by Chuck Hobermann in the USA. Given the versatility of folding grid structures there is great potential for their extensive adoption for construction projects in the future. There is considerable scope for their application for a wide variety of uses such as as an economic method of erection or as a means of providing easily adaptable or demountable and reusable structures.

Notes

1 Pérez Valcárcel, J. and Escrig, F. (1994). Pioneering in expandable structures: the Madrid 1 notebook by Leonardo da Vinci. *Bulletin of the International Association for Shell and Spatial Structures*, **35/1** (114), 33–45.
2 Escrig, F. (1993). Las Estructuras de Emilio Pérez Piñero. In *Arquitectura Transformable*, (F. Escrig, ed.) p. 26 (in Spanish). Escuela Técnica Superior de Arquitectura de Sevilla (ETSAS).
3 Hernandez, C. H. and Zalewski, W. (1993). Expandable structure for the Venezuelan Pavilion at Expo '92. In *Space Structures 4* (G. A. R. Parke and C. M. Howard, eds) vol. 2, pp. 1710–19, Thomas Telford.
4 Hernandez, C. H. (1991). Mobile and rapid assembly structure. *Engineering* (P. S. Bulson, ed.) vol. 8, pp. 237–48, Computational Mechanics Publications.
5 Loreto, A. (ed.) (1993). *Pabellon de Venezuela Expo '92 Sevilla*, Instituto de Desarrollo Experimental de la Construccion, Universidad Central de Venezuela.
6 R. Buckminster Fuller (1975). *Synergetics*. Macmillan.
7 Ulm, R. C. and Heathcote, R. L. (1959). Dome built from top down. *Civil Engineering*, December, **29** (12), 872–5.
8 Kawaguchi, M. and Mitsumune, S. (1984). A domical space frame foldable during erection. *International Conference on Space Structures*, pp. 982–87, University of Surrey, September.
9 Kato, S., Kawaguchi, K. and Saka, T. (1995). Preliminary report on Hanshin earthquake. In *Spatial Structures: Heritage, Present and Future* (G. C. Giuliani, ed.) vol. 2, pp. 1059–66, quote p. 1064, SGE.
10 Dorai, J. (1989). Indoor stadium will be ready ahead of time. *The Straits Times*, 1 March 1989, p. 39.
11 Abe, M., Aso, Y., Muto, Y., Kosaka, T., Harada, A., Kimura, I. and Shirai, T. (1993). Design and Construction of Singapore Indoor Stadium – an Example of Pantadome System. In *Public Assembly Structures from Antiquity to the Present*, Proceedings IASS Symposium, pp. 371–80, Mimar Sinan University.
12 Kawaguchi, M. and Abe, M. (1998). A structural system suitable for rational construction. In *Lightweight Structures in Architecture, Engineering and Construction*, (R. Hough and R. Melchers, eds) pp. 85–94, LSAA.
13 Escrig, F., Valcárcel, J. P. and Sánchez, J. (1995). Deployable structures squared in plan design and construction. In *Spatial Structures: Heritage, Present and Future* (G. C. Giuliani, ed.) vol.1, pp. 483–92, SGE.
14 Escrig, F. (1993). Geometría de las Estructuras Desplegables de Aspas. In *Arquitectura Transformable,* (F. Escrig, ed.), p. 93 (in Spanish). Escuela Técnica Superior de Arquitectura de Sevilla (ETSAS).
15 Pérez Valcárcel, J. B. (1993). Cálculo de Estructuras Desplegables de Barras. In *Arquitectura Transformable,* (F. Escrig, ed.), p. 125 (in Spanish). Escuela Técnica Superior de Arquitectura de Sevilla (ETSAS).
16 Robbie, R. G. (1992). The Architecture of the Toronto Skydome. In *Innovative Large Span Structures* (N. K. Srivastava, A. N. Sherbourne and J. Roorda, eds) vol. 1, pp. 52–61, The Canadian Society for Civil Engineering.
17 Allen, C. M. (1992). Toronto Skydome Roof Structure; Engineering Challenge. In *Innovative Large Span Structures* (N. K. Srivastava, A. N. Sherbourne and J. Roorda, eds) vol. 1, pp. 63–71, The Canadian Society for Civil Engineering.
18 Charalambu, H. (1992). Design of the roof moving system. In *Innovative Large Span Structures* (N. K. Srivastava, A. N. Sherbourne and J. Roorda, eds) vol. 1, pp. 82–93, The Canadian Society for Civil Engineering.

7 Future developments

In the two preceding chapters we have seen the wide variety of uses to which space grid structures can be put. Their use in deployable, foldable and retractable structures will no doubt continue to develop in subsequent years. This chapter highlights some areas where space grid structures have been little used to date but where they might be exploited to a greater extent in the future.

Polyhedral space grid buildings

It is well accepted that buildings can be composed of a continuum of polyhedral cells but it is unfortunate that the cell shape that usually springs to mind is based on the rectilinear cuboid, with parallel planes of wall, floor and ceiling. This need not be the case, as there are many more visually exciting combinations of polyhedral spaces that can form inhabitable buildings. Although practicality may have some influence on the matter it appears to be prejudice and familiarity that lead us to adopt the common rectilinear building form. More 'exotic' spaces are usually reserved for buildings of special significance, such as churches, assembly or sports halls and theatres, rather than dwellings. With some exceptions, space grids do not conform to rectilinear geometry in three dimensions.

There have been many proposals for the use of space grids, both for individual dwellings and as multi-layer grids for complete urban environments. Many of these ideas have been based on the fascination that polyhedral geometry holds for many architects and engineers. Those who question the mundaneness of the dominant rectilinear box that composes most spaces within buildings, have looked longingly at the possibilities of space filling packings of polyhedra of alternative form. In Chapter 1, the inventor Alexander Graham Bell's fascination with the strength and lightness of tetrahedra was noted. He considered that the basic tetrahedral module could be used as a building block to construct larger structures and built a house and a framework for a giant windbreak from them.[1]

There are some existing buildings that have been planned on octahedral/tetrahedral geometry. For example, large reinforced concrete space truss pavilions were built at a permanent trade fair site at New Delhi, India,

in 1982. Five pyramidal-form pavilions were constructed from in situ reinforced concrete using multi-layer grids of this type.[2,3] Nusatsum House, described in some detail in Chapter 5, shows the use of habitable multi-layer grids on the small scale.

High-rise and megastructures

Although most space grids are fabricated from steel or aluminium, they are not solely restricted to metal as the construction material. Louis Kahn's Yale Art Gallery, Yale University, New Haven, Connecticut, USA, (1950–4) was built using tetrahedral space grid floors in reinforced concrete, although the planning of the building did not really reflect the reticulation of the structure. In the middle of the 1950s, Louis Kahn was influenced very much by the ideas of Buckminster Fuller. At this time he collaborated with Anne Griswold Tyng in the design of a 188 m (616 ft) high City Tower for Philadelphia (1952–7). This work, commissioned by the Concrete Institute of America to demonstrate the innovative use of the material, was based on tetrahedral geometry and stabilized by concrete tetrahedral floors. I. M. Pei's Bank of China, 1989, has an external bracing structure, on a large scale, that encloses the high-rise building in a giant space grid. Michael Burt et al. have also proposed megacities of large space grids – Infinite Polyhedral Lattice (IPL) – constructed from elements made from small-space grids.[4,5] This is much as the Eiffel Tower is constructed from lattice elements that are assembled to produce a larger lattice structure.

Over many years, J. François Gabriel has studied the use of polyhedra in the design and construction of buildings of all sizes. He has investigated, in particular, the architecture of high-rise buildings constructed using a six-directional, multi-layer, space-filling, space grids, composed of tetrahedra and octahedra.[6] With this type of space-filling lattice it is possible to generate continuous horizontal plane grids by orientating the octahedra in two ways (a) with their long axis set vertically and (b) with one triangular face in the horizontal plane (see Figure 7.1(a) and (b)). The first of these produces a multi-layer version of the common square-on-square offset two-way space grid, whilst the latter produces the less common triangle-on-triangle offset multi-layer three-way space grid.

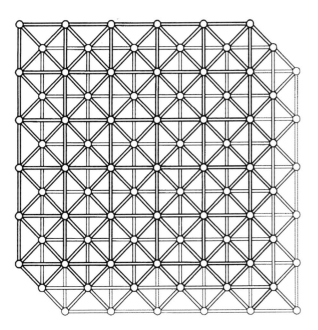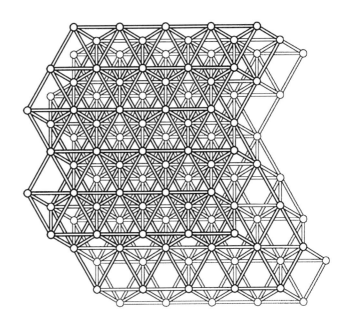

7.1
Octahedral-tetrahedral space filling lattices (a) two-way and (b) three-way (Drawing: John Chilton)

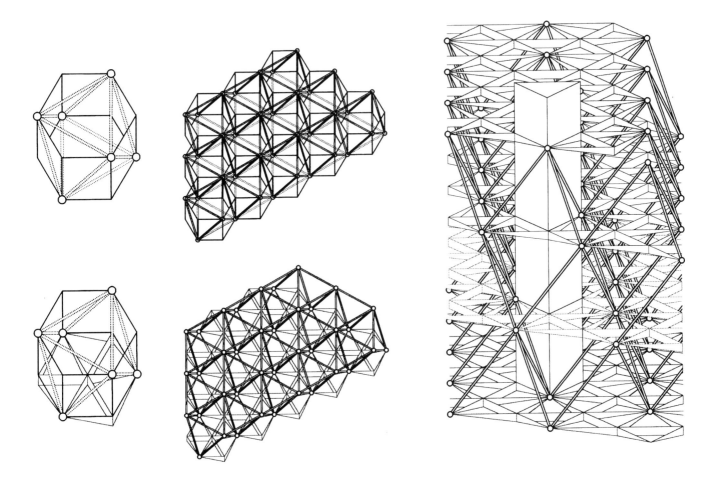

7.2
Multi-layer three-way grid modified to create structure-free 'Hexmod' cells and unobstructed spaces for vertical circulation of lifts and service ducts (Drawing: John Chilton, after J. François Gabriel)

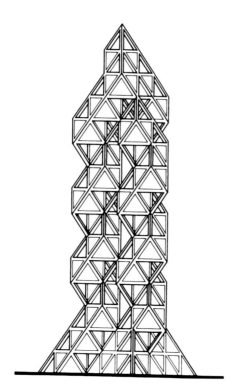

7.3
'Space town' of 126 storeys proposed by J. François Gabriel using a large-scale, three-way space grid (Courtesy J. François Gabriel)

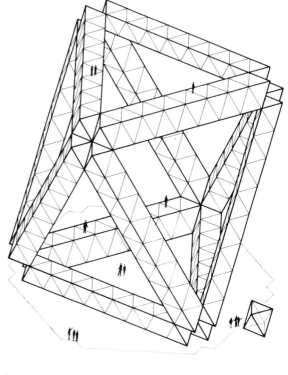

7.4
Axonometric view of one octahedral module of the megastructure. Each side is a space truss composed of eight octahedra linked by fourteen tetrahedra of side length 4 m (Courtesy J. François Gabriel)

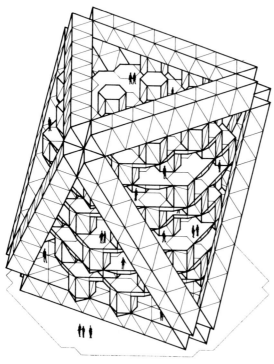

7.5
Assembly of 'Hexmod' cells to form a megastructure with hexagonal accommodation (vertical walls and horizontal floors) dispersed through the multi-layer space grid (Courtesy J. François Gabriel)

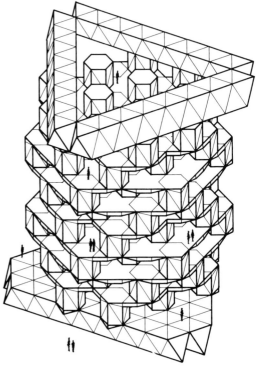

7.6
Similar assembly of 'Hexmod' cells with the diagonals of the large octahedron removed to reveal the hexagonal shape of the core building (Courtesy J. François Gabriel)

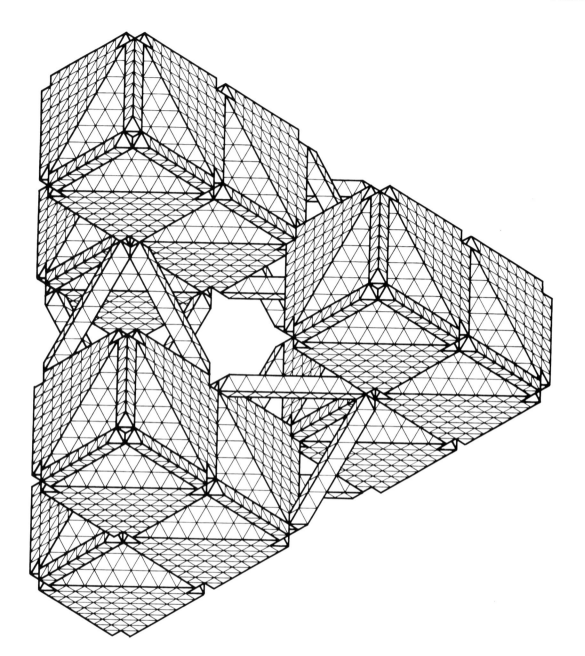

7.7
Plan view of the three identical megastructure helices used to form the 'space town'. The large octahedra are enclosed in a glass envelope and additional space trusses hold the helices together (Courtesy J. François Gabriel)

Architects are concerned with the division of space and the use to which it may be put. Within the space-filling three-way, multi-layer grid the integration of vertical circulation is a problem, therefore, J. François Gabriel has proposed a modification of the basic grid, eliminating some members whilst maintaining structural stability. This produces a spatial lattice in which a structure-free hexagonal cell or 'Hexmod' may be placed throughout and unobstructed vertical circulation (for lifts and service ducts) is also possible (Figure 7.2).

To create a high-rise, megastructure or 'space town', Gabriel has suggested the construction of a large-scale multi-layer, three-way grid in which a smaller-scale modified three-way grid containing hexagonal rooms or

'Hexmods' are provided as living and/or office space. Figure 7.3 shows his proposed 'space town' of 126 storeys in which only the octahedral sections of the macro grid are inhabited. Each of the large octahedra (Figure 7.4) is composed of twelve space trusses in turn consisting of eight octahedra linked by fourteen tetrahedra with side lengths of 4 metres (giving a storey height of 3.27 m). The large octahedron is subdivided with a smaller three-way grid of similar orientation containing the 'Hexmod' rooms (Figure 7.5), which are not allowed to protrude beyond the planes of the mega-octahedra. As can be seen in Figure 7.6 (where the six diagonal space truss members have been removed from the large octahedron) the basic building shape is also hexagonal. Due

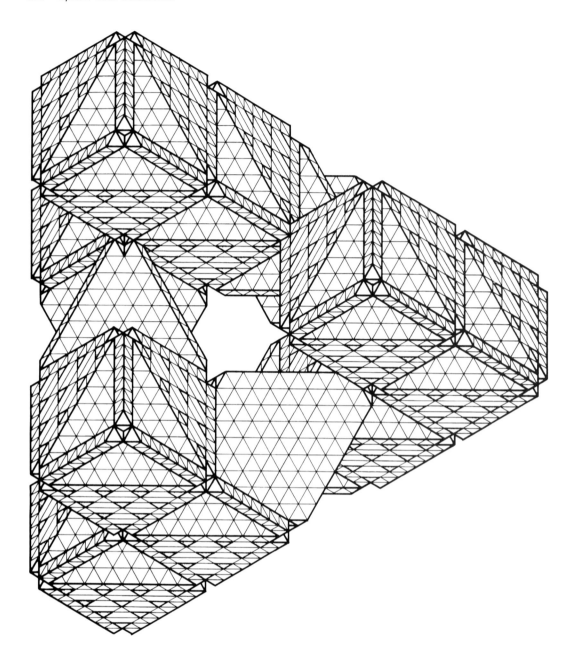

*7.8
Similar view of the
'space town' where
some 'Hexmods' have
been allowed to
penetrate the glass
envelope of the large
octahedra and
horizontal access
platforms have been
added to link the
helices (Courtesy J.
François Gabriel)*

to the geometry of the three-way grid, each hexagon (in both the small and large grid) is displaced horizontally relative to the layer below. Therefore, the structure (again at both scales) consists of linked helical spirals.

A plan view of the proposed 'space town' composed of three identical helices and with the octahedra enclosed within a glass envelope is shown in Figure 7.7. The individual helices are held together by additional horizontal space trusses. Gabriel has suggested that the hexagonal void at the centre could house high-speed lifts stopping at every ninth storey. In the similar view of Figure 7.8, some 'Hexmods' have been allowed to penetrate the enclosure of the large octahedron and horizontal access platforms have been added between adjacent

helices. These modifications are shown in detail in Figure 7.9. The adoptions of such a structural system would represent quite a radical change in the thinking of most architects and engineers as it would require the acceptance of hexagonal spaces within a octahedral/tetrahedral space grid system. An alternative that uses the more common two-way space-filling system is described below.

TRY 2004

In Japan, the Shimizu Corporation has proposed the building of a pyramidal 'city-in-the-air' (Figure 7.10) which

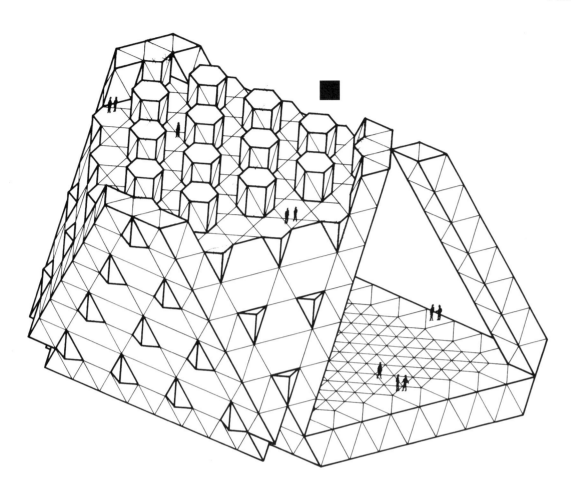

*7.9
Detail of the
'Hexmods' penetrating
the enclosure of the
large octahedra and
the access platform
(Courtesy J. François
Gabriel)*

*7.10
A pyramid 'city-in-the-
air' concept named
TRY2004 proposed
by the Shimizu
Corporation, which
uses a multi-layer grid
over 2000 m high
(Courtesy Shimizu
Corporation)*

7.11
Method of suspension of office blocks within the TRY2004 megacity space grid, i.e. vertically in the octagons of the grid (Courtesy Shimizu Corporation)

would, during working hours, contain around 1 million people. The concept, named 'TRY2004', consists of a square-based, pyramidal, multi-layer, space truss megastructure, 2800 m by 2800 m at ground level and reaching 2004 m into the sky.[7,8] The primary structure is based on octahedral units each formed by joining two 350 m by 350 m square-based pyramids, 250.5 m high, base to base. Combined together in layers, these form the well-known geometry of the octet truss.

It is not proposed to clad the complete pyramid on the external faces to form one large enclosure. However, within the primary structure individually enclosed residential, office and commercial buildings up to 100 storeys high are to be suspended. Figure 7.11 shows the method of support for a typical office building within the structure. A similar system of suspension is proposed for high-rise residential units of pyramidal/octahedral form. The residential units are to be concentrated at the lower levels

7.12
Typical 50 m diameter node within the megagrid showing the proposal for transport interchange contained within the node (Courtesy Shimizu Corporation)

and at the perimeter of the pyramid, whilst office development is to be located at the core. Leisure and commercial facilities are planned for the high levels where they command the best views.

One important reason for adopting the pyramidal shape was the improved penetration of daylight into the space grid. It was shown that annually the pyramidal form would collect 25 per cent more sunlight per unit of surface area and 81 per cent more sunlight per unit volume than would a cubic form (45 per cent and 151 per cent more respectively than would a more typical 'skyscraper'). The combination of the pyramidal form with the fully triangulated three-dimensional grid system also would provide excellent resistance to lateral loads such as wind and earthquakes.

Construction of such a multi-layer space grid would require tubular members and spherical nodes of huge proportion. It is proposed that the horizontal elements of the grid be tubes 10 m in diameter, housing transportation systems using linear induction motors. The diagonal members 16 m in diameter would generally contain services and a continuously circulating cable-car system of transport. Nodes 50 m in diameter would provide circulation between the horizontal and diagonal transportation systems and would also be used to collect sunlight for distribution by optical fibres. A typical node with the connecting horizontal and diagonal members is shown in Figure 7.12. To reduce the weight of the structure, it would be constructed using lightweight materials reinforced with glass and carbon fibres.

Assembly would be facilitated by the use of standardized components and robots to build segments that would be erected by 'push-up' methods. According to the Shimizu Corporation, such a megacity could be constructed for 88 trillion yen (1990 prices) and would require approximately seven years to complete. The concept demonstrates the eminent suitability of multi-layer space trusses for the construction of such large-scale projects, using tubular elements where the internal void may be used for transportation. Although this is still a dream (of which the desirability of realization might be questioned in terms of environmental impact and social acceptability), it represents one possible future for the use of space grids.

Composite floors

The combination of space grids with decking in floor construction is not new. In recent years there has been considerable research into composite action between a space grid and the concrete floor plate. In Chapter 5 the composite floor construction for the Milan Fair Complex was described in detail. This was developed as a system for a specific problem but there is also potential for

the use of standard space grid components in composite floor construction for multistorey buildings.

In typical modern composite floors, the overall construction depth often has to be increased to allow the passage of ventilation ducts beneath the downstand beams. The open nature of space grid structures allows the easy passage of services within the structural depth thus reducing overall storey (floor to floor) heights within the building. Potentially, this could mean an extra floor for a given building height proscribed by planning controls or the provision of the same floor space within a less tall structure. The former provides more lettable space in the same volume with little increase in construction cost (one extra floor structure), whilst the latter produces savings due to the reduced size of the building envelope.

Considerable research has taken place over recent years to develop a version of the CUBIC Space Frame as a standard system for composite floor construction. Also, the Catrus system described in Chapter 3 has two composite systems currently under development, one

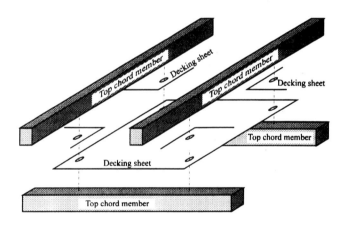

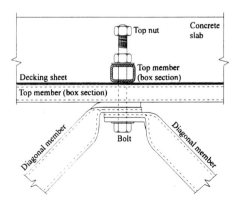

7.13
Extended upper node connection bolt, shear connector for the Catrus acting compositely with a concrete deck. The flat decking sheet is a permanent shutter for the slab concrete (Courtesy Al-Sheikh)

incorporating a concrete top slab and the other connected to a timber deck. For the composite concrete version, shear connection between the in situ slab and the space truss is provided by an extended upper node connection bolt and top nut, as shown in Figure 7.13. The use of the normal connecting bolt with an additional nut eliminates the need for welding (required for standard shear studs in traditional composite steel/concrete floor construction). Flat steel sheet decking, clamped by the node connecting bolts between the upper chords running in the two orthogonal directions, is used to support the wet concrete. Profiled decking is not required because membrane action is mobilized to provide a very economical solution.

When used with timber decking, a simple short connecting piece made from 1.6 to 2.0 mm thick cold-formed steel sheet is used. This has a single bolt hole at the centre for connection to the space grid node and four holes to permit the timber boarding to be attached.

Tensegrity and space grids

When using the combination of steel, or aluminium, and glass as structural materials, wherever possible architects try to minimize the size of the metallic structure required to support the transparency of the glass. To this end in the Musee des Beaux Arts, Montreal, Canada, Mero developed a system of glazing support using their NK joint. The structural glazing bars were supported on flying stainless steel tubular struts suspended by a grid of tension bars and connected by the modified ball joint. Thus, using a modified version of the Mero system, very light and airy glazed gallery spaces were produced (see Figure 7.14). The adoption of standard space grid components achieved economy in construction whilst allowing the architect to exploit the transparency of glass as freely as possible. Although related to tensegrity structures (described below) this was really an example of a two-way strutted beam or beam-string type structure.

Since their discovery and patenting in the early 1960s by Buckminster Fuller, Snelson and Emmerich, 'tensegrity' structures have fascinated architects and engineers alike, although there have been relatively few practical applications of the concept. (The term 'tensegrity' was coined by Buckminster Fuller to describe the system of tensile integrity). There is not space here to go into detail about geometry and behaviour of these structures where compression elements are usually held in place only by elements in direct tension. However, research is currently being carried out by Motro and Hanaor, among others, to develop double-layer tensegrity grid systems (Figure 7.15) with a view to their possible use in roof structures. Although these work in model form there are several technical and constructional problems to be over-

7.14
Tensile system supporting glazing at the Musee des Beaux Arts, Montreal, Canada (Courtesy Mero)

come before they can be used on the larger scale. However, one advantage of double-layer tensegrity grids is that they are easy to collapse and could therefore potentially be used for deployable grids.

Quasicrystal geometry: combining rods and plates

According to some designers, a negative aspect of space grids is the inflexibility of the usual member configuration patterns, these being mainly based on combinations of regular octahedral and tetrahedral forms. Recently however, the possibilities resulting from the use of alternative standard unit cells to create three-dimensional non-repeating patterns has been explored. A very exciting means of generating such patterns has derived from

7.15
Double-layer tensegrity grid where there is no direct contact between the compression elements (Photograph courtesy René Motro)

the study of forms in multidimensional mathematical space (i.e. having more than the three spatial dimensions of the real world). For example, a three-dimensional cube may be represented by a drawing on the two-dimensional surface of a piece of paper. The two-dimensional sketch of a cube is, in fact, the outline of the shadow cast by the cubic lattice. Similarly, objects of higher mathematical dimension may also be represented in lower dimensions (i.e. the 'shadow' of a four-dimensional object may exist in three-dimensional space). Exciting ideas for the use of geometries from higher dimensions have come from the studies carried out by, amongst others, Steve Baer, Koji Miyazaki and Haresh Lalvani.

One field of multidimensional geometry has led to the discovery of quasicrystals, crystal-like solid objects that can be packed together to form a continuous solid. Using the basic quasicrystal geometry it is possible to construct two different solid or wireframe cells, each with six similar rhombic faces, one 'fat' cell and one 'thin' cell. The standard rhombic face is as shown in Figure 7.16(a) and the six standard faces of the two cell types are assembled with different angles between the faces to produce the 'thin' and 'fat' versions. Figure 7.16(b) shows the 'fat' cell and figure 7.16(c) the 'thin' cell. These individual cells can be combined to produce a continuum with the property that the edges or bars of the cells form non-repeating patterns in three dimensions. The orientation of the edges or members of the cells is such that the ideal shape for the connecting nodes is a regular dodecahedron, with members perpendicular to its faces. Within the space grid, all bars have the same length between node centres and all connecting nodes have the same orientation in three-dimensional space, this being a further property of quasicrystal geometry.

Artist Tony Robbin, who works in New York, has experimented with the use of quasicrystal geometry in his art[9] and more recently in architecture. The fundamental problem with the elements of quasicrystals as architectural building blocks is that the rhombic faces are unstable as pure bar and node structures (but then so are the square faces of the cube, a very common building form!). As commented by Erik Reitzel, a structural engineer who has collaborated with Robbin, most engineers intuitively want to triangulate each rhombic face and the rhombohedral cells by introducing diagonal members to stabilize them.[10] However, this disguises the quasicrystal geometry and masks the fascinating patterns that can be generated. One alternative is to brace the structure by using fully rigid node joints; it also is possible to stiffen the rhombic faces by introducing structural plates (as, incidentally, is often done in cubic structures). To reveal the full splendour of the quasicrystal geometry, transparent plates of glass or polycarbonate sheet may be used.

A quasicrystal form was proposed for an extension to be constructed at the Technical University at Lyngby, in Denmark. Originally COAST was to be a full-scale addition to the outside of one of the existing buildings (Figure 7.17). However, despite being championed by Erik Reitzel, structural engineer for the project, in the end, due to cost restraints, only a sculptural form was built in the atrium of the administration block. The sculpture was assembled, by Tony Robbin and a team of students, over one month using over 10 000 individual parts (similar machined dodecahedral aluminium nodes and bars, all of equal length). As can be seen in Figure 7.18 all of the dodecahedral nodes in the sculptural space grid have the same orientation, as noted earlier.

An interesting quality of quasicrystal geometry is that, although it consists of a non-repeating pattern, the shadows cast when light is passed through a structure with

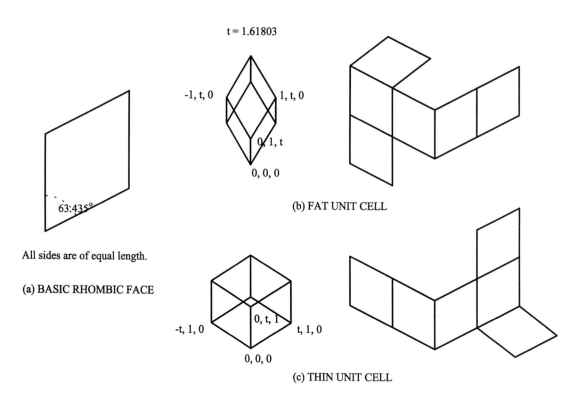

t = 1.61803

-1, t, 0   1, t, 0

0, 1, t

0, 0, 0

63:435°

All sides are of equal length.

(a) BASIC RHOMBIC FACE

(b) FAT UNIT CELL

-t, 1, 0   0, t, 1   t, 1, 0

0, 0, 0

(c) THIN UNIT CELL

7.16
Quasicrystal geometry (a) basic rhombic face, (b) the 'thin' and (c) the 'fat' quasicrystal unit cells shown as 3-dimensional cells and unfolded (Drawing: John Chilton)

that geometry can form regular patterns. For instance, Figure 7.19 shows the shadows cast on the ground at different times of the day by sunlight shining through a quasicrystal dome. The sculpture constructed at Lyngby exploits this property and, in addition to the fascinating form of the object itself, the shadows cast on the floor of the atrium mutate continuously during the day as the angle of the sunlight entering the roof changes. Because the quasicrystal geometry is not stable as a pure pin-jointed lattice structure, plates of coloured Plexiglass have been introduced at various locations throughout the sculpture to ensure its stability. These multi-hued translucent panels add to the visual excitement of the sculptural form itself and also generate fascinating combinations of colours in the shadows projected on to the floor of the atrium below.

Exploration of this exciting new geometry for use in structures is still in its infancy. However, the sculpture at Lyngby has demonstrated its potential for generating delightful architectural configurations. This stimulating construction contradicts at least two of the common criticisms levelled at space grids: the monotony of the repetitive geometry and the difficulty of producing complex three-dimensional forms using a small set of standard elements. All of the nodes of the quasicrystal space grid are similar dodecahedra that are orientated in the same way in space and all of the member lengths (between node centres) are the same. Consequently, all of the stiffening panels are the same shape and size but vary in orientation. Truly three-dimensional structural art is the outcome of this kit

of standard parts. It is possible to envisage roof structures composed of deep quasicrystal space grids partially stabilized by the double-glazing units that form the weatherproof envelope, whilst coloured panels at other positions in the structure complete the stabilizing function, filter the sunlight and produce ever-changing combinations of light and shadow. As with the pioneering sculpture at Lyngby, the challenge for the future will be to construct stable quasicrystal building structures whilst maintaining the transparency and filigree of the relatively open geometry.

What does the future hold?

In this and the previous chapter some recent developments in space grid structures have been discussed. These examples demonstrate that space grids have come of age and that from the regular modular systems developed around fifty years ago, diverse possibilities of geometry and deployability are now beginning to be explored and exploited. Computer controlled cutting, machining and drilling of space grid components means that designers are no longer restricted to standard geometries. Driven by the need for oil exploration and extraction in the oceans, oil-rigs up to around 1000 m in height and utilizing large diameter tubular steel members have been constructed. The technology and materials developed for these giant structures is now available to be used in the construction of space grid, megastructures. In office developments there is a continuing

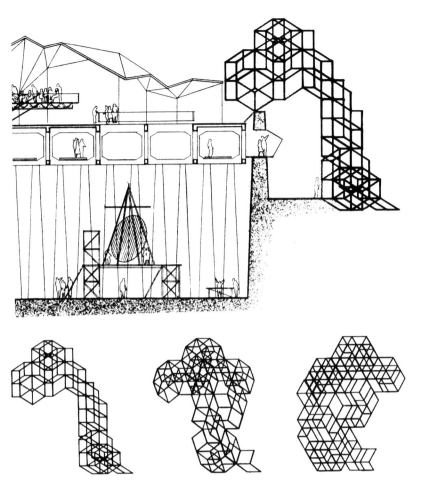

east   north   northwest

7.17
Original COAST quasicrystal building extension at the Technical University, Lyngby, Denmark as proposed by Tony Robbin and Erik Reitzel (Courtesy Tony Robbin)

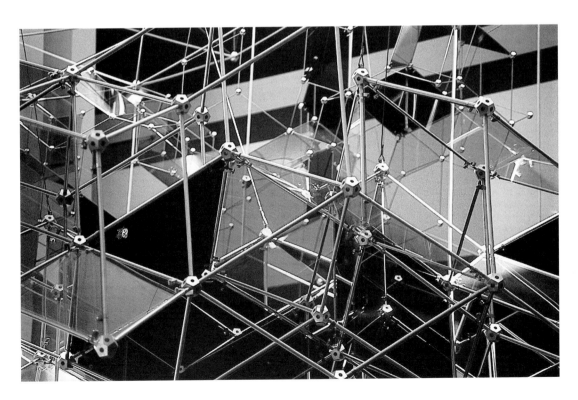

7.18
The quasicrystal sculpture in the atrium at the Technical University, Lyngby, Denmark (Photograph: John Chilton)

7.19
Diagram showing the varying shadow pattern under a quasicrystal dome as the sun passes overhead (Courtesy Tony Robbin)

demand for ever-longer floor spans to provide column free workspaces. This demand could be satisfied by the use of composite space grid floors. Lightness and transparency are fashionable qualities for architectural structures and architects continue to seek innovative structural solutions. In this area double-layer tensegrity grids and quasicrystal grids are still in their infancy with many, perhaps as yet unthought of, grid forms to be discovered. Folding, deployable and retractable structures, too, have yet to realize their full potential.

Without a doubt the future of space grid structures is assured and still developing 100 years after Alexander Graham Bell's experiments to find a more efficient structure for kites.

Notes

1   Bell, A. G. (1903). The tetrahedral principle in kite structure. *National Geographic*, **14** (6), June, 231.
2   Anon (1982). *Architects Journal*, 17 February, p. 21.
3   Anon (1982). *RIBA Journal*, July, pp. 50–1.
4   Shriftalig, D., Burt, M., Bogdanov, A., Mincovich, V. and Taran, D. (1992). I.P.L. megastructure. In *Innovative Large Span Structures* (N. K. Srivastava, A, N. Sherbourne and J. Roorda, eds) vol 1, pp. 616–26, CSCE.
5   Frances, M., Rosenhouse, G. and Burt, M. (1992). Highly regular multi-layered cylindrical shells of infinite polyhedral lattice. In *Innovative Large Span Structures* (N. K. Srivastava, A, N. Sherbourne and J. Roorda, eds) vol. 1, pp. 542–51, CSCE.
6   Gabriel, J. F. (1997). Are space frames habitable. In *Beyond the Cube* (J. F. Gabriel, ed.) p. 439, John Wiley.
7   Sugizaki, K. (1992). Super high-rise mega-city concept 'Pyramid-TRY2004'. In *Innovative Large Span Structures* (N. K. Srivastava, A. N. Sherbourne and J. Roorda, eds) vol. 1, pp. 164–74, CSCE.
8   Shimizu Corporation (1991). TRY 2004. Technical literature, Shimizu Corporation.
9   Robbin, T. (1992). *Fourfield: Computers, Art and the 4th Dimension*. Little, Brown and Co.
10 Reitzel, E. and Robbin, T. (1993). A quasicrystal for Denmark's COAST. In *Space Structures 4* (G. A. R. Parke and C. M. Howard, eds) vol. 2, pp. 1980–7, Thomas Telford.

Appendices

Appendix 1: two-way spanning structures

Considering a system of two beams of span L_1 and L_2 that intersect at right angles and are connected at their mid-span, we can determine the amount of any load applied at the intersection point that will be carried by each beam. The proportion of the applied load W carried by each will be W_1 for beam 1 and W_2 for beam 2, and the sum $W_1 + W_2$ will equal the total load W. The vertical deflection of each beam, which depends on the load and span of each, can be calculated easily for the point of contact at mid-span. Knowing that the deflection of both beams must be the same at the point where they are connected, and given the span of each beam, it is then possible to determine the proportion of load W carried by each.

Assuming that the beams have the same material and cross-sectional properties (i.e Young's Modulus E and the second moment of area I are the same for both), for beam 1 the mid-span deflection $\delta_1 = W_1 L_1^3/48EI$ and for beam 2 the mid-span deflection $\delta_2 = W_2 L_2^3/48EI$. As the two beams are connected together at their midpoint, their deflections must be equal ($\delta_1 = \delta_2$). Therefore, as the term 48EI is constant for both beams and can be cancelled from both equations,

$$W_1 L_1^3 = W_2 L_2^3 \text{ or } W_1 = W_2 L_2^3/L_1^3 \qquad \text{(Equation 1)}$$

From this equation and the fact that $W_1 + W_2 = W$, Table A.1 can be prepared to show the proportion of the total load W carried by each of the two beams for different span ratios.

Table A1

Span ratio (L_2/L_1)	1.0	1.2	1.5	2.0	3.0
Beam 1 (W_1)	0.500W	0.633W	0.771W	0.889W	0.964W
Beam 2 (W_2)	0.500W	0.367W	0.229W	0.111W	0.036W

Note: E and I constant, L_2 longer span and L_1 shorter span.

Where the beams in the two directions have different stiffness (i.e. the value of I is different for each), Equation 1 above is modified by the ratio of the two values of I and becomes:

$$W_1 = (W_2 I_1 L_2^3)/(I_2 L_1^3) \qquad \text{(Equation 2)}$$

A graphical representation of these equations is given as Figure 2.4 in Chapter 2 for ratios of I_2/I_1 of 1, 2, 3 and 5.

Appendix 2: list of manufacturers

There are many space grid manufacturers throughout the world and it would be a considerable task to list them all. Therefore, only a limited list that includes the last known addresses of the manufacturers mentioned in the text is given here.

ABBA Space Structures cc
PO Box 34409
Jeppestown 2043
South Africa

Kubik Enterprises Ltd
17 Birchwood Drive
Ravenshead
Nottinghamshire
NG 15 9EE
UK

Mai Sky System Inc.
228 East Avenue A
PO Box 1066
Salina
KS 67402-1066
USA

Mero (UK) plc
Unit 4, Ancells Court
Fleet
Hampshire
GU13 8UY
UK

Mero Raumstruktur
GmbH & Co. Würzburg
PO Box 61 69
Steinachstrasse 5
D-8700 Würzburg
Germany

NS Space Truss
Nippon Steel Co. Ltd
2-6-3 Otemachi
Chiyoda-ku
Tokyo 100
Japan

Orona S. Coop. Ltda.
Aptdo. Correos 1312
20080 San Sebastián
Spain

Ramco-YKK (Singapore) Pte. Ltd
9 Benoi Crescent
Jurong
Singapore 2262

Space Decks Ltd
Chard
Somerset
TA20 2AA
United Kingdom

Tridim Lahaye s.a.
6250 Aiseau
Belgium

Tianjin Space Frame Co.
Department of Civil Engineering
Tianjin University
Tianjin (300072)
People's Republic of China

TM Truss
Taiyo Kogyo Corporation
3-22-1 Higashiyama
Meguro-ku
Tokyo 153
Japan

Unibat International
15 rue Hégésippe-Moreau
75018 Paris
France

UNISTRUT
Space Frame Systems, Inc.
45081 Geddes Rd.
Canton
MI 48188
USA

Uskon
SSI Group Limited
PO Box 2
Whitchurch
Shropshire
SY 13 1WL
UK

Vestrut
Centro Acciai Spa
70032 Bitonto (BA)
s.s. 98 KM 78,900
Italy

Further reading

Abel, J. F., Leonard, J. W. and Penalba, C. U. (eds) (1994). *Spatial, Lattice and Tension Structures*. ASCE.

Borrego, J. (1968). *Space Grid Structures*. MIT Press.

Bunni, U. K., Disney, P. and Makowski, Z. S. (1989). *Multi-Layer Space Frames*. Constrado.

Critchlow, K. (1969). *Order in Space*. Thames and Hudson.

Eekhout, M. (1996). *Tubular Structures in Architecture*. CIDECT.

Eekhout, M. (1980). *Architecture in Space Structures*. Uitgeverij 010 Publishers.

Gabriel, J. F. (ed.) (1997). *Beyond the Cube*. Wiley.

Giuliani, G. C. (ed.) (1995). *Spatial Structures: Heritage Present and Future*. SGE.

Heki, K. (ed.) (1986). *Shells, Membranes and Space Frames*. Elsevier.

Hough, R. and Melchers, R. (eds) (1998). *Lightweight Structures in Architecture, Engineering and Construction*. LSAA New South Wales.

Nooshin, M. (ed.) (1991). *Studies in Space Structures*. Multi-Science.

Obrebski, J. B. (ed.) (1995). *Lightweight Structures in Civil Engineering*. magat® Magdalena Burska. Warsaw.

Parke, G. A. R. and Howard, C. M. (eds) (1993). *Space Structures 4*. Thomas Telford.

Pearce, P. (1990). *Structure in Nature is a Strategy for Design*, 2nd edn. MIT Press.

Pozo, F. del and Casas, A. de las (eds) (1989). *Ten Years of Progress in Shell and Spatial Structures*. CEDEX.

Pugh, A. (1976). *Polyhedra – a Visual Approach*. University of California Press.

Robbin, T. (1996). *Engineering a New Architecture*. Yale University Press.

Srivastava, N. K., Sherbourne, A. N. and Roorda, J. (eds) (1992). *Innovative Large Span Structures*. Canadian Society for Civil Engineering.

Tsuboi, Y. (ed.) (1984). *Analysis, Design and Realization of Space Frames*. IASS.

Wester, T., Medwadowski, S. J. and Mogensen, I. (eds) (1991). *Spatial Structures at the Turn of the Millennium*. Kunstakademiets Forlag Arkitekskolen.

Wilkinson, C. (1995). *Supersheds – The Architecture of Long-Span Large Volume Buildings*. Architectural Press.

Index

Note: entries given in italic refer to figure numbers.